SATAN's
TROJAN HORSE

GOD's
END-TIME
VICTORY

Also by Norman R. Gulley:
    Christ Is Coming!

To order, call 1-800-765-6955.
Visit us at www.reviewandherald.com for information on other
Review and Herald® products.

NORMAN GULLEY

SATAN's TROJAN HORSE

GOD's END-TIME VICTORY

REVIEW AND HERALD® PUBLISHING ASSOCIATION
HAGERSTOWN, MD 21740

This book was
Edited by Andy Nash
Copyedited by Delma Miller and James Cavil
Designed by Matthew Pierce/Pierce Creative
Cover illustration by Matthew Pierce
Electronic makeup by Shirley M. Bolivar
Typeset: Bembo 12/14

PRINTED IN U.S.A.
08 07 06 05 04   5 4 3 2 1

R&H Cataloging Service
Gulley, Norman R   1933-
    Satan's Trojan horse: God's end-time victory.

    1. Second Advent.   2. End of the world.   3. Seventh-day Adventists—Doctrines.   I. Title

                    236

ISBN 0-8280-1746-8

In gratitude to God for a wonderful family—

my wife, four children, and 10 grandchildren.

Each of you is very special,

and you have brought me so much joy!

CONTENTS

INTRODUCTION

The terrorist attack on America transformed the George W. Bush presidency and changed the world. September 11, 2001, catapulted America to unprecedented global leadership. The United States military shocked the world with an exponential jump in its weapons capability, with advanced delivery systems and exact precision far beyond that used in Desert Storm only 10 years before. In fact, there is sharp improvement in weapons capability over the Kosovo war, just two years before! This leaves countries around the world stunned and concerned.

In the Japanese newspaper *Financial Times* for December 8, 2001, Stephen Fidler, reporter in Washington, quotes Paul Kennedy, Yale historian, who noted that America accounts for 36 percent of all military spending in the world. No other country's weapon systems even come close. The Russian military, which had such a long drawn-out conflict in Afghanistan, predicted disaster for America in that rugged country, but the rapid collapse of the Taliban under America's withering air power shook the Russian military to the core. They are astonished at the technical prowess of the U.S. war machine.

America is so far ahead of any other country that even in the alliance against terrorism it must carry the major burden as other countries cannot contribute at the sophisticated level of America's capability. Kennedy notes that "in this alliance the U.S. does 98 percent of the fighting, the British 2 percent, and the Japanese steam round Mauritius."

This global leadership has everything to do with America fulfilling its prophetic role in last-day events. In this book we follow the theme of terrorism as one way to look at the cosmic controversy that devastates God's otherwise wonderful universe. It provides a new avenue to look into the controversy, to think through the issues and see how they relate to last-day events and how we can be ready to play our part in final battles.

May God use this book to be a means of encouragement for those who read, that each one may be found ready for the events just ahead.

Norman R. Gulley, Ph.D.
Research Professor in Systematic Theology
Southern Adventist University
January 2002

CHAPTER I

TERRORISM IN THE WHITE HOUSE OF THE UNIVERSE

September 11's horrific crash of loaded jets (fuel and passengers) into the World Trade Center's twin towers and the Pentagon and the failed attempt in Pennsylvania was an attack on America. Never since the Revolutionary War (1775-1783) has this continent been invaded. For 218 years America seemed impregnable. That all came to a shattering end with swift and utter surprise. Suddenly this shocking barbaric attack changed the course of history, and we entered a new world.

The plane that slammed into the Pentagon at full speed was likely bound for the White House. This was an attack on the headquarters of world trade and on the American presidency. It was a flagrant, all-out war on the United States and citizens of other countries who worked in the Trade Center. The suicide terrorists planned their strategy in America on American planes over a two-year period. They learned how to fly—they knew enough about the big jets to steer them. They checked out crop duster planes for biological terrorism too. They picked the most vulnerable airports to get through security (or lack of it) to board the planes. This was an inside job from visitors who entered the States and outstayed their visa expiration—and yet lived in the country without anyone checking on such illegal overstays. The visitor system was floored at the point of entrance and cries out for better tracking and identification—all possible in our sophisticated technological age. Work is under way to bring this into place to make sure it never happens again, and could have a major impact on last-day events, as we will see later.

It All Began at the Throne

It all began at the White House of the universe. War broke out against the King of the universe. It too was an inside job. In fact Lucifer was the covering cherub standing next to God. To understand the strategy of this first terrorist, and the issues involved in his attack, is to penetrate what he is doing and will do in final events.

Star Wars is more than a movie. In the universe rages a cosmic controversy that staggers the imagination. Have you noticed all the books about angels today? Good angels and bad angels? It seems that angels are working overtime. One gets the sense they have plans for the planet. The Bible presents the plan of the good angels and exposes the schemes of the bad angels. "Our struggle is not against flesh and blood, but against the rulers, against the authorities, against the powers of this dark world and against the spiritual forces of evil in the heavenly realms" (Ephesians 6:12). What's this all about? How can forces from heavenly realms be a threat? Are angels warring against us?

"There was war in heaven. Michael and his angels fought against the dragon, and the dragon and his angels fought back. But he was not strong enough, and they lost their place in heaven" (Revelation 12:7, 8). Michael defeated Satan and his army. Yet Scripture also says the red dragon's "tail swept a third of the stars out of the sky and flung them to the earth" (verse 4). Satan is described as casting his angels (stars) out of heaven because he led them into the rebellion that caused their expulsion.

Satan in Conflict With Christ

War in heaven. What a paradox! Strange that war would break out at God's throne! It began in the Most Holy Place of heaven's sanctuary. Not a likely place, for sure. In fact God's throne is the last place one would expect a fight. Right? But the throne was the focus of the battle. Possession of the throne was the mission. Two groups battled—a dragon and his angels and Michael and his angels. The dragon is Satan, the devil (see Revelation 12:9; cf. Ezekiel 28:14-17; Revelation 20:2). The Hebrew word for Michael *(Micael)* means "Who is like God." This is Christ.

Christ is called an "angel" in Scripture (Exodus 14:19; 23:20; Acts 7:30, 32; 1 Corinthians 10:1-4) and also "the archangel Michael" (Jude 9). We meet Michael in crucial moments of the cosmic controversy. Michael is first mentioned in Scripture in connection with a "great war" (Daniel 10:1). Michael helped in the struggle against Persia (see verses 13-21). In the end-time "Michael, the great prince who protects your people, will arise. There will be a time of distress such as has not happened from the beginning of nations until then. But at that time your people—everyone whose name is found written in the book—will be delivered" (Daniel 12:1). Michael is mentioned in Jude 9, where He disputes with the devil over the buried body of Moses on Mount Nebo. Satan wants to keep him buried; Christ resurrects him. Clearly Michael and the devil are at war, first in heaven and then on earth.

Do you know what happened before the war? God created the universe through Christ (see John 1:1-3; Colossians 1:15, 16; Hebrews 1:2). "For by him all things were created: things in heaven and on earth, visible and invisible, whether thrones or powers or rulers or authorities" (Colossians 1:16). This means Christ created Satan (then called Lucifer) and those who joined his side of the cosmic controversy. Rebellion was against the One who gave them existence. What ingratitude! Christ gave them life and all they had. Yet they turned on Him.

Christ's Compassion for Satan

We need to go back before the war broke out and see what led up to it. The first thing to note is all that Christ did for Lucifer. It's incredible what He gave him. Lucifer, meaning "the shining one," stood at God's throne as the "anointed guardian cherub" (Ezekiel 28:14). Like Christ (see Revelation 22:16), he was called "a morning star" (Isaiah 14:12). Imagine what this means. Christ created Lucifer as much like Himself as He could. We might call him a look-alike. In fact He was the "foremost in revealing God's purposes to the universe"[1] until pride got the better of him. This means He knew better than anyone how God is and acts. He had no excuse for doubting the One in whose throne presence he was honored to live.

13

Lucifer was endowed with special abilities to carry out the noblest of all work. He was given every opportunity, far beyond any other angel. He "held a high office in heaven, possessing a throne radiant with light."[2] To one so blessed rebellion is inexplicable. How could he treat Christ with such contempt? He acted like a spoiled kid! Christ gave Lucifer every privilege, even his own throne, and created him as much like Himself as He could, and anointed him to be His chief spokesperson in revealing His purposes to other created beings. Never has anyone been so remarkably endowed and so privileged!

Why Did He Rebel?

It's a great puzzle why one so privileged should be so ungrateful. Why did Lucifer rebel? Why did he become the devil? "You said in your heart, 'I will ascend to heaven; I will raise my throne above the stars of God; I will sit enthroned on the mount of assembly, on the utmost heights of the sacred mountain. I will ascend above the tops of the clouds; I will make myself like the Most High'" (Isaiah14:13, 14). He thought he could become God, sit on God's throne, in spite of the fact that it was Christ who had created him (see John 1:3) and given him everything—given him freedom of choice and a position as the leading guardian cherub at the throne (see Ezekiel 28:14, 15).

Lucifer was the most exalted created being in the universe. He should have been grateful and known that the One who created him was the Creator and not a created being. How many people had Lucifer created? None! He could not even make a blade of grass let alone a universe! So blind is pride.

Quiet Diplomacy

Lucifer's rebellion was not public at first. It started in his mind. That's where all sin begins. That's why Jesus spoke to this in His sermon on the mount (see Matthew 5-7). It's not just the outward act; it's the inward thought. Lucifer was becoming Satan in his mind. He mulled over the position of Christ and became jealous. He wanted to take the throne of the One who had given him his throne.

Councils convened. Angels and Christ pleaded with Lucifer. They pointed to the "justice of the Creator" and to the "sacred, unchanging nature of His law."[3] Apparently Lucifer felt Christ's position was an injustice to himself, and heaven's law unnecessary for him. This was a totally unreasonable conclusion. How could he consider himself equal with his Creator, let alone able to take His place? "To dispute the supremacy of the Son of God, thus impeaching the wisdom and love of the Creator, had become the purpose of the prince of angels."[4] Impeachment of God for all the love He had showered on him? That's the incredible darkness of pride.

Public Announcement

It was time for God the Father to act. "The King of the universe summoned the heavenly hosts before Him, that in their presence He might set forth the true position of His Son and show the relation He sustained to all created beings. The Son of God shared the Father's throne, and the glory of the eternal, self-existent One encircled both."[5] The Father announced that Christ was God. He had created the universe for the Father, and did not exalt Himself, but lived to do the Father's will. How unlike Lucifer. He hadn't created a thing and yet wanted to take the place of his Creator! The contrast was stark and stunning.

Angels burst forth in thunderous praise. The Father's focus was right. To point to Christ as Creator caused angels to sing, to rejoice, to worship. At that time in heaven all true worship came from focusing on their Creator. Satan had nothing comparable to offer. Yet Satan wanted to become God and receive worship while Christ mingled with His angels as a fellow angel. No wonder Michael means one who is like God, a quality Lucifer did not possess. For God is selfless, humble; Lucifer selfish, proud.

Mysterious Secrecy

Leaving his throne, Lucifer mingled with angels. With mysterious secrecy he diffused discontent among them and "concealed his real purpose under an appearance of reverence for God."[6] Here's the first union of the sacred and the profane—a religious veneer to cover a hatred for things religious. Hypocrisy, that's what it was! Satan is master of this strategy. He has used it throughout history, as we'll see in later chapters, and he'll use it in the end-time with great success. Like an undercover agent, he seemed supportive of Christ while distilling doubts about Him—doubts he had angels repeat and make their own. This was seed-sowing time. He looked like God's sower, but the seeds were poison.

Angels don't need law, said Lucifer. They're just as capable as God to use their own wisdom as a sufficient guide. The exaltation of Christ by the Father was an injustice to Lucifer, who thought himself also entitled to reverence and honor. "If this prince of angels could but attain to his true, exalted position, great good would accrue to the entire host of heaven; for it was his object to secure freedom for all."[7] Now that the Father had appointed Christ as an absolute ruler, even the liberty they had so far enjoyed would end. "Such were the subtle deceptions that through the wiles of Lucifer were fast obtaining in the heavenly courts."[8] Yet, while "secretly fomenting discord and rebellion, he with consummate craft caused it to appear as his sole purpose to promote loyalty and to preserve harmony and peace."[9]

Scripture says of Satan, "You were blameless in your ways from the day you were created till wickedness was found in you. Through your widespread trade you were filled with violence" (Ezekiel 28:15, 16). The Hebrew word for "wickedness" is *rekullah,* meaning trading or peddling. As Richard Davidson points out, the "widespread trade" refers to goods or to gossip. Here Satan spreads gossip about God among the angels.[10] Terrorism began with gossip, with slandering the character of God as unjust. So it was on September 11. The view that America is an evil nation was the gossip behind the ghastly attack. The attackers' view of God was wrong too. They thought He condoned the ghastly plunge of humans into the twin towers, killing all passengers and thousands of people in the buildings.

Satan's Last Chance

After the Father announced the true position of Christ, the angels responded. Even rebel angels knew Christ created them. He had given them everything. He wished them nothing but good. They responded in heartfelt worship. How about Satan? For a while "the spirit of evil seemed vanquished; unutterable love thrilled his entire being; his soul went out, in harmony with the sinless worshipers, in love to the Father and the Son. But again he was filled with pride in his own glory. His desire for supremacy returned, and envy of Christ was once more indulged."[11] How dangerous is beauty and position even in a perfect environment and much more so in a sin-cursed world. Angels pleaded with him to come back, that he didn't have a case. "Lucifer was convinced that he was in the wrong."[12] He knew but didn't admit it. He was the first individual in denial, and he threw away his future in the fires of jealousy.

"He nearly reached the decision to return, but pride forbade him. It was too great a sacrifice for one who had been so highly honored to confess that he had been in error, that his imaginations were false, and to yield to the authority which he had been working to prove unjust."[13] Through doubt Satan caused discontent and disaffection and didn't know he was drifting. He was told his destiny if he remained defiant, but he determined to continue.

Satan's Terrorist Move

God bore long with this rebel. "A compassionate Creator, in yearning pity for Lucifer and his followers, was seeking to draw them back from the abyss of ruin into which they were about to plunge. But His mercy was misinterpreted. Lucifer pointed to the long-suffering of God as an evidence of his own superiority, an indication that the King of the universe would yet accede to his terms. If the angels would stand firmly with him, he declared, they could yet gain all that they desired."[14]

Imagine the resplendent Lucifer becoming a devil! It probably took considerable time. He gradually became Satan. Satan silently and seditiously invaded heaven's peace and joy with selfishness. From sin's inception "he was a murderer from the beginning, not holding to the truth, for there is no truth in him. When he lies, he speaks his native language, for he is a liar and the father of lies" (John 8:44). With cunning craft he blamed Christ for the problem. Like a

17

lying politician, he claimed to be a better choice to run Heaven's government. His influence permeated Paradise like cancer.

A third of the angels succumbed to his deception and cast their lot with him. "Satan determined to be first in the councils of heaven, and equal with God. . . . When Satan had succeeded in winning many angels to his side, he took his cause to God, representing that it was the desire of angels that he occupy the position that Christ held."[15] Thirty-three percent is not a majority, but it was a staggering number of perfect beings who owed Christ everything but had become blinded by Satan's deceptions!

Satan denounced loyal angels as deluded slaves. But he was about to make his angels deluded slaves. After Satan assured his followers that he would win because of God's longsuffering, loyal angels persuaded many of his angels to return to Christ. But Satan had another deception. He changed his strategy to get his way. From saying that God was so merciful that they would defeat Him, he now claimed the opposite. God would not take them back. How soon a liar can change his tactic to keep his prey. "The mighty revolter now declared that the angels who had united with him had gone too far to return; that he was acquainted with the divine law, and knew that God would not forgive. He declared that all who should submit to the authority of Heaven would be stripped of their honor, degraded from their position."[16]

He knew this was sheer fabrication! It was false! He almost returned himself. He knew that "if he had been willing to return to God, acknowledging the Creator's wisdom, and satisfied to fill the place appointed him in God's great plan, he would have been reinstated in his office."[17] He must keep his angels through deception. He held out to them a brighter future of freedom, and that carried the day. He was not interested in their freedom. He was about to make them slaves forever. He was in this battle for what he could get, not for what he could give. He didn't care if these angels lost their last chance to return. What did that matter to him? He didn't care about those who followed him. He cared only about himself. Angels were disposable. He had no compassion for any of them. He only used them to advance his ambition. In time he became callous, cold, calculating, and cruel. He flung his full fury at Christ in his bid to oust Him. His angels were trapped. Satan is the first terrorist. He hijacked a third of the angels, telling them there was no way to return, that God would not accept them. He imprisoned them within his terrorist movement that hurtles through time to plunge into eternal extinction.

Terrorism and False Theology

So terrorism began with false theology. Through character defamation Satan hoped to unseat God from His throne and take His place. To do this he had to focus on God's alleged injustice, claiming that it held angels back from their true created potential. Who cares if He is Creator—if He is also unjust? No rebel angel changed sides. They all believed Satan, so powerful is gossip. Character assassination—that's what it was. It worked. And the struggle continues based upon a lie. Doubt is so powerful that even perfect angels can be blinded to the truth. Satan's terrorist strategy was to deflect attention away from Christ as Creator by questioning His justice. This is the first issue of cosmic terrorism. It worked in heaven and works on earth. Satan claims Christ hadn't leveled with them. He's keeping angels back from their destiny. Totally ignored is the fact that Christ created intelligent angels with the ability to even question His justice—the epitome of freedom!

Satan, a created being, owed everything to Christ, yet wanted to take His place. How foolish. It's like trying to take your mom's authority, as if you gave her birth instead of the other way around. But it's worse than that, for Christ is God! Satan is only a created being. How could he be omnipresent with all creation? How could he uphold all creation through an omnipotence he did not possess? How could he be omniscient when he did not even know where his rebellion was leading? How could he be eternal when he was a created being?

Mournfully come the words "How have you fallen from heaven, O morning star, son of the dawn! You have been cast down to the earth, you who once laid low the nations! You said in your heart, 'I will ascend to heaven; I will raise my throne above the stars of God;

I will sit enthroned on the mount of the assembly, on the utmost heights of the sacred mountain. I will ascend above the tops of the clouds; I will make myself like the Most High'" (Isaiah 14:12-14). Satan wanted to take Christ's place. He wanted to be like Him in position, not in character. There's no servant-leadership in his scheme. This look-alike wanted power for selfish reasons, like so many who have fallen to pride ever since. No wonder, millennia later, he urged Christ in the wilderness to fall down and worship him! (see Matthew 4:8, 9). In last-day events he'll ask you to do it too. Whether you will or not has everything to do with understanding the issues we look at in the next two chapters.

---

[1] Ellen G. White, *The Desire of Ages,* (Mountain View, Calif.: Pacific Press Pub. Assn., 1940), p. 758.

[2] *The Seventh-day Adventist Bible Commentary,* Ellen G. White comments (Washington, D.C.: Review and Herald Pub. Assn., 1953-1957), vol. 7, p. 973.

[3] White, *Patriarchs and Prophets* (Mountain View, Calif.: Pacific Press Pub. Assn., 1958), p. 36.

[4] *Ibid.*

[5] *Ibid.*

[6] Ibid., p. 37.

[7] *Ibid.*

[8] *Ibid.*

[9] *Ibid.,* p. 38.

[10] Richard M. Davidson, "Cosmic Metanarrative for the Coming Millennium," *Journal of the Adventist Theological Society,* vol. 11, Nos. 1-2, Spring-Autumn, 2000, p. 108.

[11] White, *Patriarchs and Prophets,* p. 37.

[12] *Ibid.,* p. 39.

[13] *Ibid.*

[14] *Ibid.,* pp. 39, 40.

[15] *The Seventh-day Adventist Bible Commentary,* Ellen G. White comments, vol. 7, p. 972.

[16] White, *Patriarchs and Prophets,* p. 40.

[17] *Ibid.,* p. 39.

ATTACK AGAINST THE CREATOR

The terrorist attack against Christ at God's throne in heaven's sanctuary was the beginning of a war that continues the same strategy. It calls into question God's justice and does so at the very heart of religion in holy places. We'll see this in the history of ancient Israel and Judah, the Jews in the time of Christ, the Papacy during the Dark Ages, the Medieval Crusaders' campaign against the Muslims, and the attack of Muslims on Christians, with the latter in principle the same as the September 11 attack. These all give insight into final struggles in last-day events. We'll take these up in subsequent chapters.

Our story begins on Planet Earth at creation. Satan watched the process with fiendish fascination. He saw how Christ gave everything to humans. He saw them spend their first full day of life with the Creator. He saw how happy they were to be with Christ, and how happy Christ was to be with them. He must break that dependent relationship. He must bring ruin to humans and to nature. We take up his attack on Creation itself in this chapter, his attack on humans in the next. We note the vital connection of these attacks with last-day events; war against the Creator is a major focus in final events. Finally we'll provide answers to Satan's end-time attacks.

The Creation Story

Some biblical critics believe that a number of writers wrote the book of Genesis; this is called the multiple source theory. Others toss out the Creation and Fall stories as mere myths (Bultmann) or sagas

(Barth), neither being historical. Opposed to both views, biblical students have found that the Genesis creation story is a carefully crafted account of how life came into being on Planet Earth, and must be the work of one writer. It's important that Scripture opens with the words "In the beginning God created the heavens and the earth" (Genesis 1:1). Here's the truth Satan wants to eradicate. If he can cause doubt in human minds that God created their first ancestors, then he's well on the way to breaking their dependent relationship with Him. This is the second issue in cosmic terrorism. He knows well how powerful is this dependence. For a long time he depended on God, who gave him everything he was and had, but later he twisted this to mean he lacked freedom, saying God is unjust to hold him back.

As Gordon J. Wenhem points out in the *Word Biblical Commentary,* "the material of chapters 1-11 is markedly different from that in chapter 12 onward. The opening chapters have a universal perspective dealing with all mankind. . . . Chapters 12-50, on the other hand, deal almost exclusively with Israelite concerns."[1] That's important because it places the creation record at the beginning of the human race and the Sabbath as a universal holy day and not just a day for Israel, as so many claim. As Jesus said in Mark 2:27, "the Sabbath was made for man."

Two Names for God

Two Hebrews words are used for God in the Creation record. The word *Elohiym* is found in chapter 1 (31 times) and chapter 2 (eight times); and *Yaweh* is found in chapter 2 (three times) and *Yayweh Elohiym* in chapter 2 (five times). *Elohiym* is the universal God, the one who is omnipresent, the transcendent God. By contrast, *Yahweh* is the God of the covenant, the imminent one, God up close. Genesis 1 presents the transcendent God who speaks everything into existence on each Creation day: "And *Elohiym* said" (verses 3, 6, 9, 11, 14, 20, 24, 26). The narrative structure highlights the third and the sixth days of Creation with a double announcement of the divine word "And God said" (verses 9, 11, 24, 26).

Genesis 2 presents the God up close, who stoops down and

forms Adam and Eve. In Genesis 1 the word "create" is *bara;* in Genesis 2 the word "form" is *yatsar.* The first is done by speaking from the transcendent heights; the second is done with a hands-on approach. There's a distinction between creating everything for humans and creating humans themselves. God comes close to create humans. This distinction is one that evolution of humans from animals doesn't provide.

A Correspondence Between the Two Creation Accounts

There's a correspondence between Genesis 1 and 2, and the number 7 dominates. The Hebrew words in both are multiples of 7. Thus 1:1 has seven words, 1:2 has 14 words (2 x 7), 2:1-3 have 35 words (5 x 7). Could this set the stage for the seven days? There's a correspondence between days 1-3 with days 4-6, where the first three give the areas formed by *Elohiym* and days 4-6 give the days when *Elohiym* filled those areas with His creative works.[2] Wenhem charts them as follows:

Day 1	Light	Day 4	Luminaries
Day 2	Sky	Day 5	Birds and Fish
Day 3	Land	Day 6	Animals and Man
	(Plants)		(Plants for food)
Day 7		Sabbath[3]	

So in days 1-3 *Elohiym forms* the places to be *filled* in days 4-6. And this carefully crafted structure moves to a climax—not with the creation of humans on day 6, but with the gift of the Sabbath on day 7. The narrative ends with the Sabbath in 2:1. (The chapter divisions came long after the time of writing.)

The Sabbath as the Climax of Creation

Clearly the Sabbath is not only a day of rest given to all humans by *Elohiym,* it's also the climax of the Creation story in Genesis 1. Everything in the forming and filling leads to the Sabbath, which is God's chosen memorial of Creation. With the mention of the Sabbath the word for God changes to *Yahweh,* the God up close. On the six days *Elohiym* spoke things into existence in space, but on the seventh day *Yahweh* comes to be with humans in time—up close. A work *in time* by a God up close speaks volumes of the distinction of the Sabbath compared to the works *in space* on the other days. Christ spoke everything into existence for humans. He gave them gifts in space. But on the Sabbath He gave Himself in time, to be their Creator up close. In the same way He would later come to Planet Earth "to tabernacle" among us (John 1:14). This is Immanuel, "God with us" (Matthew 1:23). Sabbathkeeping is spending time with Christ up close!

In Genesis 2:2, 3 the seventh day is mentioned three times. Wenhem rightly notes that the "threefold mention of the seventh day, each time in a sentence of seven Hebrew words, draws attention to the special character of the Sabbath. In this way form and content emphasize the distinctiveness of the seventh day."[4]

Because the worship of sun and moon was prevalent from early times, God guided Moses to use the words "greater light" and "lesser light" in place of the sun and moon respectively (Genesis 1:16). Only the Creator-God is worthy of worship, not His creation. Not only does Satan want worship instead of Christ but he inspires all worship that is not worship of Christ.

Divine Commentary on Creation

John 1:1-3 is a divine commentary on Genesis 1. "In the beginning was the Word, and the Word was with God, and the Word was God. He was with God in the beginning. Through him all things were made; without him nothing was made that has been made." Verse 14 says, "The Word became flesh and made his dwelling among us. We have seen his glory, the glory of the One and Only, who came from the Father, full of grace and truth." Genesis 1 and John 1 take us back to the beginning of Creation on Planet Earth, and show clearly that the *Elohiym* of Genesis 1 is the Christ of John 1.

Other New Testaments texts corroborate this connection. "He is the image of the invisible God, the firstborn over all creation. For by him all things were created: things in heaven and on earth, visible and invisible, whether thrones or powers or rulers or authorities;

all things were created by him and for him. He is before all things, and in him all things hold together" (Colossians 1:15-17). Christ not only created everything in heaven and on earth, but in His continued providence He keeps the world and appoints powers and authorities. God in the last days "has spoken to us by his Son, whom he appointed heir of all things, and through whom he made the universe. The Son is the radiance of God's glory and the exact representation of his being, sustaining all things by his powerful word. After he had provided purification for sins, he sat down at the right hand of the Majesty in heaven" (Hebrews 1:2, 3). Christ created more than the heavens and the earth. He created the universe with populated planets, including angels in heaven! And after Calvary, when He returned from His service of humility and suffering on earth, He ascended to the right hand of God and occupies the throne with the Father.

Satan's Studied Strategy

The Creator-Redeemer Christ is the object of Satan's continuing terrorist attacks. He schemes to hide the fact that Christ is Creator and Redeemer—that the victorious Christ, who conquered him at Calvary, is on the throne of heaven in the Most Holy Place of heaven's sanctuary. This is the throne Satan can never occupy, yet one he still aspires to take by force in a final desperate war against Christ. (See chapter 14.) Satan blindly thinks a created being can force a coup by having sheer numbers on his side. Such is the folly of depending on creaturely might. He totally ignores that only a Creator-Redeemer can be seated on that throne. Satan has no qualifications.

But Satan has a counterfeit plan of creation through natural selection, and a counterfeit plan of salvation through a system of human works—the basis of every heathen religion and of many professed Christians too. He fiendishly works to blot out the truth about Christ as Creator by natural evolution, and the truth about Christ as Redeemer by a system of human works to earn salvation. He offers Sunday, his creation, to take the place of the Sabbath, for he knows "the Son of Man is Lord even of the Sabbath" (Mark 2:28). All three constitute an outright and subtle attack on Christ to oust Him from the hearts of humans. That much he is well qualified to accomplish.

No wonder the cry goes forth to the world in the end-time to worship Christ as Creator in the context of the everlasting gospel. "Worship him who made the heavens, the earth, the sea and the springs of water" (Revelation 14:7). These words come right out of the Sabbath commandment (Exodus 20:11). The first two chapters of Genesis, the beginning of human history, contain the subject matter of Satan's final attack on Planet Earth.

Evolution as Satan's Counterfeit of Creation

We'll wait to examine Satan's counterfeit religion in which human works take the place of the work of Christ when we come to its presentation in Daniel and Revelation. We turn now to his counterfeit creation in evolutionary theories. I have written elsewhere about evolution, and its problems brought to light by molecular biology, the function of DNA, complexity at the cellular level, the human eye, absence of evidence in the fossil record, punctuated equilibrium (instant arrival of a species), and the Cambrian explosion (sudden appearance of complex animal groups).[5] I'll not repeat that material here, but focus on evolution as a human response to the evils found in nature.

Who put those evils in nature? Who deconstructs creation with bioengineering? Who pushes genetic engineering? Who desolates the good creation by producing predators and pests? Through the centuries Satan works overtime in the lab to ruin the creation of Christ. Every biological and chemical agent comes stamped with his name. Anthrax and other deadly weapons come from his inspiration. Yes, he works through human agents, too, but all evil in nature is a result of sin he introduced into Planet Earth, and he continues to work through tempest and tornado, through so-called natural disasters with their devastation. He is the first and ultimate terrorist, and the so-called acts of God are really acts of the devil.

Paul says, "The whole creation has been groaning as in the pains of childbirth right up to the present time" (Romans 8:22). This is the nature that Christ pronounced "very good" at Creation week (Genesis 1:31). Something has gone terribly wrong. Let's pull back the curtain and see what Satan is up to behind the scenes. Look at this divine commentary and its end-time significance. "While appearing to the children of men as a great physician who can heal all their maladies, he will bring disease and disaster, until populous cities are reduced to ruin and desolation. Even now he is at work. In accidents and calamities by sea and by land, in great conflagrations, in fierce tornadoes and terrific hailstorms, in tempests, floods, cyclones, tidal waves, and earthquakes, in every place and in a thousand forms, Satan is exercising his power. He sweeps away the ripening harvest, and famine and distress follow. He imparts to the air a deadly taint, and thousands perish by the pestilence. These visitations are to become more and more frequent and disastrous. Destruction will be upon both man and beast. 'The earth mourneth and fadeth away,' 'The haughty people . . . do languish. The earth also is defiled under the inhabitants thereof; because they have transgressed the laws, changed the ordinance, broken the everlasting covenant' Isaiah 24:4, 5."[6]

Note Satan's strategy. It's one he uses over and over. He causes the problem and then comes up with an assumed solution. But the solution is always to continue the attack on Christ. So he produces evil in nature, wrecking Christ's good creation, bringing contempt on the Creator. His solution is evolution. He says God couldn't have created this kind of world (which of course He didn't), so creation is the work of nature itself. Admittedly this distances the Creator from His creation. But that's the end-game. He inspires humans to distance the Creator from such a creation, and thereby distance the Creator from created humans. His goal is to break creaturely dependence upon the Creator. This is the third issue in cosmic terrorism.

Darwin's God: Evolution and the Problem of Evil, by Cornelius G. Hunter, is the best book I know that looks at evolution in the light of evil in nature.[7] Hunter notes that Darwin wondered how a God who is infinitely wise, powerful, and good could possibly be the author of nature with its evil. Darwin puzzled over the waste of tons of pollen each year, that some species are ill-adapted to their environment, that parasites feed on their victims, that ants make slaves of other ants. Darwin's letter to a friend spoke to these problems: "What a book a devil's chaplain might write on the clumsy, wasteful, blundering, low, and horribly cruel works of nature."[8]

Darwin should have known better. Even though one can question his theology professors at Cambridge University, he had access to Scripture just as readily as he had access to nature, and the scientific method requires that he give both their proper place in objective research. Creation as good followed by the Fall gives clear insight into the cosmic war in Scripture. But Darwin failed to grasp this and apply it to the problems he noted in nature. He should have seen evil in nature as evidence of its fallen state, and attributed the evils in nature to Satan, the root cause of all evil. But he didn't.

Rather, Darwin was a product of his time. The Enlightenment had long ago removed God from His world. Rationalism exalts humans and their ability to reason. In a world in which God and His revelation are banished, reasoning powers reign supreme. In Victorian times a deistic view of God, removed from the world of nature, was considered appropriate to His benevolence. History shows that reason presents humans as the crowning work of evolution. But divine revelation presents the Sabbath as the crowning work of Creation. Humans were not made from animals; they were made for God. Darwin didn't know, but could have.

Darwin Influenced by John Milton

One of Darwin's favorite books was Milton's *Paradise Lost*. At least the title should have made him think. Paradise was lost, and hence the presence of evil in nature. He had a well-worn copy of *Paradise Lost* with him for his five-year global voyage on the H. M. S. *Beagle*. Both Milton and Darwin wrestled with the problem of evil, Milton with moral evil and Darwin with natural evil, and both found a solution in distancing God from evil. Milton's book had a great impact on Darwin. It helped him see the need for distancing God from evil, and he even went beyond Milton in so doing.[9] He ended up dismissing the fact that God had anything to do with creation. He rejected the God of creation for a mechanistic view of nature in harmony with Newton's mechanistic worldview. Yet this went against the popular evidences for God's existence from nature, to which we now turn.

How Theologians Viewed Nature

It's well known that medieval theology attempted to prove God from nature. This includes the cosmological argument (everything has a cause that goes back to a first cause, God) taught by Thomas Aquinas (1225, 1274) in his theological system *(Summa Theologica)*.[10] This was challenged by David Hume (1711-1776) in his *Treatise of Human Nature (*1739),[11] and Immanuel Kant (1724-1804) in his *Critique of Pure Reason* (1781).[12] Darwin's discoveries in nature in the nineteenth century, to him, called into question the fact that there are evidences for God in nature. He wrote to a friend, "There seems to me too much misery in the world. I cannot persuade myself that a beneficent and omnipotent God would have designedly created the [parasitic wasp] with the express intention of their feeding within the living bodies of caterpillars, or that the cat should play with mice."[13] Darwin failed to factor in the Fall after the creation of the world, for there are as many evidences for the cosmic controversy in nature as there are evidences for God. But even in its pre-Fall state, nature was a mere reflection of the Creator. "In the One 'altogether lovely,' we behold Him, of whom all beauty of earth and heaven is but a dim reflection."[14] Whether Darwin knew it, Satan was the one inspiring and leading him to distance God from nature, and thereby distance Christ from humans.

The teleological argument (argument from design, with the idea of purpose: *telos* in Greek means goal) was the most popular of the arguments for God's existence. Aquinas presented this argument in his *Summa Theologica*.[15] This argument goes back to the Stoic philosopher Anaxagoras, with more extended discussions in Plato's dialogues *Timaeus* and *Philebus*.[16] Hume and Kant critiqued the argument, but we here focus on others who influenced Darwin. William Paley (1743-1805), who taught at Cambridge University, became a famous writer, and wrote *A View of the Evidences of Christianity* (1794) that was required reading to enter Cambridge University until the twentieth century. Paley was not an original thinker. He plagiarized but had the gift of communication. His book influenced generations including Charles Darwin. He was the one who popularized the famous watchmaker argument: The intricate machinery, the design of the watch, and how it works could not have come about by chance, and hence it assumed a watchmaker. Just so in nature—there are many evidences of design that presuppose a God.[17] But Darwin gave up Paley's design argument when he discovered the law of natural selection.[18]

Darwin Influenced by Sir Charles Lyell

Why did Darwin make the change? Along with *Paradise Lost* he took Sir Charles Lyell's (1797-1875) first volume of *Principles of Geology* (1830-1832) with him on his H. M. S. *Beagle* voyage. Lyell called into question the view of "catastrophism," which includes the Flood story. In its place he suggested the view of "uniformitarianism." In other words, he gave up the destruction of a world for a view that there had been no such interruption. Darwin accepted this new view,[19] not realizing its prediction in Scripture. "First of all, you must understand that in the last days scoffers will come, scoffing and following their own evil desires. They will say, 'Where is this "coming" he promised? Ever since our fathers died, everything goes on as it has since the beginning of creation'" (2 Peter 3:3, 4). Here's a direct prophecy about uniformitarianism being an end-time fact. Again Darwin, a theologically trained Cambridge University student, did not consult Scripture. He was removing God from His Word just as much as He was removing Him from His world.

Darwin Influenced by Thomas Malthus

Thomas Malthus (1766-1834) was the next to influence Darwin. In his *Essay on the Principle of Population,* which Darwin read nearly two years after his *Beagle* voyage, he gave his famous principle about population increases placing an intolerable burden upon resources of the environment: that human beings are not immune from this universal law of nature, which leads to poverty, disease, starvation, and war. Although the Anglican clergyman Malthus looked at this in the tradition of natural theology, Darwin (as a firm believer in Paley's view of design) took it out of this context and applied it to nature left to itself without God. The notion of struggle is what Darwin received from Malthus. The struggle, in Darwin's thinking, led to the principle of "natural selection," or the "survival of the fittest."

Malthus referred to breeders producing various modifications of form and color. Darwin picked this up and posited that nature did the same work as a breeder. In doing so, Darwin unwittingly attributed to nature a causation agent. He removed God as the cause, and placed the cause in nature. He assigned intelligence to nature equivalent to human breeders. He ended up critiquing Paley's design argument by exchanging chance for purpose. So things are not uncaused, but unpredictable, when specifying effects.[20] How intelligent is this?

The Problem of Distancing God From Nature

Milton distanced God from moral evil as Darwin distanced Him from natural evil. Kant, the most influential philosopher to impact subsequent philosophy, rejected the arguments for God, but at least gave some assent to the moral proof for the "existence of a moral author of the world," i.e., the existence of a God. He could even call God "a moral cause of the world." But it is the practical reason of humans that discerns this fact, for God can never be known as He is in Himself, only as He appears to humans.[21] How much better if Kant had gone to Scripture and seen the reality of God as He is in Himself given in divine revelation as the moral lawgiver (e.g., Exodus 20)!

At the end of the day, without Scripture and left to reason alone, Kant attributes moral laws not to a moral lawgiver (divine or otherwise) but to an imperative of duty. He ends up with a very subjective view of the moral condition, which is not a proof of God's existence but an evidence of an internal moral imperative. For Kant, reason is universal and hence religious belief is not necessary to act morally. It's not God who makes a duty moral, but the universalism of the duty that makes it divine. Humans are capable of moral actions that are a moral duty. In other words, a categorical duty can be done by autonomous humans without God's help. But if that's so, what's the necessity of postulating a transcendent cause? Why is there any need of God?[22]

Milton, Darwin, and Kant all distanced God from humans more

than they should have, and all of them did so because they placed reason above revelation. Evolution is thought of as scientific fact, but few see it as a worldview that has something to say about God. It's a theodicy that says God is distant from the evil in nature. That's what drives the theory of evolution. Without reference to God, what would evolution have to present? Its presuppositions expose it to be dependent upon metaphysics, and not just science, even if its science was persuasive. Milton's theodicy has God as all-good rather than all-powerful. He is virtuous and not dictatorial, and thus this lesser God is more worthy of worship.[23] But the "argument that God becomes all the more worthy of our reverence easily gives way to his loss of relevance."[24]

So Darwin's God was not necessary. Along with other Victorians he accepted Gnostic views of God removed from nature, for spirit is good and matter is evil. For Gnostics, Christ couldn't create the world nor could He become a human and suffer at Calvary. Hume and Darwin sought to give a reason for natural evil, but did so by proposing a distant God to keep Him from the responsibility of evil. It's this view of God that constitutes the basic metaphysical purpose that fuels the quest of evolutionary theory. As spirit and matter are kept separate in Gnosticism, so religion and science are kept separate in evolution.[25]

The Challenge of Science to Evolution

I will not repeat the scientific questions of evolution I have previously written (see footnote 5), but pause to first note the biochemical challenge to evolution. In his book *Darwin's Black Box,* Michael J. Behe, professor of biochemistry, observes that since the 1950s biochemistry has been examining the workings of life at the molecular level, something Darwin didn't know. "It was once expected that the basis of life would be exceedingly simple. That expectation has been smashed. Vision, motion, and other biological functions have proven to be no less sophisticated than television cameras and automobiles. Science has made enormous progress in understanding how the chemistry of life works, but the elegance and complexity of biological systems at the molecular level have paralyzed science's attempt to explain their origins."[26]

Now to another problem. How do you get from a single nut to a complex computer? It takes a lot of information to create a sophisticated IBM. Likewise, how can mutations or natural selection create new genetic information? Phillip E. Johnson, in his book *The Wedge of Truth: Splitting the Foundations of Naturalism,* notes that random mutations in genes are inactive and hence not subject to natural selection, so how can they be causing massive increases in genetic information to make evolutionary development work? [27] He refers to Lee Spetner's book *Not by Chance! Shattering the Modern Theory of Evolution,* which says the adaptive mutations that Darwinists cite as information-creating actually can experience a loss of information. For example, this occurs when a mutation makes a bacterium resistant to antibiotics, doing so by disabling its capacity to metabolize a certain chemical. Johnson likens this to hitting the case of a sputtering radio to cause a loose wire to reconnect. "But no one would expect to build a better radio, much less a television set, by accumulating such changes." [28] Nor would this help a nut toward becoming a computer.

The Challenge to Seventh-day Adventists

It's significant that Darwin actually had his 230-page *Origin of Species* (1859) written by 1844, the date when God called out the Seventh-day Adventist Church to take the first angel's message to the world, a call "to every nation, tribe, language and people" to "worship him who made the heavens, the earth, the sea and the springs of water" (Revelation 14:6, 7). God was ready to use a movement to call the world to remember the Creator-Christ and to worship Him, and the phrase "who made the heavens, the earth, the sea and the springs of water" is a repetition of part of the Sabbath commandment (Exodus 20:11).

It's vital that we sense our destiny in these last days. In a time when people have removed God from His world and His Word, we are commissioned to proclaim the truth as it is in Jesus, to point to Him as our Creator-Redeemer, to rejoice in His gift of salvation and His weekly Sabbaths, and to praise Him in heartfelt adoration. By contrast, Satan's counterfeit religion is a Christless one: it gives praise to nature instead of nature's Creator, it gives praise to human works instead of the works of Christ, it presents other days of worship instead of the Sabbath.

Scripture presents Christ as the God up close, "Immanuel," "God with us" (Matthew 1:23). The greatest evidence of creation was not in Eden. It's in Bethlehem. When Jesus was born of Mary through the Holy Spirit we have a creative act of God in history, born in Bethlehem in Judea, during the time of King Herod (Matthew 2:1). If God can create the Second Adam, the God-man Jesus, then creation of the first Adam was much easier. Evolution has nothing comparable. Its process, allegedly over billions of years, takes place before human history. It merely leads up to the beginning of human history, and hence it doesn't take place during human history, and so cannot be historically checked as can the birth of Jesus. Evolution can only demonstrate microevolution (small changes) and read this onto imaginary macro changes (evolution). Science can only help in the micro documentation; the macro is philosophy, not science. By contrast, the incarnation of Jesus is a macro kind of creation compared to the creation of Adam and Eve. Macroevolution is a theory that should be classified as philosophy, not science; a theory, not a fact. Macrocreation is a historical fact, not theory. There is a difference.

Evolution is really a theodicy, an attempt to explain natural evil by natural means rather than grasping the cosmic terrorism of Satan's deconstruction of nature. Moral and natural evil is his destructive work, the opposite to Christ's creative work. Satan pushes this counterfeit view of creation in order to distance Christ from His creative work, to distance humans from their Creator, and to do away with the Fall. For if humans are the product of an evolutionary development, then they are the pinnacle of the process. And if they can be moral in their own power, apart from God, then the process is allegedly upward without any need of salvation. There's no need of Christ as Redeemer, no need of Calvary to save us, no need of Christ's re-creative work within human lives, and no need of a future resurrection—for, like Kant, so many believe that humans are immortal. By contrast, God creates in history itself, as seen in the evidence of changed lives: for "if anyone is in Christ, he is a new creation; the old has gone, the new has come!" (2 Corinthians 5:17). Christ's creative work in humans climaxes at His second coming. "For since death came through a man, the resurrection of the dead comes also through a man. For as in Adam all die, so in Christ all will be made alive" (1 Corinthians 15:21).

When Judah forgot their Creator-God, Christ said to them, " 'Behold, I will create a new heavens and a new earth. The former things will not be remembered, nor will they come to mind. . . . The wolf and the lamb will feed together, and the lion will eat straw like the ox. . . . They will neither harm nor destroy on all my holy mountain,' says the Lord. This is what the Lord says: 'Heaven is my throne, and the earth is my footstool. Where is the house you will build for me? Where will my resting place be? Has not my hand made all these things, and so they came into being?' declares the Lord. 'This is the one I esteem: he who is humble and contrite in spirit and trembles at my word'" (Isaiah 65:17–66:2).

The Word presents Christ as the Creator who will re-create the heavens and the earth. There will be no more predators, and natural evil will be gone forever. It's this same Creator who showed His love to human rebels, carried their sins to the cross, and died to rescue them, to re-create humans into His image, to resurrect and glorify them, and to re-create a new earth one day for them. This is the Christ of the Word. How tragic that human reason led Darwin and others to miss this glorious revelation! How sad that they distanced God from the world, the very One who has the answer to the moral and natural evil of the world by being the God up close.

No wonder we are admonished, "None but those who have fortified the mind with the truths of the Bible will stand through the last great conflict."[29] We receive the Living Word through the Written Word. Happy are those that tremble at God's Word, for they will know that whatever troubles come in the end-time, "Even though I walk through the valley of the shadow of death, I will fear no evil, for you are with me; your rod and your staff they comfort me" (Psalm 23:4). Christ promised, "Never will I leave you; never will I forsake you" (Hebrews 13:5), for "surely I am with you always, to the very end of the age" (Matthew 28:20).

[1] Gordon J. Wenhem, *Word Biblical Commentary: Genesis 1-15* (Waco, Tex: Word, 1987), vol. 1, p. xxii.

[2] *Ibid.,* pp. 6, 7

[3] *Ibid.,* p. 7. Derek Kidner in Genesis (gen. ed. D. J. Wiseman, *Tyndale Old Testament Commentaries* [Downers Grove, Il.: InterVarsity, 1967]), p. 46) arranges the six days as follows:

Form		Fullness	
Day 1	Light and Dark	Day 4	Lights of Day and Night
Day 2	Sea and Sky	Day 5	Creatures of Water and Air
Day 3	Fertile Earth	Day 6	Creatures of Land

[4] Wenhem, *Word Biblical Commentary: Genesis 1-15,* p. 7.

[5] For a fuller examination of this topic see Norman R. Gulley, *Christ Is Coming!* (Hagerstown, Md.: Review and Herald Pub. Assn., 1998), pp. 375-409; "Evolution: A Theory in Crisis," *Creation, Catastrophe, and Calvary,* ed. John Templeton Baldwin (Hagerstown, Md.: Review and Herald Pub. Assn., 2000), pp. 124-158.

[6] Ellen G. White, *Counsels on Health* (Mountain View, Calif.: Pacific Press Pub. Assn., 1951), p. 461.

[7] Cornelius G. Hunter, *Darwin's God: Evolution and the Problem of Evil* (Grand Rapids: Brazos Press, 2001).

[8] Quoted from Adrian Desmond and James Moore, *Darwin* (New York,: W. W. Norton, 1991), p. 449; Hunter, p. 10.

[9] Quoted from Charles Darwin, *The Autobiography of Charles Darwin* (New York: Harcourt, Brace and Company, 1958), p. 85; *Hunter,* pp. 11, 12.

[10] Thomas Aquinas, *Summa Theologica,* trans. Fathers of the Dominican Province (Westminster, Md.: Christian Classics, 1981), vol. 1, pp. 13, 14, where he spells out five arguments for God's existence, causation being the second.

[11] David Hume, *Enquiries Concerning Human Understanding,* ed. L. A. Selby-Bigge, 3rd ed., rev. by P. H. Nidditch (Oxford, London: Clarendon, 1975), Section IV.

[12] Immanuel Kant, *Critique of Pure Reason,* trans. and ed. Paul Guyer and Allen W. Wood (Cambridge: Cambridge University Press, 1998), pp 417-421, 507-518.

[13] Quoted in Stephen Jay Gould, "Nonmoral Nature," in *Hen's Teeth and Horse's Toes* (New York: W. W. Norton, 1983), Hunter, p. 12.

[14] White, *Education* (Mountain View, Calif.: Pacific Press Pub. Assn., 1952), p. 192.

[15] Thomas Aquinas, *Summa Theologica,* pp. 13, 14. This is his fifth argument.

[16] Michael Palmer, *The Question of God: An Introduction and Sourcebook* (New York: Routledge, 2001), p. 93. For those wishing to dig deeper into the different arguments, this is a primary source.

[17] *Ibid.,* p. 96.

[18] *Ibid.,* p. 126.

[19] *Ibid.,* p. 119.

[20] *Ibid.,* pp. 119-125.

[21] Immanuel Kant, *Critique of Judgment,* trans. Werner S. Pluhar (Indianapolis: Hackett Publishing, 1987), pp. 336-353. Kant also takes up the moral argument in other works, such as *Groundwork of the Metaphysic of Morals* (trans. H. J. Paton in *The Moral Law* [London: Hutchinson and Co., 1972], p. 75); *Critique of Practical Reason,* ed. Mary Gregor Cambridge: Cambridge University Press, 1997), pp. 102-111; and *Religion Within the Limits of Reason Alone,* (trans. T. M. Greene and H. Hudson [Chicago: 1934]).

[22] Palmer, pp. 235-250.

[23] Hunter, pp. 137-146.

[24] *Ibid.,* p. 153.

[25] *Ibid.,* pp. 127–134.

[26] Michael J. Behe, *Darwin's Black Box: The Biochemical Challenge to Evolution* (New York: Simon and Schuster, 1996), p. x.

[27] Phillip E. Johnson, *The Wedge of Truth: Splitting the Foundations of Naturalism,* (Downers Grove, Ill.: InterVarsity, 2000), pp. 41–46.

[28] *Ibid.,* p. 47.

[29] White, *The Great Controversy* (Mountain View, Calif.: Pacific Press Pub. Assn., 1950), pp. 593, 594.

POWER OF DECEPTION

S atan and his angels were thrown out of heaven. Not a good start to freedom, for sure. Yes, they were angry. Seemed that they now had more evidence for Christ's injustice. He cast them out. What's wrong in wanting to better oneself, to gain more freedom, to live beyond God's law and plan one's own destiny? Thoughts crowded angel minds. They all hated Christ now. They were united in their war against Him.

Back in heaven angels knew of Christ's plan to create Planet Earth and place humans on it. That invited attention by this warring mob. Why not ruin what Christ did? Yes, that would be a good way to get back at Him. And just think, this new planet offered hope of obtaining on earth what they had lost in heaven. If only Satan could take over this world, win all of its citizens to his side, and get the 100 percent following that he failed to achieve in heaven, *then* God would have to take notice. Then Satan could use this world as his staging ground to take on the universe. This way he might still get back to heaven and seat himself on Christ's throne and rule over all the cosmos. Heady stuff indeed. Plans were laid carefully, and the mission was clear. This was a chance too good to miss. This was the only way back. This would keep his campaign alive and give hope to his cause.

All depended on the attack. He must do on earth what he had done in heaven. He must deceive. He would have to appear as a benefactor for these two humans. If he got them both, he would already have 100 percent. Deceiving just Adam and Eve made the outcome more certain compared to heaven. After all, there were myriads of angels there, and it took a long time to get a third to join him. But now there were only two. That should be easy. So Satan mused, itching to destroy Christ's plans for the planet.

Satan Watched Creation

We don't know where Satan was during Creation week. But it's a good bet he observed with fiendish interest. He saw the astonishing power of Christ as He spoke things into existence. He could only whimper by contrast. He had given orders in heaven, and angels delighted to do his bidding. But he never ordered things out of nothing. He couldn't even order life out of things at hand. He may have watched other creative acts of Christ in some far-flung reaches of space. At best he could speak of His power then, never duplicate it. It was different now. He didn't tell of His power anymore. His work was to hide that power from those who need to know about it. His work was the opposite of what it had been. He bent all his energies to disinformation and deception. His campaign instilled discontent and dissatisfaction in heaven. He must continue the same on earth.

"In the happiness and peace of the holy pair in Eden he [Satan] beheld a vision of the bliss that to him was forever lost. Moved by envy, he determined to incite them to disobedience, and bring upon them the guilt and penalty of sin. He would change their love to distrust and their songs of praise to reproaches against their Maker. Thus he would not only plunge these innocent beings into the same misery which he was himself enduring, but would cast dishonor upon God, and cause grief in heaven."[1] Here he goes again. He robbed angels of their joy in heaven, and he schemes to do the same to humans. When one is as unhappy as Satan was, one lashes out to make others unhappy too, for misery likes company. His fiendish delight, which took the edge off his misery, would be to bring misery to these humans, but especially to bring heartache to Christ.

He puzzled at the Sabbath. He squirmed at the God up close. He remembered when Christ had been up close to Him at the throne. But what's this about a Sabbath, this coming to be with humans? He looked at the three in deep, loving communion and determined that he would change all that, too. He heard that the Sabbath would be a weekly appointment. A sacred day in the week. He determined that he would destroy the Sabbath. There was no Sabbath in heaven, for all time had been holy. That is, until he launched his terrorism. Rebellion introduced the unholy in place of the holy, even in the Most Holy Place of heaven's throne room. He loved the unholy; he despised the holy. He determined to cause humans not to discern between the holy and the unholy, between the sacred and the profane. If he could achieve that, they would not want the Sabbath anyway, and they would not want Christ either. His mind was made up. He had a strategy to propose to his angels. In the war room of the enemy, plans were laid to invade the planet in the garden where the first pair lived.

Because this was such a crucial project it must be masked in deepest deception. He tried deception in heaven. It worked well. It was a good tool. No time to experiment now. This was too serious. They had to win this one. They had suffered one defeat. It was crucial that they succeed. If they failed, future plans may be dashed. Everything depended on success. Deception was a valuable asset in the arsenal of these terrorists. It must be used in the garden. So important was the outcome that Satan decided he would personally execute the plan.

Attack in Eden

Satan must choose a time when humans would least expect his visit. He must not alarm them. He must fit into the beauty as naturally as hand in glove. He must be disarming, even reassuring, for Christ had no doubt warned them about him. He was right. "Our first parents were not left without a warning of the danger that threatened them. Heavenly messengers opened to them the history of Satan's fall and his plots for their destruction, unfolding more fully the nature of the divine government, which the prince of evil was trying to overthrow."[2] In fact, "angels had cautioned Eve to beware of separating herself from her husband while occupied in their daily labor in the garden; with him she would be in less danger from temptation than if she were alone."[3] So the Christ who said, "It is not good for the man to be alone" (Genesis 2:18), no doubt said, "It is not good for the woman to be alone either."

She was alone that day, and Satan waited. He chose the most beautiful creature then known, a flying serpent whose skin dazzled with shining gold.[4] That would be his medium. We are not told how he arranged this, how he spoke through it, or whether somehow he had the ability to make himself appear as this serpent. All we know is that the serpent was curled up in the tree of the knowledge of good and evil. For Christ had said, "You are free to eat from any tree in the garden; but you must not eat from the tree of the knowledge of good and evil, for when you eat of it you will surely die" (Genesis 2:16, 17). Satan knew the testing tree, and positioned himself ready to meet the wandering Eve. As a spirit being, Satan may have darted there unnoticed when he saw her walking toward it.

As she wandered near the tree, Christ did not shout out to her and cause her to run away. Creaturely freedom means that God doesn't do that. He allows His intelligent beings to think for themselves, and to be free indeed. Now if Christ had shouted out a warning, it could have saved Him from coming to Calvary to die for human sin. But Christ does not do things to save Himself. He only saves others. How different from Satan, who does not care about others and does everything for himself. Christ was willing to enter the road of sacrifice. That's the price of freedom as seen from His perspective. From Satan's perspective, the price of freedom (so-called) was rebellion and oppression—to grasp it for himself whatever the cost to others. Markedly different, for sure!

Eve was "absorbed in her pleasing task [and] unconsciously wandered from his [Adam's] side. On perceiving that she was alone, she felt an apprehension of danger, but dismissed her fears, deciding that she had sufficient wisdom and strength to discern evil and to withstand it. Unmindful of the angels' caution, she soon found herself gazing with mingled curiosity and admiration upon the forbidden tree. The fruit was very beautiful, and she questioned with herself why God had withheld it from them."[5]

The Psychology of Satan's Temptation

Here was Satan's chance. He asked the question "Did God really say, 'You must not eat from any tree in the garden?'" (Genesis 3:1). An innocent question? So it appeared to Eve. But it came accompanied with masterful presentation and cunning flattery. The serpent spoke "in a musical voice, with subtle praise of her surpassing loveliness; and his words were not displeasing. Instead of fleeing from the spot she lingered wonderingly to hear a serpent speak."[6] What a cunning trap. He was intent on destroying her beauty, yet praised it. He spoke with a musical voice, but was about to rob her of a reason to sing. She fell for the flattery, and it must have made her think this was a very wise serpent indeed! Satan gained his point—to get her to trust him.

"The woman said to the serpent, 'We may eat fruit from the trees in the garden, but God did say, "You must not eat fruit from the tree that is in the middle of the garden, and you must not touch it, or you will die"'" (verse 3). Compare this with what God did say (see Genesis 2:17). She added "touch it" as a means to die. The multiple mistakes of Eve were (1) to brush away her fear of being alone, (2) thinking she was well able to discern by herself, (3) believing she could make it on her own, and (4) adding to God's word.

Think of it. Eve was confronted by two opposing claims. Only one could be true. Her Creator, Christ (see John 1:1-3; Colossians 1:16, 17; Hebrews 1:1, 2), gave her life, her husband, the world to have dominion over, and a beautiful garden. The crafty serpent gave her nothing except a claim that was contrary to Christ's claim. Why would she believe the one who had given her nothing and turn from the One who had given her everything?

Satan gave more than a claim. He countered God's word with apparent evidences. This is what made his counterclaim so powerful, and captured Eve. Look at the steps. The serpent was curled up in the tree "regaling itself with the delicious fruit," and was very much alive.[7] One can hear him say, "Eve, if I a serpent can speak your human language after eating the fruit, think what you, a human, can become—like God. In short, I'm not dead, but have arisen to higher heights!"

The record says, "He himself had eaten of the forbidden fruit, and as a result had acquired the power of speech. And he insinuated that the Lord jealously desired to withhold it from them, lest they should be exalted to equality with Himself."[8]

Satan continued. "God said you will die, but you won't. He said that to keep you from eating the fruit. He doesn't want you to rise to higher heights. This is an assault on your freedom. It keeps you from your full potential. It's unjust. You can become God. Go for it, Eve. Take charge."

"When the woman saw that the fruit of the tree was good for food and pleasing to the eye, and also desirable for gaining wisdom, she took some and ate it" (Genesis 3:6).

Doubting God's Word

Satan caused doubt in God's word both in heaven and in Eden. It caused the fall of angels and humans. It's important that we understand his strategy. He has emptied Scripture of revelation and confined revelation to Christ. Now, it's true that Christ is the greatest revelation of God to humans, but that's not his point. It suits Satan to have Christians believe they meet revelation outside of Scripture in a Person rather than in a Book. For if he can get Christians to look outside of Scripture, he has gotten them to look away from God's Word, which exposes him for who and what he is. It's not that he has become pro-Christ. No, he knows he can take humans captive if they become separated from the power of revelation in Scripture. Deflecting revelation to Christ is merely a cover to get people out of God's Word. This is another way to cause doubt in God's Word.

Perhaps J. S. Semler was the first to distinguish between revelation and Scripture. He said, "The root of evil (in theology) is the interchangeable use of the terms 'Scripture' and 'Word of God.'"[9] He believed that Scripture contains God's Word, but also contains much else. He could even suggest that a condensation of the Bible is possible so that it would then be God's Word.[10] To him, Scripture was no different from any other book, which led to alleging it has many contradictions.[11] The alleged contradictions themselves give cre-

43

dence to so many since Semler that Scripture could not be the Word of God.[12]

This new view is a product of the unenlightened Enlightenment. It successfully severed revelation from Scripture, so that Scripture is, at best, only a witness to revelation, but never revelation itself. This emptied Scripture of its uniqueness, and dragged it down to the level of any uninspired literary work. Those who accepted that Scripture is not revelation accepted this critical view of the Enlightenment, whether they realized it or not. This opened the way for them to look beyond Scripture for revelation, and they found revelation alone in Jesus Christ.

Christ as Revelation

Many contemporary theologies reject Scripture as the Word of God, speaking of it merely as a witness to God. All of them look to Christ as revelation as if this honors Him more than looking to Scripture as revelation. Some even think that looking to Scripture as revelation is having a paper pope.[13] But is Scripture only a *witness to God,* or a *medium for God,* rather than a *Word from God?* How would we know anything about Jesus Christ save through Scripture? Of necessity Scripture must be the written revelation of God in order for us to know anything about Jesus Christ, the living Word of God. To deny Scripture as revelation is to deny revelation about what/who it presents, including Jesus Christ. It's not possible for Jesus Christ to be God's revelation to humanity if Scripture, which tells about this revelation, is not itself God's revelation about Jesus Christ to humans. One cannot accept the one as revelation without the prior acceptance of the other. It's like the analogy of a mother and her baby. The only way the baby comes is through the mother. The baby would not be in the world without its mother and father. So, from the standpoint of human knowledge, Jesus Christ could not be God's revelation unless Scripture, which reveals this fact, is itself God's revelation.

Scripture says, "In the past God spoke to our forefathers through the prophets at many times and in various ways, but in these last days he has spoken to us by his Son" (Hebrews 1:1, 2). Note that God spoke through the prophets in the same way He spoke through

Christ. Today God speaks through the prophetic writings just as He did through the prophets, and through Christ. Christ said, "The words I say to you are not just my own. Rather, it is the Father, living in me, who is doing his work" (John 14:10). So Paul could say, "When you received the word of God, which you heard from us, you accepted it not as the word of men, but as it actually is, the word of God" (1 Thessalonians 2:13). Whether spoken or written, it was and is the Word of God.

It should be remembered that the first two heresies in the second-century Christian church were Gnosticism and Montanism, both failing to give to Scripture its proper place. Gnostics claimed to have a higher, more spiritual knowledge, a hidden gospel handed down orally from an inner group of the disciples of Christ. So Gnostics claimed to have oral teaching not found in Scripture, a claim repeated in the medieval church's placing of church tradition above Scripture. Montanists claimed to have a new revelation beyond that found in Scripture and accused church leaders of confining the Holy Spirit to a book, a claim popular among those today who look beyond Scripture to the present encountering work of the Holy Spirit or Christ as revelation.[14]

Satan's Final Deception

What does this have to do with Satan's final deception? Global terrorism impacted Eden, for the fall of Adam affected the race (see Romans 5:15). Doubt of God's Word led to disobedience. A broken relationship preceded eating forbidden fruit. Satan separates people from Christ, and this causes them to sin. This was as much a terrorist takeover as telling angels God would not forgive them. It works every time. The thrust of cosmic terrorism is to separate a person from Christ. That's the bottom line. Sins are legion, but every sin is separation from Christ. Thus, anything that separates a person from Christ is sin. Sin is fundamentally a broken relationship (Romans 14:23), and only then a breaking of God's law (1 John 3:4). That's why the Sabbath is so crucial in the Creation record. As the climax of Creation week it rejects the premise that humans are the climax of Creation. Humans do not stand alone at the pinnacle of the week. The Sabbath is the climax, and humans rest in Christ their Creator in a dependent relationship. That was so even in their pre-Fall state. Humans were made for God. In relationship with Christ there is life, but apart from this dependent relationship there is sin. It's also true that sinning continues the separation (Isaiah 59:2).

The final deception is to separate the human race from Christ. Satan has most of them. He wants them all. He must get Christians on board. Hence his appearance as Christ. If it works, he becomes ruler of all humankind. How will it take place? We have some of the facts. We can use imagination to fill in other possible details. Suppose America's war on global terrorism continues into the future. Leaders say there could be as many as 60 countries with terrorist networks linked to Osama bin Laden. If that's true, there's a lot of work to be done. Afghanistan was only the beginning. It's unwise to predict that the war on terrorism will continue until near the end. I well remember when the Moral Majority under Jerry Falwell seemed to be the movement to bring in the uniting of church and state with its final Sunday law. Its successor today is the Christian Coalition, led for years by Pat Robertson. It has the same goal and has accomplished far more. The Moral Majority is defunct. One must refrain from choosing a present movement as the final one. We don't know how long the war on terrorism will last.

We do know some things. We know troubles will increase as we near the end. The upheaval in society and in nature will escalate. Human hearts are growing colder. The world is racked by evil, both moral and natural, and Satan works through both in devastation and destruction as only a devil can do. The proliferation of nuclear know-how is of grave concern to political leaders. We think of India and Pakistan and the volatile relations between them. We think of the nuclear arsenal of the former U.S.S.R. now parceled out to the many countries that split apart, with no longer central control over the weapons. We think of the biochemical production of anthrax, and of other deadly weapons that may be in the making. How could Satan use these to his advantage in his bid for global leadership? After all, he's good at causing a problem and then showing up with a pretended solution.

If an act of nuclear terrorism should destroy a major city, as Hiroshima and Nagasaki were devastated in World War II, this could bring the world to its knees. What better time for Satan to show up as the assumed Prince of Peace! He knows how to play his cards. He's schemed with cunning craft his entrance for millennia. It's his last desperate pre-Advent attempt to take the place of Christ on Planet Earth.

Revelation as Christ

The removal of revelation from Scripture and confining it to Christ suits Satan well. It prepares for his coming as Christ, for when he comes so many Christians will see this as revelation. For those who reject Scripture as revelation, there's no point to read that Christ will be met in the air (see 1 Thessalonians 4:16-18) and not on the ground (see Matthew 24:23-27). For that's only a human writing. The fact that Christ is allegedly present in person on the ground is what constitutes true revelation to so many Christians when Satan comes as Christ. Satan has prepared well for his coming. It was Christ who said counterfeit Christs would be on earth (see Matthew 24). Satan has caused doubt in these words by transferring revelation from these words of Christ to revelation as Christ. What a deception!

Satan's Coming as Christ

Satan's approach to Eve in the beginning of human history is the same approach in last-day events. It worked so well once that he'll do it again. Scripture says, "Satan himself masquerades as an angel of light" (2 Corinthians 11:14). He spoke through a shining serpent in the tree; he comes in brilliance as Christ in the final deception.

"As the crowning act in the great drama of deception, Satan himself will personate Christ. . . . In different parts of the earth, Satan will manifest himself among men as a majestic being of dazzling brightness, resembling the description of the Son of God given by John in the Revelation. Revelation 1:13-15. The glory that surrounds him is unsurpassed by anything that mortal eyes have yet beheld. The shout of triumph rings out upon the air: 'Christ has come!

Christ has come!' The people prostrate themselves in adoration before him, while he lifts up his hands and pronounces a blessing upon them, as Christ blessed His disciples when He was upon the earth. His voice is soft and subdued, yet full of melody. In gentle, compassionate tones he presents some of the same gracious, heavenly truths which the Savior uttered; he heals the diseases of the people, and then, in his assumed character of Christ, he claims to have changed the Sabbath to Sunday, and commands all to hallow the day which he has blessed. He declares that those who persist in keeping holy the seventh day are blaspheming his name by refusing to listen to his angels sent to them with light and truth. This is the strong, almost overmastering delusion." [15]

As in Eden, Satan questions God's word. Back then "You will not surely die" (Genesis 3:4) replaced Christ's word "You will surely die" (Genesis 2:17), and in the future "Keep Sunday" replaces "Remember the Sabbath day by keeping it holy" (Exodus 20:8). Satan's deception in the end-time will be so powerful that only those who know Christ and their Bibles will remain unmoved. "Only those who have been diligent students of the Scriptures and who have received the love of the truth will be shielded from the powerful delusion that takes the world captive. By the Bible testimony these will detect the deceiver in his disguise. To all the testing time will come. . . . Are the people of God now so firmly established upon His word that they would not yield to the evidence of their senses? Would they, in such a crisis, cling to the Bible and the Bible only?" [16]

The issue is this: Is our belief in God's Word stronger than apparent evidence to the contrary? Doubt in God's Word led to the fall of angels. Doubt in God's Word led to the fall of the human race. Doubt in God's Word is the final pre-Advent hijack of humanity by Satan. He'll take the world captive, except for a few. Satan's strategy is "seeing is believing." He appeals to the senses without any reference to God's Word, and contrary to it. God's solution is "believing is seeing." Believing God's Word is seeing through the deception. Only the power in God's Word can unmask the powerful deception of the enemy.

End-time Christians are in need of discernment just as was Eve.

She thought "she had sufficient wisdom and strength to discern evil and to withstand it."[17] What a tragic mistake! Not even sinless beings had the ability to withstand Satan's great deception alone. Angels had not, nor did humans. How much more is this true for fallen sinners! Have you ever compared the third chapter of the first and last books of the Bible? The Fall of humans and the final delusion have so much in common. When Adam and Eve sinned they knew they were naked (see Genesis 3:7). Not so the end-time church. Like Eve, it feels no concern. It has need of nothing, and doesn't even know it is naked (see Revelation 3:17). Just as Eve lacked discernment, so does the end-time church. That's why Christ longs to give it eye salve that it might see (see verse 18).

Satan's studied strategy is to separate created beings from Christ. When he accomplishes this, the rest is easy. He has them trapped. They are his. Eve thought she could go it alone; so does the end-time church as described in Revelation 3, for Christ is kept outside. He is standing at the door knocking, hoping to gain entrance (see verse 20). How do we get discernment? How can we be prepared for the end-time delusion? Scripture in our minds is one way; the other is to let Christ in. For when He comes within, He brings discernment so that biblical study can fortify the mind and prepare it to withstand the nearly overmastering delusion. It's not one without the other. Biblical study without Christ suits Satan well. Anything without Christ is to be without the necessary protection from his deceptions. It is "Christ in you, the hope of glory" (Colossians 1:27).

---

[1] E. G. White, *Patriarchs and Prophets,* p. 52.

[2] *Ibid.,* p. 52.

[3] *Ibid.,* p. 53.

[4] *Ibid.*

[5] *Ibid.,* pp. 53, 54.

[6] *Ibid.,* p. 54.

[7] *Ibid.,* p. 53.

[8] *Ibid.,* p. 54.

[9] J. S. Semler, *"Abhandlung von freier Untersuchung des Canon," Texte zur Kirchen-und Theologiegeschichte* (Güetersloh, 1967), vol. 5, pp. 43, 47, 55, 58ff.; Gerhard Maier, *The End of the Historical-Critical Method,* trans. Edwin W. Leverenz and Rudolph F. Norden (St. Louis: Concordia, 1974), p. 15. "Holy Scripture and Word of God are very much to be distinguished, because we know the difference; just because someone has not previously seen that difference, that is no prohibition against us seeing it." (in Gerhard Maier, *Biblical*

Hermeneutics, p. 298).

[10] Gerhard Maier, *Biblical Hermeneutics,* trans. Robert W. Yarbrough (Wheaton, Ill: Crossway Books, 1994), p. 298.

[11] *Ibid.,* p. 11.

[12] Maier, *The End of the Historical-Critical Method,* p. 47.

[13] For example, the theologies of Karl Barth, Emil Brunner, Thomas Torrance, Hans Frei, Paul Tillich, G. Stroup, George Lindbeck, G. C. Berkouwer, Stanley Grenz, Avery Dulles, James Barr, David Tracy, David Kelsey, and Donald Bloesch.

[14] For a very helpful book on these matters and more, see Roger E. Olson, *The Story of Christian Theology: Twenty Centuries of Tradition and Reform* (Downers Grove, Ill.: InterVarsity, 1999), pp. 28-39.

[15] White, *The Great Controversy,* p. 624.

[16] *Ibid.,* p. 625.

[17] White, *Patriarchs and Prophets,* p. 54.

GREAT DEBATES

I s God just? This is the issue in the cosmic controversy. Satan says God is not just. Angels in heaven and Eve on earth believed him. Cosmic terrorism is a campaign against the justice of God. When we look at Christian history it seems Satan is winning. Disinformation is the name of the game. The devil deliberately spreads disinformation about God. He once was the chief communicator about the purposes of God. Now he is the chief distorter of the purposes of God. He knows that God is transcendent, almighty, and powerful. So he twists this into a God who is removed from humans, disinterested in their joys, unmoved by their cries, unaffected by their prayers, predestining some to salvation and the rest to hell. Humans are disposable. He'll gain great delight by throwing the masses into eternal torment. What a horrible picture of God! It's really a picture of Satan. The enemy transfers his own evil and hatred onto God.

Satan knows God is compassionate and caring, a God up close. So he twists this to mean God needs the world and humans. He is evolving with nature, and is dependent on nature for His presence in the world (process theology). He is also dependent upon humans to know the future, for He doesn't know all the future. He waits for humans to decide so He can know the future about them (open theism). If He's sovereign in the first picture, He's imminent in the second. If He determines future destinies for all humans in the first, He doesn't know human destinies in the second. These ideas are not only out in the world, but are held by Christians. That's how successful Satan's disinformation about God has been! In fact it's among Christ's professed followers that some of the worst ideas of God have been proclaimed. All the examples in this chapter come from professed believers.

Putting these together, God as sovereign doesn't know the future from foreknowledge but predetermines what will take place. Contradictory views of God, but they serve Satan's strategy well. Confusing views give God bad press. They question His justice. That's the next issue in cosmic terrorism. In war the enemy is demonized. In cosmic terrorism the devil demonizes the Deity. He's either a ruthless, uncaring, heartless being who delights in eternal hell or a dependent, diminished, nonsovereign being who doesn't know much about the future. Either way He's not a person you can trust. Either He'll throw you into everlasting burning or He doesn't know all that's coming. How can you depend on Him for assurance in the future? He's not the kind of person you would want to live with. And that's the point. Distorted views of God keep humans distant from Him. That's the aim of cosmic terrorism—to distance created beings from their Creator.

Does God Determine Destiny?

Is it a waste of time to study last-day events? It is if it doesn't make any difference. Imagine if God determined from eternity that you will be lost, no matter your decisions, no matter your dreams, no matter your efforts to prepare for heaven. Your life doesn't count. It's ignored. If God doesn't want you in heaven, you'll not be there. It's as simple as that. Moreover, He'll do nothing to help you get there. You feel unwanted, unloved, very much alone. You are left to the utter dread of a future you cannot escape, no matter how much you try. Imagine if you heard God say that "this is just," because He created you and has a right to decide where you will spend eternity. He is boss, and has a right to do this as much as you have a right to make decisions about objects you make. You feel that you are a thing, less than a person, a throwaway piece of junk. Right?

Imagine if you heard that God lavishes help upon those He chooses to save. He has favorites. He decides in eternity that He'll get them to heaven. They cannot be lost. They have guaranteed protection from hell. It's only the ones He does not choose that He damns. Why could He not leave the damned alone in eternity as He leaves them alone in history? Why not let them cease to exist? This would be more merciful to those He doesn't want. Why throw them into unending torment just because He didn't choose them? But He did choose them. He chooses to give them life, life without Him. Why did He choose to give them life to endure endless suffering? How would you respond to this God? You would hate Him. You would fear Him. You would ache at the thought of endless burning, for this infliction would be His work. No one else could do it. It's a miracle. He must keep you alive to suffer forever, for fire consumes. What utter injustice! This is worse than the extermination of the Jews in gas chambers. At least their misery ended.

What a grotesque monster! He needs to be destroyed. Satan laughs as he sees multitudes repulsed by these distorted views of God. He gloats as preaching proclaims these views. He works to blot out the true picture of God. The greatest debate today among evangelicals is whether God fully knows the future or not, or whether God is absolutely sovereign. This was the central focus of the Evangelical Theological Society convention in Colorado Springs in November 2001. Besides many papers and plenary speakers a long discussion ensued way into the night. An indecisive vote followed the next day.

The contenders have a common problem. Neither side takes into consideration the biblical context of the cosmic controversy. When God's justice is seen as the issue in the cosmic controversy, then it becomes of paramount importance that God be understood as just by the evidence of His relationship to all created beings.

Questions

Scripture speaks of a "determinate counsel" (Acts 2:23, KJV), "predestination" (Romans 8:30), "good pleasure" (Ephesians 1:9), "election" (1 Thessalonians 1:4, KJV) and "foreknowledge" (1 Peter 1:2). Does God determine all that transpires in human history, and thus in last-day events? Did He decide in eternity the destiny of everyone, some to heaven and others to hell? How does the universality of the gospel relate to the particularity of election? In fact, why does the gospel invitation need to be given in human history if God determined who will be saved in His eternal decree? If all human acts are foreordained, what's the purpose of the final judgment? These are questions that remain outside the debate, yet crucial to it.

What's the relationship between divine predestination and human freedom? Is human destiny predetermined without reference to human response? Does Scripture single out one attribute of God from which all of His acts toward this world and humankind can best be understood? Does God operate out of love or out of will? If love is primary, what does this do to His will? If will is primary, what does this do to His love? Is His relationship with humans personal or impersonal? Do we accept the justice of God on the basis of faith, or do we accept it on the basis of reason too? The present debate must think through these questions carefully for they have determinative influence on the way we understand last-day events.

The issue in the cosmic controversy is the justice of God. It can be resolved only if humans are truly free to understand the justice of God, so that He is not merely declared just because He is God, but is seen as just on the basis of evidence. Last-day events include human destiny. Is that destiny decided in God's eternal decree or in human history? Much of the debate fails to take history seriously, and yet history must be taken seriously if intelligent beings are to decide about God's justice.

We'll look briefly at influential Christian leaders who promote distorted views of God because they don't take seriously the cosmic terrorism against Him.

Augustine of Hippo, 354–430

Augustine says, "God has the lordship over men's wills" "to bestow kindness on some, and to heap punishment on others, as He Himself judges right by a counsel most secret to Himself, indeed, but beyond all doubt most righteous."[1] How can such contrary actions be deemed beyond all doubt righteous merely by saying they are? Do such actions seem just to God even if they seem unjust to others? Throughout the Christian Era, Christian leaders claim that God is just because He is God. But if the cosmic controversy is about the justice of God, it requires that God be seen as just by humans. Merely saying He is just doesn't count. After all, humans are the ones who must decide. These writers only assume what needs to be demonstrated.

Nor is it good enough for Augustine to say, "God works in the hearts of men to incline their wills whithersoever He wills, whether to good deeds according to His mercy, or to evil after their own deserts"[2] Where is the freedom of human willing now? (He proclaims it elsewhere.)[3] Augustine's theology has an internal inconsistency. Humans either have freedom of the will, or God's will (read secret decree) denies them that freedom. He makes it clear that "if not a single member of the race had been redeemed, no one could justly have questioned the justice of God"[4] He claims that it's only an exercise of mercy that He saves any. But the question presses, If He doesn't exercise mercy for all, is He just? That question is never raised or answered by Augustine. He merely assumes that a limited mercy is sufficient. But in the light of the cosmic controversy over the justice of God, no such assumption is adequate.

Thomas Aquinas, 1225–1274

The greatest Catholic theologian next to Augustine is Thomas Aquinas. Together they form an important basis for Catholic theology. Aquinas speaks of justice. He says, "The order of the universe, which is seen both in effects of nature and in effects of will, shows forth the justice of God." Hence God's justice can be manifested. What God "does according to His will He does justly." Parting somewhat from Augustine, Aquinas allows mercy to go beyond the saved. For "even in the damnation of the reprobate mercy is seen, though it does not totally remit, yet somewhat alleviates, in punishing short of what is deserved."

God's attributes of mercy and justice are linked to election and reprobation, respectively, in Aquinas as they are in Augustine. Note that hell is linked to justice! Human destiny is linked to God's gratuitous action. Aquinas says He doesn't owe humans anything.

Hence, "In things which are given gratuitously a person can give more or less, just as he pleases (providing he deprives nobody of his due), without any infringement of justice. This is what the master of the house said: 'Take what is thine, and go thy way. Is it not lawful for me to do what I will?' (Matthew 20:14, 15)." Aquinas misses Matthew's point. The passage has nothing to do with election/ reprobation, in which some are rewarded with salvation and others rewarded with damnation, for all receive the same reward. That's the point of the parable. All receive the same good reward for different amounts of work done, for they all receive the same wages even though some came later in the day to begin work.

If this illustrates the kingdom of heaven, as verse 1 suggests, then it illustrates salvation for all kingdom workers, even though some only became workers in the kingdom just before the Second Advent. This indeed shows the justice of God. The idea of reprobation is not in the parable. Furthermore, the will to work was present with each one who went to work. There's no hidden will in the owner that was responsible for the willing in the minds of those who chose to come to work. On all counts the passage fails to sustain the point Aquinas is making.

Like Augustine, Aquinas uses the word "justice" in reference to reprobation. But that's an assumption that cannot be made when the question of God's justice is before the universe to decide. If a person is thrown into eternal hell merely because God never chose them to be saved, does this not appear arbitrary rather than just? To give it the name justice does not make sense to human reason, and it's human reason that has to decide on God's justice in the final judgment, even though it is human reason responding to divine revelation.

Martin Luther, 1483–1546

In Romans Luther discovered "the just shall live by faith" (Romans 1:17, KJV). Finally the freedom of the gospel broke through. It's my contention that this freedom was not fully realized because of the doctrine of the eternal decrees espoused by Luther and Calvin. If God decides in eternity who will be saved, then to that extent the freedom of the gospel is called in question.

One of the greatest works, if not the greatest, written by Luther was *The Bondage of the Will*. After stating that " 'free-will' is a downright lie,"[5] Luther says, "God foreknows nothing by contingency, but that He foresees, purposes, and does all things according to His immutable, eternal, and infallible will. By this thunderbolt, 'free-will' is thrown prostrate, and utterly dashed to pieces. Those, therefore, who would assert 'free-will,' must either deny this thunderbolt, or pretend not to see it, or push it from them."[6] "From which it follows unalterably, that all things which we do, although they may appear to us to be done mutably and contingently, and even may be done thus contingently by us, are yet, in reality, done necessarily and immutably, with respect to the will of God. For the will of God is effective and cannot be hindered; because the very power of God is natural to Him, and His wisdom is such that He cannot be deceived. And as His will cannot be hindered, the work itself cannot be hindered from being done in the place, at the time, in the measure, and by whom He foresees and wills."[7]

That's because of "the impotency of our depraved will"[8] on the one hand, and belief in His promises on the other hand. Luther grants that free-will is used "in respect only of those things which are below" a person, but "not in respect of those which are above him." For, "in things which pertain unto salvation or damnation, he has no 'free-will,' but is a captive, slave, and servant, either to the will of God, or to the will of Satan."[9] Luther likens the human will to a beast, upon which God or Satan rides. "Nor is it in the power of its own will to choose, to which rider it will run, nor which it will seek; but the riders themselves contend, which shall have and hold it."[10] So the human will is passive to the active wills of God and Satan. If that's true, how could any human freely choose which side of the cosmic controversy to be on? If that choice is relegated to the two antagonists in the controversy, then how can any passive will have the ability to judge whether God or Satan is just? If both the will of God and the will of Satan override the freedom of the human will, would not that human will consider both God and Satan to be equally unjust?

John Calvin (1509-1564)

More than Augustine, Aquinas, and Luther, Calvin speaks about the eternal counsel of God. He calls it "the secret counsel,"[11] "determinate counsel,"[12] "hidden counsel,"[13] "eternal and immutable counsel determined once for all,"[14] and the "inaccessible tribunal."[15] Whereas Luther wished he had never been born when contemplating the decree,[16] Calvin said, "The decree, I admit, is dreadful; and yet it is impossible to deny that God foreknew what the end of man was to be before he made him, and foreknew because he had so ordained by his decree."[17] Both Luther and Calvin had a view of God that put fear in them, a hidden decree that was irreversible, determinative, and final about the destiny of humans, one that did not take into consideration human freedom of choice.

Calvin defines the decree. "By predestination we mean the eternal decree of God, by which he determined with himself whatever he wished to happen with regard to every man. All are not created on equal terms, but some are preordained to eternal life, others to eternal damnation; and accordingly, as each has been created for one or other of these ends, we say that he has been predestined to life or to death."[18] This is a chilling outlook. No wonder Luther and Calvin had such torturous thoughts! Humans don't even start the same. They come into the world doomed to damnation or elected to salvation. They have no choice in the matter. The choice resides solely with God's good pleasure. This has to be the most discouraging outlook to anyone not included in the elect. They would have every right to ask why God so chose. Why did He even give me life? Why will God damn me forever when I have no chance to change from a reprobate to an elected person? If God's decree is unchangeable, then all are locked into their destiny from eternity, and their human lives have no contribution whatsoever. This is a picture of an arbitrary, unjust God. That's cosmic terrorism of the worst kind! And God is terrorist, while Satan laughs all the way to his next scheme.

Nevertheless, Calvin speaks of "the strictest justice" with reference to God.[19] "It properly belongs to the nature of God to do judgment" so "he must naturally love justice and abhor injustice."[20] Like so many before him, Calvin appeals to Romans 9:20, 21, in which

God, as the potter, makes one vessel unto honor and another unto dishonor. He confines this passage to election/reprobation. But the choice of Jacob over Esau had nothing to do with their eternal destiny; rather it was a choice for mission. Jacob, who became Israel, was chosen to be the nation through whom God could reach all nations with the gospel, just as Mary was the instrument through whom Jesus came as the Savior of humanity. In different ways, they were chosen as an avenue to bring salvation to the world.

Yet Paul uses the word "election" (Greek, *eklogē*) in this context (Romans 9:11). What we have here is a broader definition of election. God's choice is not limited to matters of salvation. It also includes matters of mission. It also includes the distribution of gifts (Ephesians 4:7, 11-13; 1 Corinthians 12:4-11, 28-31). It's vital to understand that the choice for mission, and the giving of the gifts for mission, are all for the benefit of others, and not for the benefit of the recipient. Israel was chosen to bless the world (Genesis 12:3; 28:14); the gifts are given to bless the church (1 Corinthians 12:7; Ephesians 4:12, 13). That's different from election for personal salvation and reprobation for personal damnation.

Does God Lack Future Knowledge?

I first encountered this question when a doctoral student at the University of Edinburgh. Some of my peers and I took a walk in the Scottish countryside. They were concerned with personal freedom. They didn't buy the idea of a sovereign God as described above. The fact that the Reformers held to these views was of no consequence to them, for their view of God was a being who valued the freedom of His intelligent created beings, and didn't violate their freedom of choice either by an eternal hidden decree or by the way He related to them in daily decision making. They had a conviction: "If God knows the future of each one of us, we aren't free."

What do you do with that? Here's a different level of concern from the salvation/damnation discussion above. The God of Augustine, Aquinas, Luther, and Calvin knows the future, and there is no human freedom involved. That's true. But that's because He determines the future, and it will happen because He makes it happen. Knowledge of destinies is not based upon foreknowledge, but upon predestination. The students' question was not about predestination, which violates human freedom. It was about God knowing the future. They thought even foreknowledge robs humans of freedom. That's an important part of the contemporary debate.[21]

Gregory Boyd's Contribution

One contributor to the debate about God's foreknowledge comes close to understanding the cosmic controversy. Gregory A. Boyd's *Satan and the Problem of Evil* (2001)[22] shows evil originated with Satan. He rejects Calvinistic foreordination of evil, as this makes God responsible. He opts rather for an open view of God—that He doesn't exhaustively know the future, and so couldn't know that evil would come, and so cannot be held responsible for it. The origin of evil is owing to the wrong use of creaturely free will.[23]

He presents six theses in a carefully constructed order, each building on what has gone before. The first three are (1) love entails freedom, (2) freedom entails risk, (3) risk entails moral responsibility. I concur with Boyd's focus on God's love and His giving angels and humans freedom to choose. I don't agree that God took a risk in granting this freedom in the sense that He didn't know the outcome.[24]

Before the Incarnation, Christ with the other members of the Trinity knew the outcome, so there was no risk for Them to create beings free to choose. But the fact that the Trinity knew the outcome and still went ahead and created beings with freedom of choice magnifies the level of commitment They had to freedom, for They believed in it so totally that They created free beings, angelic and human, even though it would bring great suffering to Them, particularly in the life and death of Jesus. Boyd misses this depth of commitment to creaturely freedom in his risk focus. And the risk focus is a major one for those who think God doesn't know what will happen each new day. It's a mistake to equate absolute foreknowledge with absolute control.[25] God's absolute foreknowledge has nothing to do with controlling events. It's confined to knowing free choices, and not causing them.

Boyd rejects predestination as opposed to human freedom, yet accepts hell, which is the ultimate invasion of human freedom! He's not alone in this. Some persons on both sides of the "divine sovereignty/human freedom" debate accept unending torment in hell. Boyd believes, with others, that sin against God deserves eternal punishment because He is God. But God tells us to forgive (Matthew 6:12-15; 18:21, 22; 2 Corinthians 2:7; Ephesians 4:32; Colossians 3:13). Does He fail to practice what He teaches? Christ said on Calvary, "Father, forgive them" (Luke 23:34). Jesus said that He came to reveal the Father (see John 14:9). God is love (see 1 John 4:8, 16). He forgives. Theology must look at hell in the light of Calvary.

Theology must also look at hell in the light of the first temptation of humans. God said that they would die if they ate the fruit (see Genesis 2:16, 17), not that they would live forever in rebellion. The wages of sin is death (see Romans 6:23). Christ died on Calvary, and the final judgment will be death—the ultimate separation from God. Such a separation is merciful, an act of love. Sin brings separation (see Isaiah 59:2), and sinners want to be separate (see Genesis 3:8; Revelation 6:15-17). So the final judgment is God allowing sinners to have their choice, which is the real evidence that God honors creaturely freedom to choose. This demonstrates His love in a way that eternal torture cannot. Hell is a place of burning until sinners are consumed (see Matthew 10:28), and hence Scripture includes texts on annihilation (see Matthew 7:19; 13:40; John 15:6; Hebrews 10:27; 2 Peter 2:3, 6) as well as those on hell (see Revelation 14:9-11; 19:19, 20).

Besides this, the soul cannot be immortal because only God has immortality (see 1 Timothy 6:16), and the gift of immortality is given at the Second Advent (see 1 Corinthians 15:52-54) and not before. Boyd's idea that hell must be eternal because souls are eternal[26] fails to apply this reasoning to salvation. Is salvation given because souls are eternal, or because Christ died to give immortality as a future gift? Inherent immortality does not need the death of Christ. The idea of immortality of the soul originated with Satan's words to Eve "You will not surely die" (Genesis 3:4). Scripture reads, "The soul who sins is the one who will die" (Ezekiel 18:20). Here the word "soul" (Hebrew *nephesh*) is the word used of the soul in other passages. If the soul can die, it is not inherently immortal. The point is Scripture knows no dichotomy between soul, spirit, or body. Neither does modern medicine. The soul stands for the total person, just as body can do the same. Thus we speak of souls won for Christ and somebody in particular as one of these souls. Rather than inherent immortality Scripture speaks of "those who by persistence in doing good seek glory, honor and immortality" (Romans 2:7). Christians seek immortality as they look forward to the Second Advent when it will be given to them.[27]

There are two other beliefs of Boyd that must be questioned. His view that animals died before the Fall of humans is predicated upon the evolutionary theory of origins.[28] But the biblical creation view of human origin clearly places death after the Fall of humans (see Genesis 1–3). Scripture concurs that the wages of sin is death (see Romans 6:23). Death is not natural, nor is it a part of the creation process—for then the Creator would be responsible for death, rather than sin being responsible. The other problem is the indeterminate nature of physics at the quantum level.[29] Because humans cannot predict the movements at that level says nothing about whether God can or not. Boyd believes molecular indeterminacy demonstrates God's future knowledge as limited, but it really speaks of human knowledge as limited.

I commend Boyd for a well-thought-out argument in much of his book. He's made an important contribution by calling attention to a cosmic controversy. But he doesn't say why there's a war. Nowhere does he speak about the issue in the war. God's justice being called into question is missing. But this issue in the cosmic controversy is vital to its understanding. If God doesn't respect creaturely freedom, this is sufficient evidence that He is unjust. If God elects only some to be saved and damns the rest, this is sufficient evidence that He is unjust. The issue before the universe, whether God is just or not, is the worldview within which the debate on God's foreknowledge versus the openness view of God must be decided. In all of the above, the justice of God must be clearly demonstrated so that God is seen to be love. So often predestination runs roughshod over the biblical definition that "God is love" (1 John

4:8, 16), as if it really says, "God is will." Boyd rightly rejects the overriding of God as love by the will of God, but needs to be consistent in this when he comes to his understanding of hell.

Any suggestion that something unreasonable to human minds is reasonable to the divine mind, because God transcends humans, begs the question. For it was God who invited humans to "come now, let us reason together" (Isaiah 1:18). Also, if there is an eternal hell, then the cosmic controversy will never end, because those suffering in the flames will forever sin against God.

Cosmic terrorism includes blaming God for angelic rebellion. "Satan and his emissaries represent God as even worse than themselves, in order to justify their own malignity and rebellion. The deceiver endeavors to shift his own horrible cruelty of character upon our heavenly Father, that he may cause himself to appear as one greatly wronged by his expulsion from heaven because he would not submit to so unjust a governor."[30] He blames hell on God. Most churches preach this doctrine of the devil, and millions recoil from such a God. "The theory of eternal torment is one of the false doctrines that constitute the wine of . . . Babylon, of which she makes all nations drink. Revelation 14:8; 17:2."[31] This happens in the end-time.

There's no doubt that hell is an invention of Satan, and speaks volumes of what he would attempt to do if he occupied heaven's throne. Thrusting hell onto God makes Him into the image of Satan. More important, if God keeps angels and humans alive to writhe in unending agony, this would be the worst terrorist attack ever! Then God would be the consummate terrorist, not Satan.

---

[1] Augustine, in *Nicene and Post-Nicene Fathers* (Grand Rapids: Ferdmans, 1987), First Series, vol. 5, p. 461.

[2] *Ibid.,* p. 463.

[3] *Ibid.,* vol. 2, p. 282.

[4] *Ibid.,* vol. 3, pp. 268-272.

[5] Martin Luther, *The Bondage of the Will,* trans. Henry Cole (Grand Rapids: Baker, 1981), p. 17.

[6] *Ibid.,* pp. 38, 39.

[7] *Ibid.,* pp. 39, 40.

[8] *Ibid.,* p. 41.

[9] *Ibid.,* p. 43. Luther charges Erasmus with being no better than Epicurus in believing the future life to be a mere fable (p. 55).

[10] *Ibid.,* p. 74.

[11] John Calvin, *Institutes of the Christian Religion,* trans. Henry Beveridge (London: James Clarke, 1962), vol. 1, book 1, chap. 16, sec. 2, p. 173.

[12] *Ibid.,* vol. 1,book 1, chap. 16, sec. 4, p. 76.

[13] *Ibid.,* vol. 2, book 3, chap. 23, sec. 1, p. 227; cf. vol. 1, book 1, chap. 16, sec. 9, p. 180.

[14] *Ibid.,* book 3, chap. 21, sec. 7, p. 210.

[15] *Ibid.,* book 3, chap. 22, sec. 6, p. 217.

[16] "But it is this, that seems to give the greatest offence to common sense or natural reason—that the God, who is set forth as being so full of mercy and goodness, should, of His mere will, leave men, harden them, and damn them, as though He delighted in the sins, and in the great and eternal torments of the miserable. To think thus of God, seems iniquitous, cruel, intolerable; and it is this that has given offence to so many and great men of so many ages. And who would not be offended? I myself have been offended more than once, even unto the deepest abyss of desperation; nay, so far, as even to wish that I had never been born a man" (Martin Luther, p. 243).

[17] Calvin, vol. 2, book 3, chap. 23, sec. 7, p. 232.

[18] *Ibid.,* book 3, chap. 21, sec. 5, p. 206.

[19] *Ibid.,* book 3, chap. 23, sec. 3, p. 228.

[20] *Ibid.,* book 3, chap. 23, sec. 4, p. 229.

[21] Some of the contributors include Clark Pinnock, Richard Rice, John Sanders, William Hasker, David Basinger, *The Openness of God: A Biblical Challenge to the Traditional Understanding of God* (Downers Grove, Ill.: InterVarsity, 1994); James K. Belby and Paul R. Eddy, eds., *Divine Foreknowledge: Four Views* (Downers Grove, Ill.: InterVarsity, 2001); Thomas R. Schreiner and Bruce A. Ware, eds., *Still Sovereign: Contemporary Perspectives on Election, Foreknowledge, and Grace* (Grand Rapids: Baker, 2000); R. K. Wright, *No Place for Sovereignty: What's Wrong With Freewill Theism* (Downers Grove, Ill.: InterVarsity, 1996); David Basinger, *The Case for Freewill Theism: A Philosophical Assessment* (Downers Grove, Ill.: InterVarsity, 1996); Gregory A. Boyd, *God of the Possible: Does God Ever Change His Mind?* (Grand Rapids: Baker, 2000); Bruce A. Ware, *God's Lesser Glory: The Diminished God of Open Theism* (Wheaton, Ill.: Crossway, 2000); Paul Helm, *The Providence of God: Contours of Christian Theology* (Downers Grove, Ill.: InterVarsity, 1993); John Sanders, *The God Who Risks: A Theology of Divine Providence* (Downers Grove, Ill.: InterVarsity, 1998); Norman L. Geisler and H. Wayne House with Max Herrera, *The Battle for God: Responding to the Challenge of Neotheism* (Grand Rapids: Kregel, 2001).

[22] Gregory A. Boyd, *Satan and the Problem of Evil: Constructing a Trinitarian Warfare Theodicy* (Downers Grove, Ill.: InterVarsity, 2001).

[23] *Ibid.,* pp. 50-84.

[24] *Ibid.,* pp. 85-115.

[25] *Ibid.,* pp. 155-158.

[26] *Ibid.,* p. 326.

[27] There are two dimensions of eternal life. In the present, through Christ, Christians have eternal life (1 John 5:11-13), but they do not receive immortality until the Second Advent (1 Corinthians 15:52-54).

[28] Boyd, p. 255

[29] *Ibid.,* p. 71.

[30] Ellen G. White, *The Great Controversy,* p. 534.

[31] *Ibid.,* p. 536.

GREATEST TIME OF TROUBLE

W hen is the greatest time of trouble? After the close of probation? During the plagues? The time of the death decree? The answer is yes concerning the future, but no concerning the greatest time of trouble ever since the inception of cosmic terrorism. The worst time was 2,000 years ago when Christ came to Planet Earth. All hell broke loose. Satan threw everything he had at Christ. Imagine Christ coming as a helpless babe behind enemy lines. Satan feared Him in the war in heaven. But not now. "I will kill Him," said Satan. And thousands of babies died in the attempt under Herod (see Matthew 2:3-18).

The Hardest Life Ever Lived

Can you imagine the fiendish expectation of Satan? *Oh, just let me get my hands on Him. I will lash out and get even! I'll teach Him for ejecting me from heaven. I'll show Him who is boss on this planet. I'll dog His footsteps from birth onward. I'll never let Him out of my sight. I'll stalk and terrorize Him. I'll set traps through church leaders. I'll bring Him hardship, hatred, harassment. I'll make Him misunderstood, misinterpreted, maligned. I'll criticize and condemn. I'll cause heartache and loneliness. I'll make His life a pathway of suffering.*

Christ was God with a divine face. He would become a Jew, with a Jewish face. But that's not all. He sacrificed His beauty to save others. As a human, "He had no beauty or majesty to attract us to him, nothing in his appearance that we should desire him" (Isaiah 53:2). He looked ordinary, homely. "He was despised and rejected by men, man of sorrows, and familiar with suffering. Like one from whom men hide their faces he was despised, and we esteemed him not" (verse 3). He left the adoration and worship of heaven to be despised and rejected on earth. Jesus, the only human who has been homesick for heaven—for He knew what He left, and He longed to go home.

No one understood this Child. He was different. Siblings probably chided Him. "Trying to be a goody, that's what You are! Who do You think You are, anyway? You don't fit in. Why don't You mingle with us, play our games, and take it easy. What's all this about praying, and reading, and sharing Your lunch with others? You better look after Yourself, and not try to act better than the rest of us."

Public Ministry

He labored from morning till night. Long days, crowds, noisy voices, and needy people filled His day. Multitudes clamored around Him to be healed. The blind, the deaf, lepers, demoniacs, cripples, all followed and pressed upon Him. Jesus saw in them the result of Satan's work. But the evil in the heart, the conniving, criticism, contempt—all exposed a deeper, deadlier disease. Heart trouble, that's what it was. Minds held captive by a devil that sought only to destroy. Jesus was moved with compassion for those who needed physical and spiritual healing. How often they sought the first and ignored the second. They wanted to feel better but not be better.

A large group gathered at the Temple early one morning. Right before the crowd they dragged her and dumped her in front of Christ. "She's an adulterer," they shouted, wanting everyone to hear. "Caught in the very act. We saw her. Moses said she should be stoned. What do You say, Jesus?" Yes, Leviticus 20:10 did state her fate. Christ knew the Scriptures. But He looked beyond the words to the disheveled, fear-ridden waif of a girl thrown down in front of Him. His love didn't break the law, but kept it. For the law hangs on devotion to God and compassion to humans (see Matthew 22:36-40). He had compassion on her.

"Cast the first stone if you are sinless," He replied. Jesus knew they were frauds. They covered up their sins, but exposed hers before everyone. Yet in doing so they denounced themselves. No, Jesus didn't condone sin, but He didn't condemn the sinner, either. Fearfully she cowered, expecting a rock to crash into her frail body at any moment. But none came. After a seemingly eternal silence she heard the welcome words "Neither do I condemn thee; go, and sin no more" (John 8:11, KJV).

Imagine when Mary Magdalene shuffled, head down, for the seventh time into the presence of Infinite Purity. Did Jesus say, "You again! Why, I have helped you six times already. You're hopeless and need to be locked up. That will cure you"? No, Jesus sent her away forgiven—clean. Moreover, on Resurrection morning He "appeared first to Mary Magdalene, out of whom he had cast seven devils" (Mark 16:9, KJV). He treated her as she needed, not as she deserved.

Zacchaeus was a despicable IRS man. He worked for the hated Romans, extorting exorbitant taxes from his fellow countrymen. Perhaps he had become rich at their expense. Jewish society regarded people of his type as outcasts. But Zacchaeus felt drawn to the Man under the tree. "Come on down, Zacchaeus, for I'm going to dine at your house." Just hear the bystanders exclaim, "Lunch with Zacchaeus! I wouldn't be seen dead with such a cheat! Jesus, You must be crazy! Don't You know what he has done to us? Command that he cease. Punish him for robbery." But Jesus treated him as he needed, not as he deserved. Salvation came to Zacchaeus that day, and restitution to others.

Here comes blustering, unpredictable, self-centered Peter. "Yes, he can be My disciple. Come, Peter, and follow Me." But impetuous Peter had his own way of doing things.

"Lord, is that You out there on the water? Just call me to join You." Eagerly he waited, then made a mighty leap into the sea. Rising like a cork, he got up on the water, and as if it were concrete, strode forth. "Wow, how exciting! I'm walking on the surface of the sea—the first man to do it other than Jesus." Peter may have felt like one ready for the *Guinness book of World Records*. "Look at me, fellows!" He may have turned to show off to his stunned colleagues. One thing we know, he took his eyes off Christ and was afraid of the wind and waves. His faith turned to doubt. He began to sink and cried out, "Lord, save me." Christ rushed to the rescue, reached down His strong arm, and pulled Peter up to safety, treating him as he needed, not as he deserved (see Matthew 14:28-31).

Remember Peter's remarks another time? "No, Lord, I'll never do that. Of course I won't deny You! I'll even die for You. That's what I'll do" (see Matthew 26:33-35). An assertive, cocksure blunderer, Peter had the last word. He often had the first and the middle ones, too.

Yet later . . . "Peter followed Jesus from a long way off" (see verse 58)? What happened to his promise to become a martyr for Christ?

"Oh, I don't know Him. Never heard of Him. Who is He, any-way?" And the language that rolled from that fisherman's lips would make even black ink blush red. He spoke in the language un-known—unused by Jesus.

But Christ chose him to speak in another tongue—to be the great Pentecostal preacher just six weeks later (see Acts 2:14-40), treating him not as he deserved, but as he needed. Peter's denial crushed him, broke him to the core. He felt unworthy to be a dis-ciple. And really he was. But Jesus, after coming from the tomb, sent a special message to Peter (see Mark 16:7) and asked him three times whether he loved Him, in order to reinstate him fully before his peers—one affirmation for each denial. That's Jesus. He didn't deny the one who had denied Him.

Then there's Judas, keeper of the moneybag and a thief. Watch him carefully during two feasts. Simon, once a leper (see Matthew 26:6; Mark 14:3), probably held the first one in Bethany in gratitude for his healing from Christ. Who else could heal a leper, save Christ and His disciples? A Pharisee, Simon belonged to that group that masterminded Christ's death (see Matthew 21:45; John 7:32; 12:10; 18:3), against whom Christ spoke His most scathing words (Matthew 23; Luke 11:39-52; 14:7-10). Yet Simon held a banquet for Him when the priests' hatred of Christ had plummeted to its most bitter depths, because of the recent resurrection of Lazarus. Although the Pharisees schemed to kill Lazarus (see John 12:10), still Simon invited Jesus, His disciples, Martha, and Lazarus to the feast (see Matthew 26:6-13; John 12:1-8).

Mary, a former prostitute, came in and poured costly spikenard ointment on Jesus' feet and head. The anointing became obvious as the scent permeated the whole room. "What a waste," the disciples complained. "This should have been given to the poor" (see Matthew 26:8). "Some murmured" (see Mark 14:4), perhaps indicating that others also joined in questioning Mary's action. But Scripture singles only one out by name for criticizing her—Judas (see John 12:4).

How typical of treasurer Judas to launch the question and cloud the room with a different atmosphere. Perfume of love and words of hatred—the two met that night in Simon's home and filled the room. "Why, of all things! This ointment could have been sold for at least 300 pence and given to the poor." That's as much as a whole year's wages. What an utter waste of money! Judas pretended concern for the poor. Yet, right after the feast, he went out to sell Jesus for 30 pieces of silver (see Matthew 26:14, 15; Mark 14:10), or about a third of the price of the ointment.

While Mary gave a year's wages in love for Jesus, Judas received four months' wages to get Him murdered. Our Savior knew it, but did not unmask Judas. He longed to save His disciple. He treated him as he needed, not as he deserved.

Five nights later Jesus with His disciples met in an upper room. Judas arrived the richer, four months' wages stuffed into some secret pocket. Christ stooped down and washed His betrayer's dirty feet— but longed far more to wash his polluted heart. If only He could stop him! What good would four months' wages be when he was dead? How tragic any momentary gain in exchange for eternal loss! Jesus said to the group, "Woe to the man who will betray Me" (see Luke 22:22). "It would even be better had he never been born" (see Mark 14:21). Each statement speeded through the air as a rescue rope to pull His disciple back from his terrifying plunge over the abyss.

Jesus said, "I give this sop to My betrayer," and handed it to Judas to jolt him to his senses and save him from going over the precipice to perdition. But the disciple went out. No one else in the room understood what Jesus meant when He stated, "What you do, do quickly." They thought He referred to something their treasurer had to buy for the feast (see John 13:26-30). But either Judas couldn't understand all of Christ's agonizing words of warning, or he chose to ignore them. The words came packed with compassion, just as had His act of washing Judas' feet. Jesus did not expose Judas in either case. He treated him as he needed, not as he deserved.

The Greatest Terrorist Attack of All Time

Come now and consider His greatest time of trouble. "Overcome evil with good" epitomized Christ's mission. Yet, strangely, many despised, hated, and hurt Him, trying to overcome good with evil. Jewish leaders lunged at Him out of professional jealously. Herod harassed Him because of personal pride and depravity. Pilate gave Him up to scourging and crucifixion as political expediency. No matter the reason, the result was the same. Jesus, the kindest man who ever lived, suffered undeserved treatment from the very ones He came to save.

Ridicule, mockery, blasphemy were mercilessly heaped on Christ. Our tenderhearted Prophet, Priest, and King went as a lamb to the slaughter while wretches laughed, jeered, and gibed at Him. "Some prophet You are. Here, throw this bag over His dumb head. That's it. Hit Him. OK, prophet, who flung his fist in Your face? Tell us now. Come on, quick!"

"Then did they spit in his face, and buffeted him; and others smote him with the palms of their hands, saying, Prophesy unto us, thou Christ, who is he that smote thee?" (Matthew 26:67, 68, KJV). Some yanked out parts of His beard (see Isaiah 50:6).

Twice they mocked Jesus as king, once led on by Herod, the other time by Pilate. The unfeeling soldiers and the unruly rabble took full advantage. Such chances didn't come often to them. "Herod with his men of war set him at nought, and mocked him, and arrayed him in a gorgeous robe" (Luke 23:11, KJV).

"We'll teach You to talk. Fancy a king sitting on a throne unable to speak!" Soldiers roared great guffaws of laughter. "Dumb king He is! Hail, speechless Pontiff! We will do everything You say." Their derision fell, as it were, on deaf ears. Jesus suffered every insult imaginable from people who would not give Him a chance to really be their King.

Pilate did no better. "Take Him to the common hall. Bring the whole band of soldiers, strip Him, and put on the scarlet robe." Wrenching His raiment from Him and robing Him in scarlet shot pain throughout His lacerated and bleeding back. They wove a crown of thorns and shoved it deep into His temples, causing extreme anguish and a flow of blood down His cheeks and beard. "Here, O Your Majesty. Here is Your royal insignia." They thrust a reed into His hand. "OK, fellows, bow the knees." Some half bowed, others half curtsied. Several fell over in jest. "Hail, King! Live forever—at least till we get through with You," they shouted. "Don't die yet, King. We have to let You feel our presence."

"And they spit upon him, and took a reed, and smote him on the head" (Matthew 27:30, KJV). "He was despised and rejected by men, a man of sorrows, and familiar with suffering. . . . Surely he took up our infirmities and carried our sorrows" (Isaiah 53:3, 4). All he could say was "Scorn has broken my heart and left me helpless; I looked for sympathy, but there was none, for comforters, but I found none" (Psalm 69:20). As Prophet, Priest, and King, Christ came to give men what they did not deserve, but in exchange He received from them what He did not deserve.

Gethsemane and Calvary surround the disgraceful farce of a trial. They constitute the worst terrorist attack on a helpless victim ever undertaken anywhere at any time in history. Satan flung his full force against Jesus with tireless and relentless energy. He brought all his cunning and craft to break His dependency on His Father. He weighed in upon Him with such pressure that discouragement and despair filled Him with utter dread. The weight of the world's sin pierced His soul to the depths. It was killing Him. He feared that He would not make it.

The Horrors of Gethsemane

For Jesus in Gethsemane, it was as if the Father shut the door of heaven and left Jesus alone with the devil. He became the sin-bearer for every sinner. Even one's own sins are enough to crush a person, let alone the sins of billions of people! Never before was Christ so utterly sad and silent. His form swayed as if He would fall. Sin was separating Him from His Father. Like an earthquake fault, a deep gulf appeared, so broad, so black, so deep, that His spirit shuddered before it. He must suffer the consequences of human sin. He must receive divine justice in their behalf. He plunged into intense heartache and suffering. "As Christ felt His unity with the Father broken up, He feared that in His human nature He would be unable to endure the coming conflict with the powers of darkness."[1]

He was filled with dread of separation from God. "Satan told Him that if He became the surety for a sinful world, the separation would be eternal. He would be identified with Satan's kingdom, and would nevermore be one with God."[2] What pressure! Satan once told angels in heaven that God would not forgive. He was essentially saying the same to Jesus. "If You become the sin-bearer for humans, You will become captive to my side of the controversy. You will forfeit heaven." How hard it was for Christ to hear these words when He longed for the peace and security of heaven and His Father's presence again.

"The sins of men weighed heavily upon Christ, and the sense of God's wrath against sin was crushing out His life."[3] It was so hard for Him to receive the wrath of the One who had loved Him from eternity. "Behold Him contemplating the price to be paid for the human soul. In His agony He clings to the cold ground, as if to prevent Himself from being drawn further from God. The chilling dew of night falls upon His prostrate form, but He heeds it not. From His pale lips comes the bitter cry, 'O My Father, if it be possible, let this cup pass from Me.'"[4]

This was superhuman agony! Christ was going through hell. "Terrible was the temptation to let the human race bear the consequences of its own guilt, while He stood innocent before God."[5] His face was so changed. Disciples hardly knew Him. Anguish aged Him. He was haggard. Sins of a world on Him were crushing out His life. The weight of human guilt caused unimaginable pain. He was seized by superhuman agony. Fainting, exhausted, He staggered with great drops of blood falling from His face. The Creator of the universe wrestled alone with the powers of darkness. "He was like a reed beaten and bent by the angry storm."[6]

He longed for companionship, but the disciples slept, and God was withdrawing His presence. His face was marked by bloody sweat and agony. Many "were appalled at him, his appearance was so disfigured beyond that of any man and his form marred beyond human likeness" (Isaiah 52:14). No one can understand the depths of suffering involved, changing visage and causing blood to flow. Jesus was overcome by the horror of a great darkness. "The humanity of the Son of God trembled in that trying hour. He prayed not now for His disciples that their faith might not fail, but for His own tempted, agonized soul. The awful moment had come—that moment which was to decide the destiny of the world. The fate of humanity trembled in the balance. Christ might even now refuse to drink the cup apportioned to guilty man. It was not yet too late. He might wipe the bloody sweat from His brow, and leave humans to perish in their iniquity. . . . His decision is made. He will save humans at any cost to Himself."[7]

The greatest pain, making the physical hardly felt, was heart pain. How could Satan be so cruel? How could sin be so terrifying? How could He save the world when so few would want to be saved? How could He endure the loss of the majority? Was it really worth it? How horrible the loneliness, the Godforsakenness, of sin. How empty was life without the Father. How terrible the broken relationship sin inflicts. He tasted it all, to the utter depths. He drained the dregs. He plunged into the deepest depths of substitution, taking our punishment so that we can go free. Through it all God the Father suffered with His Son. I can see Him sobbing as His Son suffered to become your Savior and mine. It broke His heart to see Him suffer for sinners as if alone, Godforsaken.

The Loneliness of Calvary

The crowing work of Creation was the Sabbath. Christ loved humans so much that He came to Adam and Eve as the God up close to give Himself to them in time for a full day of fellowship and communion. That gift began on Friday at sunset. By contrast, on another Friday, His people gave Jesus the cross. Yes, they collaborated with Romans because there was no other way. But they gave Him up to die. They had no King but Caesar. They rejected Jesus and put Him away. He was ostracized from society, a common criminal, to hang on the wood as a curse (see Galatians 3:13). He was nailed to the tree stark naked. There was no more degrading, humiliating, and anguishing death than crucifixion. He would not experience a God up close. He would be dead on the Sabbath.

Creation Friday and Crucifixion Friday. Two Adams. The first full day of life for one, the last day of life for the other. Christ gave life to Adam that first Friday. He was giving life to all the redeemed the other Friday. It was hands-on creation and hands-on crucifixion. There was no other way. He could not say "Let there be" in either case. He came up close to make it possible both times. Imagine: The God of the universe, the eternal one, the one who has never had a beginning, was about to die. It took His death to give us eternal life. There was no other way. He had to pay the price to give us this gift. He owned the universe but could not pay for salvation. He couldn't give things. He had to give Himself. Wonder, O heavens, and be astonished, O earth, that the Creator of the universe, who flung stars into space and called worlds into existence, populated planets, hung helpless on the cross, a victim, yet a willing substitute, dying the death that we should die, paying the price that we should pay, in order to give us a second chance. On Crucifixion Friday the human race had a new beginning.

"Did You think you were a priest? How come You're hanging on a cross then? Priests save others. Can't do that when You're dead. Some priest You are! You think You can save others, but You can't even save Yourself" (see Mark 15:31). Heartless to the end, religious leaders rejected Christ because they were devoid of a relationship with God or humans. That's the length to which loveless legalism goes. It's not only life apart from Christ; it crucifies Him.

At the very time He received the terrible weight of the world's sins upon Him, Jesus could no longer see the Father. "The withdrawal of the divine countenance from the Savior in this hour of supreme anguish pierced His heart with a sorrow that can never be fully understood by man."[8] This was Satan's opportunity. He had tried to break Christ's dependent relationship on His Father all his life. Now was his final attempt. Jesus felt so very much alone, and

Satan would tell Him He would remain alone forever if He went through with being the substitute for humans. Christ cried out, "My God, my God, why have you forsaken me?" (Mark 15:34).

"Satan with his fierce temptations wrung the heart of Jesus. The Savior could not see through the portals of the tomb. Hope did not present to Him His coming forth from the grave a conqueror, or tell Him of the Father's acceptance of the sacrifice. He feared that sin was so offensive to God that Their separation was to be eternal. Christ felt the anguish which the sinner will feel when mercy shall no longer plead for the guilty race. It was the sense of sin, bringing the Father's wrath upon Him as man's substitute, that made the cup He drank so bitter, and broke the heart of the Son of God."[9]

Think of it, Jesus cried out to the Father, "If I can never be with You again in becoming the substitute for humans, if they can be redeemed to heaven in My place, so let it be." And He plunged into the abyss and perished. That's the depth of His substitution. He was willing to let humans take His place with the Father He loved—if that's what it took to redeem them. There's no greater love than this, so selfless, so deep. How different was Satan's scheme. He wanted to wrench Christ from His throne and rule there in His place. But Jesus was willing to give up the throne and allow fallen sinners to sit on the throne in His place (see Revelation 3:21).

There's no greater contrast between Christ and Satan than at Calvary. Jesus gave His life to save others. Satan murdered Christ in utter selfishness. Calvary reveals the love of God and the hatred of Satan. Christ triumphed; Satan was defeated. Calvary is the climax of cosmic terrorism.

Satan's Attack

Satan hates defeat. In denial, he lunges forth to make Calvary of no effect. This is the next issue in cosmic terrorism. Yes, he does say the law was nailed to the cross. But he does more. He works to hide the cross, and make it of no effect. He hopes that Christ's death will be a waste of time. He cannot change Christ's victory, but he can cause humans not to accept it. (We'll say more about this in another chapter.) Satan couldn't get Christ to sin, but he can spread the word that He didn't sin because He was God. Christ didn't show that created beings can keep the law because He lived on earth as God. This way Christ contributed nothing to the question of God's law.

Here's deception going into high gear again. Satan knew that Christ had a double mission in coming to Planet Earth. True He came to live and die to save humans. But He also came to show that the law can be kept by created beings in a dependent relationship on God. Satan blamed Christ for creaturely rebellion. The law was too high. It needed to be changed. Christ came to Planet Earth as a human to show that the law can be kept, that God isn't unjust in giving the law to created beings. Satan had to admit that Christ did live a law-abiding life. He couldn't deny that any more than he could deny Calvary. So through many major theologians the word went out that Jesus lived on earth as God—and therefore He couldn't help keeping the law. His life proved nothing about what created beings can do.

Early councils said Christ was fully God and fully man, but never spelled out the relationship between the two. So for a thousand years theologians said Jesus lived on earth as God. This continued among the Reformers in the sixteenth century. Martin Luther believed that the divine-human natures were comingled, so that the humanity was divinized and the divinity humanized, forming a third person neither divine nor human. Such gave Christ an advantage over humans in lawkeeping. Later John Calvin had Christ's divinity on the throne of the universe while He lived as a human on earth, so He had a distinct advantage over other humans. But the reality is that Christ lived on earth as a man, totally dependent upon His Father in heaven. No wonder He came "at the risk of failure and eternal loss." [10]

In the previous chapter we noted the contemporary debate questions God's full future knowledge and focuses on the risk He takes with humans every day, not knowing their decision. That is a diminished God. He takes no risk in the sense that He doesn't know the outcome. This is what makes Christ's creation of humans so awesome. He knew full well the cost their creation would be to Him, but He loved them more than Himself, and willingly created them. The same is true with His creation of Lucifer. He knew that cosmic terrorism would plague the universe, and plunge Him into great suffering, but He went ahead. So great is His love for others. The only time Christ took a risk was in becoming a man, and living a dependent life in enemy territory where Satan threw everything at Him.

---

[1] Ellen G. White, *The Desire of Ages*, p. 686.
[2] *Ibid.*, p. 687.
[3] *Ibid.*
[4] *Ibid.*
[5] *Ibid.*, p. 688.
[6] *Ibid.*, p. 689.
[7] *Ibid.*, pp. 690-693.
[8] *Ibid.*, p. 753.
[9] *Ibid.*
[10] *Ibid.*, p. 49.

GOD'S WAR STRATEGY

When Christ faced Calvary, Peter thought He needed help. The mob moved into Gethsemane to arrest Him. It was time for Peter to act. He took his sword and lopped off the ear of the high priest's servant. It was precision delivery, suggesting a well-trained swordsman. Peter was ready for battle—why else would he have his sword with him? We do not read of Christ's disciples as armed militia. But Peter sure acted as one that early morning.

Jesus quietly said to Peter, "Put your sword back in its place, . . . for all who draw the sword will die by the sword. Do you think I cannot call on my Father, and he will at once put at my disposal more than twelve legions of angels?" (Matthew 26:52, 53). Jesus was teaching a vital lesson. Don't fight. Let God do the fighting. A Roman legion was 6,000 footmen and 700 horsemen, or a total of 6,700 men.★ Twelve legions would be 80,400 men! Christ was saying What's one sword compared to 80,400 powerful angels! Christ put His trust in God, not in human plans. He demonstrated that this is what His followers should have done throughout their history. Their repeated failures had everything to do with failure to trust in God.

The Exodus

It never was God's plan to have His people fight. His plan was to fight for them. It all began in Egypt. They were slaves. There wasn't much they could do but work. God sent the plagues. God destroyed the firstborn. God brought them out of Egypt.

They came to the banks of the Red Sea. How would they get

across? They couldn't swim. There were no boats. There was no bridge. Besides that, the Egyptian army was in hot pursuit. They were trapped. No way of escape. "As Pharaoh approached, the Israelites looked up, and there were the Egyptians, marching after them. They were terrified and cried out to the Lord" (Exodus 14:10). God spoke through Moses, "Do not be afraid. Stand firm and you will see the deliverance the Lord will bring you today. The Egyptians you see today you will never see again. The Lord will fight for you; you need only to be still" (verses 13, 14). What a mandate. You need only to be still. How hard it is for humans to do this. But it's the only plan God has for humans. He wants His people to trust Him alone.

God opened the way through the Red Sea. The walls of water were pushed to each side, and Israel went through on dry ground. Now there's something for Israel to do. Step in and walk across. But that's all. It was not their job to keep the waters back. That was God's job. It's important to know God's work and humans' work. So often humans try to do the work that belongs to God alone. Of course, they can never do this work, and end up in failure. As the Israelites trudged across the path through the Red Sea, "the angel of God, who had been traveling in front of Israel's army, withdrew and went behind them. The pillar of cloud also moved from in front and stood behind them, coming between the armies of Egypt and Israel. Throughout the night the cloud brought darkness to the one side and light to the other side" (verses 19, 20). The angel and the cloud protected Israel, and separated them from the pursuing enemy.

Who was the angel of God? Later God would say, "I am sending an angel ahead of you to guard you along the way and bring you to the place I have prepared . . . my Name is in him" (Exodus 23:20, 21). God says the angel was God. Scripture shows that it was the preincarnate Christ. On another occasion, "An angel appeared to Moses in the flames of a burning bush" and He said, "I am the God of your fathers" (Acts 7:30, 32). The Exodus is specifically linked to God's presence. "He brought you out of Egypt by his Presence and his great strength, to drive out before you nations greater and stronger than you and to bring you into their land" (Deuteronomy

4:37, 38). Note how God's presence, not Israel's, was to drive out the nations.

In looking back Paul could say, "I do not want you to be ignorant of the fact, brothers, that our forefathers were all under the cloud and that they all passed through the sea. They were all baptized into Moses in the cloud and in the sea. They all ate the same spiritual food and drank the same spiritual drink; for they drank from the spiritual rock that accompanied them, and that rock was Christ" (1 Corinthians 10:1-4).

No wonder it says, "The Lord looked down from the pillar of fire and cloud at the Egyptian army and threw it into confusion. He made the wheels of their chariots come off so that they had difficulty driving. And the Egyptians said, 'Let's get away from the Israelites! The Lord is fighting for them against Egypt'" (Exodus 14:24, 25). Here's the preincarnate Christ helping His people, and even the Egyptians realized they were fighting more than men.

Go Possess the Land

It all began much earlier. When God called Abraham He promised, "I will make you into a great nation and I will bless you" (Genesis 12:2). He said to Abraham, "All the land that you see I will give to you and your offspring forever. I will make your offspring like the dust of the earth" (Genesis 13:15, 16). There may have been battles in early times for which we have no record. Melchizedek said to Abraham, "And blessed be God Most High, who delivered your enemies into your hand" (Genesis 14:20). And God said to Abraham, "Do not be afraid, Abram. I am your shield, your very great reward" (Genesis 15:1). Clearly from the beginning it was God's plan to fight for His people, and He encouraged them to look to Him for help and therefore to be unafraid.

So the great rescue at the Red Sea was not the first battle God had fought for His people. But it's the most famous battle, and it became the great event that stands behind all the history of Israel and Judah in the Old Testament. Later leaders repeatedly refer back to this marvelous deliverance. The Exodus is to the Old Testament what the resurrection of Jesus is to the New Testament. These are two great acts that only God could do, and both had saving value for His people.

As Israel came to the borders of the Promised Land, they were reminded. "See, I have given you this land. Go in and take possession of the land that the Lord swore he would give to your fathers—to Abraham, Isaac and Jacob—and to their descendants after them" (Deuteronomy 1:8). "Do not be terrified; do not be afraid of them. The Lord your God, who is going before you, will fight for you, as he did for you in Egypt, before your very eyes, and in the desert. There you saw how the Lord your God carried you, as a father carries his son, all the way you went until you reached this place" (verses 29-31).

When the spies went into the land they spoke of the Anakites, who were strong giants (verses 19-28). God did not want them to look to the height or strength of the enemy any more than He wanted David to be impressed with Goliath. God wanted them to see *Him*. He is so much more powerful than any human enemy. "You may say to yourselves, 'These nations are stronger than we are. How can we drive them out?' But do not be afraid of them; remember well what the Lord your God did to Pharaoh and to all Egypt. You saw with your own eyes the great trials, the miraculous signs and wonders, the mighty hand and outstretched arm, with which the Lord your God brought you out. The Lord your God will do the same to all the peoples you now fear. Moreover, the Lord your God will send the hornet among them until even the survivors who hide from you have perished. Do not be terrified by them, for the Lord your God, who is among you, is a great and awesome God" (Deuteronomy 7:17-21).

"Hear, O Israel. You are now about to cross the Jordan to go in and dispossess nations greater and stronger than you, with large cities that have walls up to the sky. The people strong and tall—Anakites! You know about them and have heard it said, 'Who can stand up against the Anakites?' But be assured today that the Lord your God is the one who goes across ahead of you like a devouring fire. He will destroy them; he will subdue them before you. . . . The Lord your God will drive them out before you, to accomplish what he swore to your fathers, to Abraham, Isaac and Jacob" (Deuteronomy 9:1-5).

Promise Renewed to Joshua

After the death of Moses, Joshua became the leader of Israel. The God who is the same today and forever renewed His commitment to Joshua. "As I was with Moses, so I will be with you; I will never leave you nor forsake you. Be strong and courageous, because you will lead these people to inherit the land I swore to their forefathers to give them. Be strong and very courageous. . . . Do not be terrified; do not be discouraged, for the Lord your God will be with you wherever you go" (Joshua 1:5-9).

"When you go to war against your enemies and see horses and chariots and an army greater than yours, do not be afraid of them, because the Lord your God, who brought you up out of Egypt, will be with you. . . . Do not be fainthearted or afraid; do not be terrified or give way to panic before them. For the Lord your God is the one who goes with you to fight for you against your enemies to give you victory" (Deuteronomy 20:1-4).

"The Lord your God himself will cross over ahead of you. He will destroy these nations before you, and you will take possession of their land. . . . Be strong and courageous. Do not be afraid or terrified because of them, for the Lord your God goes with you; he will never leave you nor forsake you. . . . The Lord himself goes before you and will be with you; he will never leave you nor forsake you. Do not be afraid; do not be discouraged" (Deuteronomy 31:3-8).

Looking Back From the Time of Isaiah

Isaiah lived in a time when Israel and Judah were prosperous but in crisis. They had forgotten God and no longer relied on Him. It was the eighth century B.C. Isaiah reviewed God's goodness to His people. "In all their distress he too was distressed, and the angel of his presence saved them. In his love and mercy he redeemed them; he lifted them up and carried them all the days of old. . . . Then his people recalled the days of old, the days of Moses and his people—where is he who brought them through the sea, with the shepherd of his flock?" (Isaiah 63:9-11).

Sennacherib's Invasion

Sennacherib, king of Assyria, invaded Judah and laid siege to fortified cities. He wanted to conquer them for himself (2 Chronicles 32:1). Hezekiah, king of Judah, said to the troubled Jews, "Be strong and courageous. Do not be afraid or discouraged because of the king of Assyria and the vast army with him, for there is a greater power with us than with him. With him is only the arm of flesh, but with us is the Lord our God to help us and to fight our battles'" (verses 7, 8).

Sennacherib sent a message to the Jews. "Do you not know what I and my fathers have done to all the peoples of the other lands? Were the gods of those nations ever able to deliver their land from my hand? Who of all the gods of these nations that my fathers destroyed has been able to save his people from me? How then can your god deliver you from my hand?" (verses 13, 14). God had an answer. "Therefore this is what the Lord says concerning the king of Assyria: 'He will not enter this city or shoot an arrow here. . . . I will defend this city and save it.' . . . That night the angel of the Lord went out and put to death a hundred and eighty-five thousand men in the Assyrian camp" (2 Kings 19:32-35). What an awesome God! He knows how to fight. It always went better when His people allowed Him to do what He does best.

Where Are You Looking?

So many are afraid of last-day events. They look to giants such as the Sunday law, the great time of trouble, and the death decree. What will it be like to live at a time when probation has closed and Satan has full control of the finally impenitent? What will it be like when the whole world worships the beast and all must comply with Sunday deference? What will it be like when there is no more mediation in heaven and the Spirit has been withdrawn from the world? Some respond, "I don't believe in eternal hell, but that will be hell for a time."

Did you notice in the texts above that God repeatedly told His people He was going to be with them to fight their battles, and hence they need not fear? Further, He would carry them through the experience and bring them victory. Did you notice that He is the God of miracles so that appearances are deceptive? It's nothing for Him to open up a sea to let His people pass over on dry ground, or to destroy a mighty Egyptian or Assyrian army. He specializes in the seemingly impossible. He calls His people to look beyond the crisis to Him, the Christ.

What is the issue in this chapter? Cosmic terrorism deflects attention away from Christ to the crisis. Satan specializes in causing people to see troubles. He knows that if he can get them fixated on the problems, he will capture them. If he can get them to take their eyes off Christ, they will panic at the coming crisis. The name of the game is to replace Christ in this arena too. Satan replaces Him with the bad news. The coming crisis removes from view the coming Christ. People get discouraged and afraid. They capitulate to the demands of rulers in the end-times.

Our success in last-day events is dependent upon our focus. If we refuse to be deflected by the crisis, and cling to Christ, we will triumph. But if we fail to keep focused on Christ, we will be overwhelmed. There is no middle ground.

The Final Exodus

The exodus at the Red Sea is a type of the exodus through final events. Just as Israel was trapped by the enemy, so will God's people be in the end-time. All the world will wonder after the beast (see Revelation 13:3). God's people are surrounded by a world in rebellion. They will feel helpless as did Israel at the banks of the Red Sea. There is no human way out. But God provides a way. He will do it again. He will miraculously open up a way through final events from the Sunday law to the coming of Christ.

Again it is essential that we keep our eyes on Christ and not on the crisis. We will look at the light in the trenches with us, and not at the walls of water towering over us. We will focus on the promises of God given in this chapter. This is the way God prepares His people for the battle. They rest in His presence. They let Him carry them through. They do not try to fight. To rest in Christ is our battle. It takes all we have to be so resigned in the face of danger.

But it's an essential contribution that we can and have to make. Christ will even help us in this. We can plead for Him to make us willing to depend upon Him, and He can make it happen.

Jesus practiced this Himself. He knew in Gethsemane that swinging the sword was wrong. "Not My will, but Thine be done" prepared Him for the final battle. He kept His eyes upon His Father. That's why it was so hard for Him when He felt Godforsaken. The Father had to withdraw from Him when He took on the sins of the world. Christ hated sin, yet He had to carry it to become our Savior. He hated it because of its evil, but more than that, He hated the separation from the Father, the first and only separation in Their eternal relationship.

Jesus lived the life of a dependent human. It was something new for Him. Since the first creation of intelligent beings Christ had given orders. But as a human He had to learn to be dependent on His Father. He will teach His people to be the same. He experienced God's forsakenness so that we do not have to in the end-time. He promises us, "Never will I leave you, never will I forsake you" (Hebrews 13:5). He paid an enormous price to make that promise possible. His was the greatest time of trouble because He was Godforsaken, but the coming time of trouble will find none of His followers Godforsaken. Christ will be walking through final events with them.

Jesus kept His eyes on the goal. "For the joy set before him [He] endured the cross" (Hebrews 12:2). For the hope of being with Christ forever, we can endure last-day events. Look to Christ to fight your battles in the end-time, and you are well on the way to victory.

Summary of Issues in Cosmic Terrorism
1. Deflect attention from Christ as Creator by questioning His justice.
2. Cause doubt that Christ created first ancestors and break dependent relationship on Him.
3. Distance Creator from created beings.
4. Cause doubt in God's Word by appealing to the senses.
5. Disseminate views of God that question His justice.

6. Make Calvary of no effect.
7. Teach that Christ lived on earth as God, not as man, so His lawkeeping did not prove that created beings can keep God's law.
8. Deflect attention from Christ to the crisis.

---

* *The Seventh-day Adventist Bible Commentary,* vol. 5, p. 604.

WHERE ARE YOU LOOKING?

E verything depends upon focus. God knew that. He wanted the Jews to remember the Exodus—that He was the one who fought for them. He was the great deliverer. They need not fight their own battles. That is God's department; it was He who opened up the way through the Red Sea and kept the waters back. Their work was to simply trust Him, and rest in Him. That's the only battle they had to fight. That's the only battle any follower of Christ must fight. But it's a real struggle. It's a battle often lost, and such loss characterizes the history of God's ancient people. That battle is harder to win than volleying forth with swords at the ready.

That's why God asked His people to remember the Sabbath. It's a whole day resting in Him. The Sabbath provides the rest needed to resist the urge to fight. If they had entered into a dependent relationship with Christ during the Sabbath, it would have schooled them to continue that relationship during the week. That's why the Sabbath was the first full day of life for Adam and Eve. Christ knew that it was vital for even perfect humans to begin their life with a full Sabbath of resting in Him their Creator.

But the Jews forgot to remember the Exodus and the Sabbath, with disastrous results. God's chosen people became two nations, Israel the northern kingdom and Judah the southern kingdom. Their separation from each other was a result of a deeper separation from Christ. They fell onto a slippery slope that plunged toward Calvary. Their purpose as a nation terminated when they crucified Christ, and it all began with losing their focus.

The Importance of Focus

Have you read the record in Kings and Chronicles? So many kings did evil in the sight of God. Ahab "did more evil in the eyes of the Lord than any of those before him" (1 Kings 16:30). He served and worshiped Baal, and built a temple for Baal in Samaria (see verse 32). Wondering whether to go to battle, Ahab and King Jehoshaphat of Judah (who "did what was right in the eyes of the Lord" [1 Kings 22:43]) sat in their royal robes on their thrones at the entrance gate of Samaria, listening to the prophets who urged them to go to battle in Ramoth-gilead. But Micaiah, God's prophet, "saw the Lord sitting on his throne with all the host of heaven standing around him on his right and on his left" (verse 19). He told them not to go to war. Both kings ignored Micaiah and listened to the prophets' lies. They went to battle, and Ahab died (see verses 29-38). Both kings lost their focus on the King of kings. God says that Israel crafted idols and offered human sacrifices, "But I am the Lord your God, who brought you out of Egypt" (Hosea 13:4). They lost sight of the God of the Exodus.

King Jehu of Israel killed all the relatives of Ahab, as well as his chief men, close friends, and priests (see 2 Kings 10:11). He also tore down the temple of Baal (see verse 27). "Yet Jehu was not careful to keep the law of the Lord, the God of Israel, with all his heart" (verse 31). It was easier for him to kill all the enemies than to surrender fully to Christ. That's precisely why God did not want His people to fight. It would be easy for them to depend upon their success and not depend on Him. It was their success that separated them from Christ. So it was with Jehu.

Many kings did what was right in God's eyes, but not fully. They did not remove the high places where people continued to offer sacrifices and burn incense to other gods. So it was with Joash (see 2 Kings 12:3), Amaziah (see 2 Kings 15:3, 4), and Jothan (see verses 34, 35), all kings of Judah. Pluralism was a peril to Judah in its decline. Even good kings didn't conduct a thorough reformation. They failed to eradicate false worship.

It got worse. Ahaz, king of Judah, "even sacrificed his son in the fire" (2 Kings 16:3), and took "silver and gold found in the temple of the Lord" and sent them as a gift to the king of Assyria (verse 8). He introduced a new altar into the sacred temple (see verses 10-18). During his reign Israel went into Assyrian captivity because they "sinned against the Lord their God, who had brought them up out of Egypt. . . . They worshiped other gods and followed the practices of the nations the Lord had driven out before them, as well as the practices that the kings of Israel had introduced. . . . They built themselves high places in all their towns" (2 Kings 17:7-9).

God fought against the nations and gave their lands to the Jews. But instead of being grateful and looking to Him above anyone else, they looked at the worship of the nations that God defeated and adopted that worship, even though their gods had been defeated by the only God! What a tragic loss of focus. They had every reason to worship God for His mighty acts of deliverance, but instead they worshiped the gods who had been defeated! It doesn't get any worse than that! King Hezekiah "gave him [the king of Assyria] all the silver that was found in the temple of the Lord" and "stripped off the gold with which he had covered the doors and doorposts of the temple of the Lord, and gave it to the king of Assyria" (2 Kings 18:15, 16).

The God of the Exodus who destroyed the entire army of Egypt to launch the history of Israel did it again at the close of Israel's history. He destroyed the entire army of Sennacherib, the Assyrian king (see 2 Kings 19:35). The sad history of Israel is played out between these two mighty battles that God fought for His people. They lost sight of the God of the Exodus, the God of the Red Sea, and while the captivity to Assyria was under way, God rose up and gave them one more view of His mighty power before their permanent demise. If only they had kept their focus on, and trust in, the God of the Exodus, then the victory over Sennacherib would have been one of a series of God fighting for His people.

The Last Days of Judah

King Manasseh worshiped the gods of the nations that the God of Israel defeated for His people. What's the good of worshiping defeated gods instead of the victorious God? What's the point? Sin is blind. In fact, in "both courts of the temple of the Lord, he built altars to all the starry hosts. He sacrificed his own son in the fire, practiced sorcery and divination, and consulted mediums and spiritists" (2 Kings 21:5, 6). "He took the carved image he had made and put it in God's temple" (2 Chronicles 33:7). Manasseh led them astray, so "they did more evil than the nations the Lord had destroyed before the Israelites" (2 Kings 21:9). They sank lower than the heathen nations. God said, "You have been more unruly than the nations around you" (Ezekiel 5:7).

Looking back over the entire history of Israel-Judah, God mournfully assessed, "They have done evil in my eyes and have provoked me to anger from the day their forefathers came out of Egypt until this day" (2 Kings 21:15). Throughout their history they forgot the great act of God in the Exodus, and no wonder the prophets often reminded them (see chapter 6), but to no avail. "The Lord, the God of their fathers, sent word to them through his messengers again and again, because he had pity on his people and on his dwelling place. But they mocked God's messengers, despised his words and scoffed at his prophets until the wrath of the Lord was aroused against his people and there was no remedy" (2 Chronicles 36:15, 16). Finally God would send His Son, and they didn't recognize Him for who He was. They murdered their deliverer because they had never accepted Him by being dependent on Him and looking to Him as they had at the banks of the Red Sea.

Imagine becoming worse than the nations God defeated on their behalf! That was the result of accepting their gods. To both Israel and Judah the principle is true: "They followed worthless idols and themselves became worthless" (2 Kings 17:15). It's dangerous to lose our focus on God. This leads to "no remedy," as we read above. Immediately following the words "no remedy," it says, "He brought up against them the king of the Babylonians" (2 Chronicles 36:17). This brings us to the first verses of Daniel. "Nebuchadnezzar king of Babylon came to Jerusalem and besieged it. And the Lord delivered Jehoiakim king of Judah into his hand" (Daniel 1:1, 2). How tragic that the book whose theme is God's deliverance has to begin with God's deliverance of His people into enemy hands. That's because they had chosen the gods of the defeated nations, and worshiped these defeated gods, so God allowed them to experience the defeat of such nations and gods, for they had turned away from Him, the God who defeated these former enemies. Now they were defeated by Babylon, and entered a 70-year captivity.

By beholding we become changed (see 2 Corinthians 3:18) is another principle at work in Israel-Judah. The verb tense is in the present continuous: "By beholding we are becoming ever more like that which we gaze upon." God's people could have continually gazed upon the wonders of God's mighty deliverance in the Red Sea and experienced deliverance themselves. But they looked at the defeated nations, accepted their defeated gods, and by continually looking at them became defeated themselves.

Yes, I know they were stupid. They even sank so low that they sacrificed their children to these gods. Yes, they had forgotten that the God of the universe would send His Son to become a sacrifice for them! Sacrificing their children was an utter waste of life! But so were their own lives of apostasy! But don't be too hard on them, as horrible and incredible as they were, for in last-day events so many Adventist Christians are scared of what's coming, as if they worshiped defeated gods. I find this is true throughout the Adventist world. In my last-day events presentations in various countries I find the fear factor is high among those who contemplate coming times of trouble. They say, "It's all trouble! Help! I wish I could go to heaven via the resurrection and skip all the trouble." Have you ever felt that way?

The problem is focus. They look at the crisis instead of to Christ. They fixate on what is coming instead of who is coming. Their god is not the God of the Exodus. They may not know it, and would certainly deny it, but they have a replacement God, a lesser god, a god that isn't on the throne of the universe as the great deliverer! For no focus on the God of the Exodus brings fear. The God of the Exodus is the delivering God who destroys the enemy and delivers His people. When people fixate on this truth, it sets them free (see John 8:32)—free from fear of final events! And countless thousands of Adventists have experienced this change.

You Are What You Think

Yes, you are what you eat. But you are what you think too. Do you choose your thoughts as carefully as you choose your food? It's just as important. Think big thoughts, as some captives did in Babylon. It would be natural to be frustrated, not able to go home for 70 years. That's like serving a life sentence, especially for those beyond their teens. For a 20-year-old, that meant no homecoming until they were 90! (That is, if they made it until then.) They could fill their minds with sadness, homesickness, and despair. But what good would those be to them? How much would they add to their life in captivity? They would be imprisoned by their thoughts, which is an even greater captivity! Much better to think of the God who was with them in their plight, and who longs to make life in captivity a life free in Him.

You've heard it said—prisoners can look at bars or stars. That can be a flippant statement. It's not easy to be imprisoned for life, with no hope of parole, and no future freedom in sight. I would not underestimate how cruel and devastating that can be. I would hate to be in that state myself. But even there God has not forgotten. He understands and cares, for the God of the Exodus is also the God of Gethsemane and Calvary, and He was willing to die, even if He never came home again, in order that *we* can come home in His place. It doesn't get harder than that; Jesus lived eternally in His home, greatly loved, adored, and worshiped, and only came on this mission to a rebel planet because He wanted humans home with Him in heaven forever.

Satan said that Jesus would be eternally forsaken if He took human sin, and out of the depths of His Godforsakenness Christ made the decision to plunge into the abyss forever in ultimate substitution. It was only later, in sheer faith, that He commended Himself to the Father in His expiring breath (see Luke 23:46) and triumphed because of His focus. He looked above the present crisis to the joy set before Him and endured the cross (see Hebrews 12:2). He focused on the throne, the redeemed gathered there, the peace and harmony of the universe restored. That's the only focus for end-time saints to endure the coming crisis.

Those who fill the mind with that future can sense Christ with them in the present. They say with Paul, "I am convinced that neither death nor life, neither angels nor demons, neither the present nor the future, nor any powers, neither height nor depth, nor anything else in all creation, will be able to separate us from the love of God that is in Christ Jesus our Lord" (Romans 8:38, 39).

Counterfeit Worship

Counterfeit worship caused the Captivity. Counterfeit worship is a recurrent challenge in captivity. Daniel, Hananiah, Mishael, and Azariah came from royalty or nobility (see Daniel 1:3, 6) and demonstrate that leaders who keep God in their minds and hearts can rise to any heights. How unlike most of the kings of Israel and Judah they were! They were unafraid to ask to be given an exception. Daniel asked for a 10-day test to eat vegetables instead of the royal food and wine. He said it would make them look healthier and better than the others. And it worked (see verses 11-16). After three years of academic training the four were "in every matter of wisdom and understanding . . . ten times better than all the magicians and enchanters in his whole kingdom" (verse 20). I believe each one studied with much prayer and asked God to give them the wisdom and understanding that made them better than the rest. God delights to honor such prayers, and if you pray, God can prepare you for big things in the end-time.

When King Nebuchadnezzar had a dream he forgot, yet wanted his astrologers to tell him the dream and the interpretation, they replied in fear, "There is not a man on earth who can do what the king asks! . . . No one can reveal it to the king except the gods, and they do not live among men" (Daniel 2:10). Nebuchadnezzar was mad and issued an order to kill them. This is the first of many death decrees in the book of Daniel (see verses 12, 13). Daniel and his friends were to die too, yet they hadn't been asked to tell the dream. When Daniel found out, he didn't hesitate but went in before the king and asked for time. Daniel rushed home and gathered his friends and "urged them to plead for mercy from the God of heaven" (verse 18).

"During the night the mystery was revealed to Daniel" (verse 19). God came through because Daniel and his friends were in a trust relationship with Him. They didn't suddenly know how to pray in this emergency. No, they prayed to a God well known. He had blessed them during the three years of their training. We never know what God has in store for us, and even in school the foundation is being laid to give us the experience to stand when crises come. Many are afraid of the future because they do not know God now. We must get to know Him now if we ever hope to be ready for the crisis when it comes. God didn't let His faithful servants down. They had been in daily conversation and worship, and this crisis was but another experience along the way. He revealed the dream just as He had given them wisdom in their studies before. It was not a miracle out of the blue, but part of an ongoing relationship.

Daniel's first response was to worship God. "Praise be to the name of God for ever and ever; wisdom and power are his. He changes times and seasons; he sets up kings and deposes them. He gives wisdom to the wise and knowledge to the discerning. He reveals deep and hidden things; he knows what lies in darkness, and light dwells with him. I thank and praise you, O God of my fathers: You have given me wisdom and power, you have made known to me what we asked of you, you have made known to us the dream of the king" (verses 20-23). It was natural for Daniel to worship and praise His God. He rejoiced in yet another evidence of His love and blessings to him.

Daniel gave God full credit. "No wise man, enchanter, magician or diviner can explain to the king the mystery he has asked about, but there is a God in heaven who reveals mysteries. He has shown Nebuchadnezzar what will happen in days to come" (verses 27, 28). The dream spanned from God giving Nebuchadnezzar dominion in the present to the time when "the God of heaven will set up a kingdom that will never be destroyed" (verse 44). Daniel emphasized the transitoriness of human rule compared to the eternal rule of Christ. The rock to smash the final kingdoms was cut out without human hands (see verses 34, 45). God is in control. "The great God has shown the king what will take place in the future" (verse 45). So

Daniel pointed the king beyond the passing human kingdoms to the coming kingdom of God!

Nebuchadnezzar was convicted. "Surely your God is the God of gods and the Lord of kings" (verse 47). A heathen king had grasped what most kings of Israel and Judah failed to understand. He focused on the God they failed to see.

He Lost his Focus

God gave the vision of His image to Nebuchadnezzar in the second year of his reign (see verse 1). When did the king build his counterfeit image? Daniel does not give the year. But 2 Kings 24, 25 gives important data. Nebuchadnezzar invaded Judah during the third year of King Jehoiakim, and Jehoiakim was a vassal for three years (see Daniel 1:1; cf. 2 Kings 24:1). In the eighth year of Nebuchadnezzar's reign (see 2 Kings 24:12), or six years after he received God's image dream (Daniel 2:1), he took King Jehoiachin of Judah captive and "removed all the treasures from the temple of the Lord" (2 Kings 24:13), just as a few years before he took "some of the articles from the temple of God" (Daniel 1:2). He appointed Zedekiah as a vassal king. Zedekiah did evil in the eyes of the Lord (see 2 Kings 24:18, 19) and later rebelled against Babylon, so Nebuchadnezzar in the ninth year of Zedekiah came against him and lay siege to Jerusalem. The siege lasted for two years. Zedekiah was captured, his eyes were put out, and he was bound in bronze shackles and taken to Babylon.

In the nineteenth year of Nebuchadnezzar, Nebuzaradan, commander of the Imperial guard, "set fire to the temple of the Lord, the royal palace and all the houses of Jerusalem. Every important building he burned down" (2 Kings 25:8, 9). It had been 17 years since God gave His original vision of the image to Nebuchadnezzar. The king had accomplished many great exploits since then. Human success filled the screen of his mind, shutting out the vision of God.

"How come my kingdom is only a passing one?" What an unwelcome idea to Nebuchadnezzar, who had accomplished so much since he had the image dream. Satan told him he was a great king, and surely his kingdom would survive. Had not Nebuchadnezzar defeated Judah? He destroyed the capital city, burned the Temple, burned the palace, and burned every important house. He had taken kings captive, and most of the inhabitants of Judah were taken to Babylon. That's an impressive victory against the God of heaven! Surely it's Babylon that will last forever, not God's kingdom. After all, God doesn't even have a kingdom now.

It was time for Nebuchadnezzar to set the record straight. The image of God claimed that God's kingdom would be forever. But that was 17 years before, and Nebuchadnezzar had changed all that, or so he thought. Nebuchadnezzar reasoned that his kingdom would be forever, and ordered an image to be constructed—an image made of all gold, not just a head of gold. For his golden kingdom had proved invincible even against God. The image was immense, 104 feet high—probably 52 feet of image itself with a pedestal of 52 feet.★ It was placed on the Plain of Dura, and stood tall for all to see. Nebuchadnezzar was exceedingly pleased. This was his view of future history. God's view of history was no longer relevant. Nebuchadnezzar trusted more to his own works than the Word of God. He lost his focus on the God who could recall a forgotten dream as well as tell its meaning. He no longer looked to that God, but to his own alleged successes against that God. How often pride hides the truth, as it did for Satan in heaven.

The Voice of the Conqueror

"I know what I'll do," said the king. "I'll gather the leaders of my kingdom and have them come to a dedication ceremony." The crowd gathered in awe at the immense and shining image. How it glistened in the noonday sun! The king's order was given. "When the music sounds, bow down and worship the image." It really was bowing to worship Nebuchadnezzar, the one whose kingdom it represented. Here was the king of Babylon calling for worship that only the God of heaven should receive. "Bow or burn" was the king's order, and peoples from all nations and languages bowed down and worshiped (see Daniel 3:7).

But not the three Hebrews. They stood tall, unwavering, unafraid. The king was furious. This was a personal affront by captives of all people! He had decimated their nation. They of all people should bow down. "What god will be able to rescue you from my hand?" screamed the king. Then they replied to the king, "O Nebuchadnezzar, we do not need to defend ourselves before you in this matter. If we are thrown into the blazing furnace, the God we serve is able to save us from it, and he will rescue us from your hand, O king. But even if he does not, we want you to know, O king, that we will not serve your gods or worship the image of gold you have set up" (verses 16-18). The king was as mad as a hornet and ordered the furnace heated seven times hotter.

They didn't bow down, so strong soldiers bound them and cast them into the furnace. The king watched. "Look!" he said. "I see four men walking around in the fire unbound and unharmed!" (verse 25). Christ was in the furnace with them! He fought the battle for them. All they did was trust Him. They would rather die than worship other gods. And Christ rewarded them by standing with them in the flames.

The End-time Test

In the future the whole world will be called to false worship (see Revelation 13:12-15). All will bow except a few. "Bow down to Sunday or die." That's the decree. Sunday looks like Saturday; both have 24 hours. But only one is the Sabbath of the Lord. Only the Sabbath is made by God. The other day of worship is made by humans. Likewise, the image of different metals and materials was a "God-made" vision, and the golden image was made by Nebuchadnezzar. When the whole world is ordered to bow down and worship Sunday, Christ will stand with those who stand up for the Sabbath. When the whole world turns on them with a death decree and they are thrown into the final fiery furnace of the great time of trouble, Christ will be in the middle of the flames with them to give them the victory that resting in Him alone can bring (see Matthew 28:20; Hebrews 13:5).

★ *The Seventh-day Adventist Bible Commentary,* vol. 4, p. 780.

SATAN'S TROJAN HORSE

Joseph Stalin and Adolf Hitler share much in common. They were angry tyrants that ruled over a nation as absolute dictators and killed millions of people. They were nationalists, and hated the Jews. Both wrote as revolutionaries, Stalin for the Georgian Marxist Journal called *Brdzola* ("The Struggle"), and Hitler a book called *Mein Kampf* ("My Struggle"). Both promised to be orderly when coming to power, but both discarded that for dictatorship. They were terrorists. They remind me of Satan, who promised so much in heaven and in Eden but only as a cover for his absolute despotism to take over the planet. This is cosmic terrorism, for behind the Stalins and Hitlers of this world stands Satan, who captured them and made them tools for his reign of terror.

Stalin, meaning "man of steel," had no feeling. As Myron Rush put it, "Stalin ruled by terror during most of his years as dictator." His rule was from 1929 to 1953. He executed or jailed all who helped him rise to power, and was "responsible for the death of millions of Soviet peasants."[1] He didn't allow dissent, and ruthlessly killed to get his way, until the military leadership was decimated when Germany invaded the country in World War II.

What about Hitler? First a word about Germany. Defeated in World War I, Germany was bankrupt, with millions out of work. The Versailles Treaty confiscated a lot of land from Germany, and demanded payment for war damages. Hitler's *Mein Kampf* laid out plans for the nation's future, including recapture of lost lands and the takeover of Austria, Czechoslovakia, and parts of western Russia.

"Hitler promised the aging president, Paul von Hindenburg, that he would act lawfully if he were named to head the government." The president did this on January 30, 1933. The Nazis (Hitler's party) burned the parliament building the next month (February 27, 1933), and Hitler blamed the Communists and "persuaded Hindenburg to sign a law 'for the protection of the people and the state.' This law wiped out individual rights in Germany and allowed the Nazis to jail anyone without a trial."[2]

Hitler hated non-Germans, especially Jews and Slavs. He was steeped in Eastern mysticism and hypnotized the masses. He was a dictator for 12 shocking years (1933-1945). Six million Jews were incarcerated and burned in gas chambers just because of their ethnicity. What butchery! This barbaric and brutal hatred of people mirrors Satan, who possessed him. A time bomb narrowly missed taking Hitler's life on July 20, 1944, at his headquarters. In angry revenge he "had at least 4,980 persons executed. On his orders, some of them were strangled slowly with piano wire. Movies were taken of their suffering so Hitler could watch."[3]

Stalin and Hitler were once helpless babes. What a blessing they could have become. Many factors led them otherwise. One thing they had in common were harsh and brutal fathers. Stalin's dad was "a drunkard who was cruel to his young son."[4] Hitler was a poor student in high school. "His low grades angered his father, who was harsh and had a bad temper."[5] Both went far beyond their dads to become the most brutal men in modern times.

Hidden Dictator Dominates Israel

As Hitler hated the Jews, so did Satan. They were God's chosen avenue to bring salvation and the Savior to the world. Satan did everything to wipe them out, but with hidden subtlety. Undercover terrorism is the most insidious. He caused them to feel independent while taking over as dictator. They didn't know it, nor did Stalin and Hitler. Satan's stealth campaign is to work from within. Any life separate from Christ is already captive to cosmic terrorism, whether one knows it or not. Anyone without Christ within is a potential Stalin or Hitler. The Jews didn't realize they would murder Christ.

Because Christ wanted to use them to reveal truth to the world, Satan used them to distort that revelation. Satan denigrated their religion, desecrated their Temple, and destroyed their mission. They ended up killing Christ rather than revealing Him.

Their worship deteriorated into a system of works to appease idols, even to sacrificing their children. Working to save oneself is the basis of every heathen religion, and became the basis of the religion of Israel and Judah. They lost sight of the gift of salvation in the coming death of Christ, because they lost sight of victory as a gift in God's fighting their battles. When they went to war and did the fighting, it was often interpreted as a victory through human prowess. Thus Satan's subtle strategy worked. They became victims of cosmic terrorism.

Their worship was more about what they did than what their idols did. After all, their idols did nothing. Imagine worshiping idols of carved wood or molded metals. That's no different from worshiping the image on the Plain of Dura. Scripture says, "All the leaders of the priests and the people became more and more unfaithful, following all the detestable practices of the nations and defiling the temple of the Lord, which he had consecrated in Jerusalem" (2 Chronicles 36:14). Had Nebuchadnezzar invited everyone to worship his golden idol, the nation of Judah would have obeyed. Satan controlled these captives long before their Babylonian captivity. This makes the response of the three Hebrew worthies so remarkable. They were a loyal remnant in last-day events of Judah before the Babylonian captivity.

Ezekiel, a contemporary of Daniel, gives further insight into the decadent worship in Judah. "You have defiled my sanctuary with all your vile images and detestable practices" (Ezekiel 5:11). God took Ezekiel in vision to Jerusalem and showed him the inner court where the idol of jealousy stood (see Ezekiel 8:3-5). Ezekiel explains, "Then he brought me to the entrance to the court. I looked, and I saw a hole in the wall. He said to me, 'Son of man, now dig into the wall.' So I dug into the wall and saw a doorway there. And he said to me, 'Go in and see the wicked and detestable things they are doing here.' So I went in and looked, and I saw portrayed all over the walls all kinds of crawling things and detestable animals and all the idols of the house of Israel. In front of them stood seventy elders of the house of Israel. . . . Each had a censer in his hand. . . . He said to me, 'Son of man, have you seen what the elders of the house of Israel are doing in the darkness, each at the shrine of his own idol?'" (verses 7-12).

God showed Ezekiel women sitting at the entrance of the north gate of the Temple mourning for Tammuz, a Babylonian god of vegetation (see verse 14). Ezekiel continues, "He then brought me into the inner court of the house of the Lord, and there at the entrance to the temple, between the portico and the altar, were about twenty-five men. With their backs toward the temple of the Lord and their faces toward the east, they were bowing down to the sun in the east" (verse 16). Idolatry gripped Judah for a long time. They offered incense to many gods. Repeatedly God sent prophets to them but they did not listen (see Jeremiah 44:4, 5). Jeremiah was one of them. The men of Judah told him straight: "We will not listen to the message you have spoken to us in the name of the Lord! We will certainly do everything we said we would: We will burn incense to the Queen of Heaven and will pour out drink offerings to her just as we and our fathers, our kings and our officials did in the towns of Judah and in the streets of Jerusalem" (verses 16, 17). They claimed that worship of the Queen of Heaven made their crops successful, but unsuccessful when they didn't worship her.

The worship of Tammuz, the sun, and the Queen of Heaven, together with a desecrated temple, made Judah a type of the papal power introduced in Daniel 8. Just as Satan hijacked the religion of God in Judah (and Israel before) so he hijacked the religion of God in the Christian Era. This background helps us to better understand what Satan is doing today, and will do in last-day events. We will address this in coming chapters. His approach has always been to work from within, taking over by stealth, a vintage Trojan horse maneuver. Judah was as surely captured by satanic terrorism as Russia and Germany were in modern times. This is the background for the book of Daniel.

How to Understand the Book of Daniel

The book of Daniel makes a significant contribution to last-day events and to the question of worship, both genuine and counterfeit. It's important to understand the structure of the book, how it's put together. There's a type/antitype relationship between the historical section (chapters 1-6) and the last-day events section (chapters 7-12). The examples from history are local but typical of the global events in the future. We saw one example in the previous chapter. Worship of the golden image made by Nebuchadnezzar typifies worship of a human-made Sunday in the end-time. Both are counterfeit worship. Both are forced worship under penalty of a death decree. Just as God's three Hebrews were delivered from the fiery furnace, so will God's people be delivered from the final fiery furnace (see Daniel 12:1). From a human perspective, there seemed no way out of the dilemma, but God miraculously intervened, and will do it again globally in the end-time.

It's important to understand the Hebrew way of thinking. Unlike the Western way of thought, where a story unfolds chronologically until its conclusion, the Hebrew way of thinking is the reverse. The conclusion of the story is given first, and only then are the steps given that lead to the conclusion. Thus chapters 9 and 8 are steps in the story, whereas chapter 7 is the conclusion. The steps cover less history, the conclusion stretches from the beginning to the end.

Chapter 9 _____

Chapter 8 _____

Chapter 7 _____

Chapter 9: 490 years, 457 B.C.-A.D. 34
Chapter 8: Babylon to 1844
Chapter 7: Babylon to Second Advent

The best book I know on Daniel, which illustrates the Hebrew way of thinking, is William Shea's commentary.[6] Shea presents chapters 7 to 9 in the reverse order, so as to get the story from a Western perspective. I will follow him in this arrangement. We will look at these chapters from the perspective of cosmic terrorism. I call them "The Tale of Two Desecrations of the Jerusalem Temple" (Daniel 9), "The Desecration of the Heavenly Temple" (Daniel 8), and "The Judgment From the Heavenly Temple" (Daniel 7). It's fitting that the temples dominate these three chapters, as the heavenly temple is where cosmic terrorism began, and the temples on earth were devastated by the satanic terrorists as tragically as were the twin towers in New York. The devastation was first spiritual and then physical. Deflecting attention from dependence on Christ is just as potent a vehicle as planes plunging into buildings.

Chronologically, the three chapters (Daniel 9; 8; 7) take us on a journey (1) from Judah's time of trouble to her last-day events, and (2) through the Christian Era to final events on Planet Earth. The journey includes some dates and details that help us grasp the timeline as cosmic terrorism works through religions to destroy Christ's plan for the planet.

Daniel as a Type of the End-time Saints

Daniel and his companions knew how to worship God. Daniel also gives us insight into how to pray. He was not deterred by the decree of Darius to pray only to him for 30 days or be thrown to the lions (see Daniel 6:7). This is the second death decree to enforce counterfeit worship in the book of Daniel. It's also a type of the end-time global decree to worship the beast or die (see Revelation 13:12-15). Daniel opened his windows toward Jerusalem, toward the Temple, and "three times a day he got down on his knees and prayed, giving thanks to his God, just as he had done before" (Daniel 6:10). He was not afraid of the death decree. He ignored it. Furthermore, he thanked God. Here is a person who does not allow crises to separate him from Christ. He daily gazed on Christ seated on the throne of heaven and had no fear of any human king. That's the way to be ready for any terror attack of the enemy.

Even king Darius recognized Daniel's consistent prayer life: "May your God, whom you serve continually, rescue you!" (verse 17). Daniel spent the night with hungry lions, but "God sent his angel, and he shut the mouths of the lions" and "no wound was found on him" (verses 22, 23). Daniel didn't worry. God had taken four praying captives and made them 10 times fairer and wiser, and He had given and interpreted visions to Daniel for another king— so why be concerned about this latest royal challenge? It was consistent communion with Christ that kept Daniel unafraid. When you daily bend low before the King of kings, you can stand tall before any other king.

Daniel's Prayer

Look at Daniel's prayer in chapter 9:4-19. "O Lord, the great and awesome God, who keeps his covenant of love" (verse 4). What a way to begin a prayer. Daniel had a clear picture of God on the throne of heaven, an awesome God, a God who loves His people. But he could have begun the prayer a different way. He had just read in Jeremiah 29:10 that Judah's captivity in Babylon would be 70 years (see Daniel 9:2). That was less than two years away. So what's the problem? The problem is the number he heard in Daniel 8:14—2,300 evenings and mornings! Any extension like that of the 70 years was too much! After all, he was nearing 90 years of age, and longed to go home before he died. He could have prayed, "God, how come the time has been extended? You said it was 70 years in Jeremiah. I thought You never changed Your word. How can we depend on You?" But he didn't. For nearly 70 years he had prayed to God in captivity, and they were so close that he knew there was a good answer. He knew God could be trusted. His God had explained two dreams for Nebuchadnezzar. He could explain the 2,300 number, too.

Then Daniel did something incredible. He allied himself with the rebellious people of Judah that did all the terrible things we noted above. He said, "We have been wicked and have rebelled. . . . We have not listened to your servants the prophets" (Daniel 9:5, 6). By contrast, he says, "Lord, you are righteous" (verse 7). He repeats this in verses 9-11 and then says, "God is righteous in everything he does; yet we have not obeyed him" (verse 14). As Stalin, Hitler, and Judah reflected Satan, so Daniel reflected the Christ who "bore the sin of many, and made intercession for the transgressors" (Isaiah 53:12). Like Jesus, he had a burden for others that transcended any fear for himself. This is crucial in final events. Beholding Christ changes one, and being separate from Him changes one. Eternal destiny hangs on our connection or disconnection with Christ. To break that dependent connection is the primary thrust of cosmic terrorism.

Besides his burden for Judah, Daniel is burdened over the Temple in Jerusalem, the temple toward which he prays three times a day. "Under the whole heaven nothing has ever been done like what has been done to Jerusalem" (Daniel 9:12).

"Now, O Lord our God, who brought your people out of Egypt with a mighty hand and who made for yourself a name that endures to this day, we have sinned, we have done wrong" (verse 15). Here is the key to Daniel's success. Unlike most of the others in Israel and Judah, he never forgot the God of the Exodus. He kept that great act of God clear in his mind. It kept him on course. How could those rescued by that mighty act of God ever turn to idols who cannot act at all? It doesn't make sense! How could Aaron make a golden calf and the people say, "These are your gods, O Israel, who brought you up out of Egypt" (Exodus 32:4)? It wasn't even made before they crossed the sea!

Daniel is burdened. "O Lord, look with favor on your desolate sanctuary. Give ear, O God, and hear; open your eyes and see the desolation of the city that bears your Name. We do not make requests of you because we are righteous, but because of your great mercy. O Lord, listen! O Lord, forgive! O Lord, hear and act! For your sake, O my God, do not delay, because your city and your people bear your Name" (Daniel 9:17-19). Daniel is jealous for the name, or reputation, of God. He knows that enemies who worship idols believe their idols are more powerful than the God of the universe, for had not Babylon with its idols apparently destroyed God's city and Temple in Jerusalem? End-time saints will have the same burden. They want God's name to be honored in final events. They plead not for personal salvation but for God's name to be vindicated when all the world is caught up in counterfeit worship.

Gabriel's Contribution
Gabriel is the covering cherub who once stood with Lucifer at

heaven's throne and, since the fall of Lucifer, took his place. He came to give Daniel "insight and understanding." The closeness between Christ and Daniel is seen in Christ's response. Gabriel conveyed it saying, "As soon as you began to pray, an answer was given, which I have come to tell you, for you are highly esteemed" (verse 23). Daniel says, "You are an awesome God," and God says, "You are highly esteemed, Daniel." How they love each other! There is a deep bonding between the two, and that's what it takes to go through final events. There's no substitute for relationship. Anything less is no better than a lifeless idol. Jesus said, "This is eternal life: that they may know you, the only true God, and Jesus Christ, whom you have sent" (John 17:3). To "know" in this verse doesn't come from the Greek word *allos* (to know about, like knowing about President Bush) but *givosko* (to have a relationship with). They were bonded friends. The three prayers a day were not a routine but a reveling.

Gabriel came to interpret the vision (Daniel 9:23). Which vision? There are two words used for vision in the book: *hazon* and *mareh*. *Hazon* means the entire vision, and *mareh* is a sub-element of the vision. The word "vision" in verse 23 is *mareh*. The *hazon* is 2,300 years (see Daniel 8:14) and *mareh* is 490 years (see Daniel 9:24-27). Daniel 9 has to do with the 490 years cut off (see verse 26) from the 2,300 years, "cut off" signifying cut off from its beginning, the first segment.

Don't get lost here. We want to make this simple. Information about the 490 years is a response to Daniel's prayer. "For your sake, O my God, do not delay" (verse 19). Help, God, please don't let it be 2,300 years! God answers that it will be 490 years. No adding of some 2,300 years to the 70 years of captivity. No way—that would be devastating news! No! The good news is that Judah is not about to end; it has 490 years more! Now that's worth hearing when you come from Judah! Now the rest of the news is a mixed bag. In this time there will be a restoration (see verse 25) and another destruction (see verse 26) of the Temple.

Daniel must have been overjoyed to hear the Temple would be restored, but saddened to know that within 490 years it would be destroyed again. He must have pondered long on that. Between these two events at the Temple, the preincarnate Christ He knew so well in prayer and in the reading of Messianic prophecies would come to earth.

In His coming, Christ was appalled that the sacred Temple was a secular place of merchandise. Humans had turned a holy place of worship, in which worshipers should be able to meet in quietness and sense the presence of God, into a well-oiled system of salvation by works. The poor weary pilgrims traveled great distances. Some longed to worship at the holy Temple. But it wasn't simple. Their money had to be changed into Temple shekels, and the exchange rate was outrageous. The exorbitant prices were in stark contrast to the free gift of salvation. The priests became rich through selling sacrifices. Twice Christ threw out the money changers, at the beginning (see John 2:12-22) and the close (see Matthew 21:12-16, 23-46) of His ministry.

Extortion and fraud fueled the commerce. The people were told that God wouldn't bless them if they didn't sacrifice. The atmosphere was one of sharp bargaining, angry disputation, and such confusion that worshipers were drowned out by the uproar.[7] Since the first cleansing of the Temple, the "condition of things was even worse than before. The outer court of the temple was like a vast cattle yard. With the cries of the animals and the sharp clinking of coin was mingled the sound of angry altercation between traffickers, and among them were heard the voices of men in sacred office. The dignitaries of the temple were themselves engaged in buying and selling and the exchange of money. So completely were they controlled by their greed of gain that in the sight of God they were no better than thieves."[8]

Toward the end of the 490 years Christ will atone for sins (Daniel 9:24). He will be "cut off and will have nothing" (verse 26). The original language here actually does not say He will have nothing, but He will have no one.[9] "I have trodden the winepress alone; from the nations no one was with me" (Isaiah 63:3). Christ dies alone (see Matthew 27:46). He is the one Jew who had an unbroken relationship with God the Father, who totally depended on Him for everything, and who is the ultimate model of end-time saints who have no earthly support but rest in Christ alone. He understands their needs, from His own experience, and they will abide in Him as He abode in His Father.

There are two more important points in Gabriel's explanation about this 490-year period. "The Anointed One, the ruler" refers to Christ (Daniel 9:25). This is a double title. William Shea logically sees the two titles continued in verse 26. Thus, "the Anointed One will be cut off" (Calvary) and "the people of the ruler" (Christ) "will destroy the city and the sanctuary." It's God's people who destroyed both city and Temple.[10] They did not invade city and Temple as the soldiers did. But they invaded the Temple by polluting it with idols and false worship, which caused its coming destruction. The rank rebellion that Daniel's prayer mentions brought it about. If they had remained true to God, the physical destruction would never have taken place. That's why Daniel said the Lord delivered Temple articles into the hand of Nebuchadnezzar (see Daniel 1:1, 2), a principle that applies to the later Roman invasion too. Furthermore, William Shea notes that some Jewish troops entered the Temple in the battle, using it as a fortress, which led to an attack on it by Roman soldiers, a final abomination in that Temple, and its destruction.[11]

The second point is the sealing up of vision and prophecy in Daniel 9:24. This is the terminus of the 490-year period. Stephen is giving his final speech before the Sanhedrin, the Jewish leaders. As in Daniel's prayer, Stephen refers to the great Exodus at the Red Sea (see Acts 7:36). All the remnant in Old Testament times remembered that mighty deliverance. The end-time remnant must too. He speaks of idolatry leading Judah into Babylonian captivity (see verses 42, 43). "Was there ever a prophet your fathers did not persecute? They even killed those who predicted the coming of the Righteous One. And now you have betrayed and murdered him" (verses 51, 52). "When they heard this, they were furious and gnashed their teeth at him. But Stephen, full of the Holy Spirit, looked up to heaven and saw the glory of God, and Jesus standing at the right hand of God. 'Look,' he said, 'I see heaven open and the Son of Man standing at the right hand of God'" (verses 54–56).

This was Stephen's final day of his last-day events. He looked into heaven's temple with God and Christ at the throne. How appropriate to see the crucified Christ seated on the throne in heaven's temple! That's where cosmic terrorism began. That's the temple to be attacked next in Daniel 8, because that's where Christ is. The focus will shift from the Temple in Jerusalem to the temple in heaven. Stephen's temple vision was the last prophetic message that the Jews ever received. This is the meaning of "to seal up vision and prophecy" in Daniel 9:24. The prophetic ministry came to an end in the vision of Stephen.[12] Even though the Jews rejected Christ as King at Calvary, choosing Caesar instead (see John 19:15), Christ bore long with His people until this final appeal in Stephen's view of the throne room. How merciful is the heart of God compared to the cruelty of dictators!

It was the throne room scene that lifted Stephen above the present crisis and caused him to say, "Lord, do not hold this sin against them" as they lunged into his body with stones that killed him (Acts 7:59). Like Daniel he was burdened for his fellow Jews more than for himself. How marvelous the change that comes through a connection with Christ. How unlike the enslavement of satanic terrorism that kills millions as disposable items, as seen in Stalin and Hitler! You are becoming like one or the other. There's no third choice. Stephen reflected the crucified Jesus: "Father, forgive them, for they do not know what they are doing" (Luke 23:34).

As the final vision to Judah was a view of the crucified on the throne of heaven's temple, so it must be the focus of end-time saints. That's why the enemy does everything he can to eradicate that view, as we see in the next chapter.

---

[1] Myron Rush, "Joseph Stalin," *World Book Encyclopedia* (1973), vol. 18, p. 648. Information on Stalin comes from this article, pp. 648, 648d.

[2] William A. Jenks, "Adolf Hitler," *World Book Encyclopedia*, vol. 9, p. 238a. Information on Hitler comes from this article, pp. 236-238b.

[3] *Ibid.*, p. 238b.

[4] Rush, p. 648a.

[5] Jenks, p. 237.

[6] William H. Shea, *The Abundant Life Bible Amplifier: Daniel 7-12*, gen. ed. George R. Knight (Boise, Idaho: Pacific Press Pub. Assn., 1996), vol. 2.

[7] Ellen G. White, *The Desire of Ages*, p. 155.

[8] *Ibid.*, p. 589.

[9] Shea, pp. 73, 74.

[10] *Ibid.*, pp. 74–76.
[11] *Ibid.*, p. 81.
[12] *Ibid.*, pp. 58, 59.

COUNTERFEIT SYSTEM

There's a significant change in Daniel 8. Nations are represented by tame beasts (ram, goat) rather than wild beasts (lion, bear, leopard, terrible), as in Daniel 7. These beasts are sanctuary animals, indicative that the burden of Daniel, in chapter 9, over the desolate temple is continued in this chapter. The temple, however, is in heaven. Has something happened to that temple? Is it desolate too? What terrorist did this? When did it happen? Is it still desolate today? These questions are the central concern of Daniel 8.

The story begins with the two-horned ram beast, or Media-Persia (verse 20). Babylon is defeated. It happened at Belshazzar's feast (see Daniel 5:30). Darius the Mede conquered Belshazzar the Babylonian. Nebuchadnezzar's kingdom was finished. Then Greece (goat, Daniel 8:21) conquers Media-Persia. Its large horn was broken and "in its place four prominent horns grew up toward the four winds of heaven" (verse 8). Here is sanctuary altar language (four horns). A small horn (sanctuary language) rises from the four winds. This is pagan Rome, which becomes papal Rome in verse 10.

Papal Rome

Papal Rome "grew until it reached the host of the heavens, and it threw some of the starry host down to the earth and trampled on them" (verse 10). When Satan and his angels were cast out of heaven by Christ (see Revelation 12:7, 8), Satan "swept a third of the stars out of the sky and flung them to the earth" (verse 4). In both cases Satan did not literally do this, but is responsible for a literal fall of angels and a literal deflection of attention from heaven to earth, from the real temple with Christ as high priest to a substitute system of priests on earth.

The Papacy "grew." Two things are happening. First, papal Rome expands its influence territorially, for the government center of Rome moved to Constantinople, leaving the church to fill the vacuum in Rome, and the city became as great a religious center as it had been a civil center. So the Papacy expands its influence horizontally. But it also expands its influence vertically. Heaven's temple had become the center of focus in the New Testament after the resurrection of Christ—for Christ was seated at the right hand of the Father, as Stephen saw in his vision. Numerous New Testament writers testify to this fact (see Mark 16:19; Acts 2:25; 5:31; 7:55, 56; Romans 8:34; Ephesians 1:20; Colossians 3:1; Hebrews 1:3, 13; 8:1; 10:12; 12:2; 1 Peter 3:22). The New Testament calls Christians to look up to the throne, where Christ is in control, continues to unfold the plan of salvation, and ever liveth to make intercession for His people.

Satan hates that focus because he knows it breaks his power every time. So in consummate craft he hijacked a Christian church to cause Christians to look to a counterfeit system on earth. Those on board do not know where they are headed. The journey is just as deadly as planes plunging into towers. As long as he can keep Christians looking down to a system on earth, he has successfully deflected their attention from where the action takes place at heaven's throne. As long as he causes Christians to depend on humans in place of Christ, they are captured. Now I want to be very clear. I love Catholics, and so does Christ. The Seventh-day Adventist Church considers true Christians in the Catholic Church as brothers and sisters in Christ. There are so many genuine saints among them who really love Christ, and He looks forward to having them with Him in heaven. However, Scripture speaks about the papal system, and it is that, and that alone, that is the cause of concern in Daniel.

The papal system "set itself up to be as great as the Prince of the host; it took away the daily sacrifice from him, and the place of his sanctuary was brought low" (Daniel 8:11). There are two words for prince in Daniel. *Nagid* refers to Christ on earth (see Daniel 9:25, 11:22), but *sar* refers to Christ in heaven. It's the heavenly prince, the ascended Christ, that's the focus of attack in this verse. The New International Version says this power "took away the daily sacrifice from him." The word "sacrifice" is not in the original. It should read "daily" *(tamid),* which refers to much more than sacrifice. It refers to everything done in the sanctuary services each day (Exodus 22:20, 21; 25:30; 28:29, 38; 30:8; 1 Chronicles 16:6). It means Christ's daily ministry, His intercession for sinners, His forgiving of sins, His dispensing of gifts—all these functions were brought low in that attention is deflected from them in heaven to their substitute in the papal system on earth. The papal system has priests interceding, priests forgiving sins, and priests dispensing Christ.

These actions are rebellion, and cause truth to be thrown to the ground (see Daniel 8:12). For Christ alone can do these things for humans. This is one of the cleverest terrorist attacks since the ascension of Christ. Satan was defeated at the cross, so he bends every energy to hide Calvary from view. He knows that Christ is in heaven to apply the benefits of the cross to His followers. He knows that without those benefits it will be as if the cross had not taken place. Satan hides that greatest gift, and smothers it in a works system to earn salvation. Believers are taught that they must come to Mass often, a service in which Christ is crucified each time by the priest, His body and blood dispensed as food for the souls of participants. Every day Christ is crucified in millions of places all over the Catholic world in the Mass. This does such disservice to the awesome death of Christ. It trivializes it, as if human priests can make it happen again and again with the mere saying of words.

Has Rome Changed?

A great number of Protestants believe the Catholic Church has changed since the Vatican II Council (1962-1965). They point to the Mass being said in the language of the people instead of Latin. That's a change, for sure. But it's only a superficial change, because it's still the Mass that's said in the different languages. The Mass itself needs to be changed, for Christ is not crucified again and again on a daily basis. Scripture says, "Christ was sacrificed once" (Hebrews 9:27). His death is as unrepeatable as His birth.

Reading through the sixteen *Documents of Vatican II* and sections of the *Catechism of the Catholic Church* (1994) gives evidence that the daily ministry of Christ is still deflected by the system of the pope and priests in their ministry on earth. I have written about this in *Christ Is Coming!* and will not repeat it here.[1] Suffice it to say, although a case can be made for some change at Vatican II, the change has nothing to do with removing the substitution of Christ's heavenly priesthood and ministry. Such a substantive change would call into question the very essence of the papal system.

Compare the Temple worship of Judah with that of the Papacy. The buying of sacrificial animals with Temple shekels became a system of salvation by works just as buying indulgences did. The importing of idols into the Temple is much the same as introducing saints, for both receive prayers of worshipers. The sacrificing of humans is similar to priests sacrificing Christ, both human works in place of Christ's self-sacrifice. Worshiping the sun is similar to worshiping on the day of the sun, both human ideas. Praying to the queen of heaven is the same as praying to Mary, who is called the queen of heaven. Both systems were produced by professed followers of Christ, and both systems hide the truth of the plan of salvation as God's gift to humans, hence antichrist—"in place of" Christ and therefore "against" Him.

Mary at the Throne of God

In many respects Mary has taken the place of Christ in the papal system. Satan wanted to sit on Christ's throne in His place. He knows Mary is dead in the grave. But it suits his strategy to exalt Mary to depreciate Christ. How he must rejoice to see Mary elevated to that throne, and often in place of Christ as far as Catholic devotion to Mary is concerned. Yes, Mary is the mother of Jesus, but more is made of this than should be. In Vatican II it says, "The Blessed Virgin was eternally predestined, in conjunction with the incarnation of the divine Word, to be the Mother of God. By decree of divine Providence, she served on earth as the loving mother of the divine Redeemer, an associate of unique nobility." She "was united with Him in suffering as He died on the cross. In an utterly singular way she cooperated by her obedience, faith, hope, and burning charity in the Savior's work of restoring supernatural life to souls. For this reason she is mother to us in the order of grace."[2]

Note the added works they give to Mary. She is an "associate" with Christ. She was united with Him in His suffering at Calvary. She uniquely works with Christ in restoring supernatural life to souls, and as she was a mother to Jesus she is a mother to believers (meaning she can supply their needs). This is why Mary is prayed to so much. True the official position is that Mary doesn't detract from the one mediation of Christ, but in reality that's precisely what she does. Vatican II says, "The maternal duty of Mary toward men in no way obscures or diminished this unique mediation of Christ, but rather shows its power. For all the saving influences of the Blessed Virgin on men originate, not from some inner necessity, but from the divine pleasure."[3] Note that Mary has a maternal duty toward men, interpreted as "saving influences." These statements give her a mission as co-Redeemer.

No wonder "Mary is united with her Son, the Redeemer, and with His singular graces and offices. By these, the Blessed Virgin is also intimately united with the Church." She is even called the "new Eve." She not only gave birth to Christ, but in the birth of all members of the church "she cooperates with a maternal love."[4] Note how she even takes the place of Christ in the following focus: "In the most holy Virgin the Church has already reached that perfection whereby she exists without spot or wrinkle (cf. Ephesians 5:27). Yet the followers of Christ still strive to increase in holiness by conquering sin. And so they raise their eyes to Mary who shines forth to the whole community of the elect as a model of the virtues. Devotedly meditating on her and contemplating her in the light of the Word made man, the Church with reverence enters more intimately into the supreme mystery of the Incarnation and becomes ever increasingly like her Spouse."[5]

It's by beholding Christ that we become changed. Nowhere does it say in Scripture that we become changed by beholding Mary.

Catholic doctrine affirms that Mary ascended to heaven just as Jesus did. Son and Mother are there together. She was "exalted by divine grace above all angels and men. Hence the Church appropriately honors her with special reverence. Indeed, from most ancient times the Blessed Virgin has been venerated under the title of 'God-bearer.' In all perils and needs, the faithful have fled prayerfully to her protection." Note how the church hasn't changed. "This most holy Synod deliberately teaches" "the liturgical cult, of the Blessed Virgin, be generously fostered. It charges that practices and exercises of devotion toward her be treasured as recommended by the teaching authority of the Church in the course of centuries, and these decrees issued in earlier times regarding the veneration of images of Christ, the Blessed Virgin, and the saints, be religiously observed."[6]

How could a mere human being give help to all believers on the planet? How could she hear all their prayers, let alone dispense to them gifts? She would have to be God. In spite of this, Vatican II admonishes, "Let the entire body of the faithful pour forth persevering prayer to the Mother of God and Mother of men. Let them implore that she who aided the beginnings of the Church by her prayers may now, exalted as she is in heaven above all the saints and angels, intercede with her Son in the fellowship of all the saints."[7]

We find more insights in the latest *Catechism of the Catholic Church*. We noted above that Calvary is trivialized by the daily repetition of it in the Mass. We know Satan hates the cross, because he was defeated at Calvary. There's no way he can get to the throne now. So what does he do? He puts Mary on the throne, sharing in the work of salvation with her Son as if she were a fourth member of the Godhead, as if the Trinity made way for a fourth person. But Satan does more. He reduces the agony of the cross and the awesomeness of Christ being our sin-bearer, an act that no other human could ever do, by stating that Mary participated in that death. "Thus the Blessed Virgin advanced in her pilgrimage of faith, and faithfully persevered in her union with her Son unto the cross. There she stood, in keeping with the divine plan, enduring with her only begotten Son the intensity of his suffering, joining herself with his sacrifice in her mother's heart, and lovingly consenting to the immolation of this victim, born of her: to be given, by the same Christ Jesus dying on the cross, as a mother to his disciple, with these words: 'Woman, behold your son.'"[8]

It's well-known that Mary is considered sinless from birth, in order for Christ to be sinless in His humanity. It's called the Immaculate Conception. Clearly Mary gets the credit for providing that possibility for Christ. No wonder so many look to her as a co-Redeemer, and pray to her to intercede with her Son. No wonder Catholic icons love to picture Mary with Jesus as a babe or a boy. Where is Christ as God in all this? He's replaced by Mary and by images of mother and Son. Of Mary's assumption to heaven we read, "Finally the Immaculate Virgin, preserved free from all stain of original sin, when the course of her earthly life was finished, was taken up body and soul into heavenly glory, and exalted by the Lord as Queen over all things."[9] As such she is not only mother of Christ, but mother of the church and mother of all humans. In the papal system there are three Kings and one queen at the throne in heaven's temple.

Clearly, according to Catholic theology, Mary never needed a Savior, went to heaven on the basis of who she was, and today is queen of heaven, just as Christ is a King. Apparently she is one human who has become divine. Yet Scripture says nothing about Mary being different from other humans, let alone honored, prayed to, and necessary to Christ in His work of redemption. In fact, Scripture says, "Salvation is found in no one else, for there is no other name under heaven given to men by which we must be saved" (Acts 4:12). This is an attempt to replace Christ, and it's worked in the devotion of so many who adore and worship Mary, as if she can understand humans better than her Son, as mothers usually do. Scripture says all humans have sinned and come short of the glory (see Romans 3:23). It also says that there is no life after death (see Deuteronomy 31:16; 2 Samuel 7:12; 1 Kings 2:10; John 11:11-14; Acts 13:36; 1 Corinthians 15:51; 1 Thessalonians 4:13, 14), and that the righteous must wait for the final resurrection (1 Thessalonians 4:16-18).

When a person came to Christ and said His mother and brothers wanted to speak to Him, He replied, "'Who is my mother, and who are my brothers?' Pointing to his disciples, he said, 'Here are my mother and my brothers. For whoever does the will of my Father in heaven is my brother and sister and mother'" (Matthew 12:48-50). In this remarkable statement Christ didn't treat Mary any differently than any other sinner needing salvation—and needing to be obedient to His heavenly Father.

One more comment from the *Catechism*. "This motherhood of Mary in the order of grace continues uninterruptedly from the consent which she loyally gave at the Annunciation and which she sustained without wavering beneath the cross, until the eternal fulfillment of all the elect. Taken up to heaven she did not lay aside this saving office but by her manifold intercession continues to bring us the gifts of eternal salvation." [10]

Christ's Concern

"Never were those repelled that sought His grace. A homeless wanderer, reproach and penury His daily lot, He lived to minister to the needs and lighten the woes of men, to plead with them to accept the gift of life. The waves of mercy, beaten back by those stubborn hearts, returned in a stronger tide of pitying, inexpressible love. But Israel had turned from her best Friend and only Helper. The pleadings of His love had been despised, His counsels spurned, His warnings ridiculed. The hour of hope and pardon was fast passing; the cup of God's long-deferred wrath was almost full. The cloud that had been gathering through ages of apostasy and rebellion, now black with woe, was about to burst upon a guilty people; and He who alone could save them from their impending fate had been slighted, abused, rejected, and was soon to be crucified." [11]

Jesus could see that future and beyond. He saw the parallels between the Jewish system and the papal system. He knew that He would be replaced again in the system to come as He was in the system before Him. He saw weary members in both, caught up in a round of ceremonies that brings no peace to the soul, no comfort to the weary, and leaves one empty. That emptiness He longed to fill. But He remained outside, unwelcome. They had no place for Him, the only one who could help them.

Israel turned away from Christ and replaced Him with Baal, and were scattered to many countries through the Assyrian captivity. Judah was God's last hope in the Old Testament. Satan entered the heart of their Temple worship and introduced perversion that destroyed a sense of the sacred presence of God. The profane will always do that. The tree of good and evil is a fit symbol of Satan's strategy. He mixes the unholy with the holy, the profane with the sacred, falsehood with truth, and drags truth to the ground. The mixture never improves truth but changes it to a lie. The mixture always ends in a takeover in which Satan replaces God, just as He wanted to do in heaven's temple at the throne. He accomplished in the sacred temple of God in Jerusalem what He failed to complete in heaven. The history of Judah is a sorry testimony to this fact, and was the reason why they went into captivity, and gave Christ to crucifixion.

Christ felt the venom of the enemy every day of His life on earth. It was the religious leaders who dogged His every footstep, eager to trap Him and hasten His demise. The temple reflected Satan more than God, because the enemy had infiltrated the system and changed it from within. Christ suffered because His own church gave Him over to the Romans to be killed. He heard them say, "We have no king but Caesar." They were right. He had not been their king for a very long time. They thought more of human kings. He longed to be their king and to be their Savior, but they had high regard for achieving everything human, including working to save themselves. It seemed the decent thing to do. There was no place for Christ.

"O Jerusalem, Jerusalem, you who kill the prophets and stone those sent to you, how often I have longed to gather your children together, as a hen gathers her chicks under her wing, but you were not willing! Look, your house is left to you desolate" (Luke 13:34, 35). The Temple was desolate long before it was destroyed. It was empty of meaning, for human ideas pushed out the divine. Because there was no room for God in Temple worship, there was no room for Christ in the temple hearts of most in Judea. They were professed believers without a profession. Their hearts were empty of Christ, discernment, and compassion, as one day Crusaders, Muslims, Stalin, and Hitler would be. It did not faze citizens of Judah to give Christ to be crucified, for that is the point. Counterfeit religion replaces

Christ. And the ultimate of replacement is crucifixion, or death. There's no room for Him in the human scheme of things.

There was one brief apparent exception. As He rode on the donkey, they thought He was about to fit into their human yearning—become a king and release them from the hated Romans. Now that was worth supporting. Jesus had finally caught on, and the fickle crowd shouted hosannas. Jesus allowed them to give their praise, but it was worship based on a false premise. It was like a knife to Christ's heart. They wanted Him for what they could get out of Him, not for who He was. When Jesus came to the brow of the hill and looked over Jerusalem, He stopped. He took in the long history of the city, and looked into the future too. It was a city doomed to destruction in 40 years.

Suddenly the onlookers "are surprised and disappointed to see His eyes fill with tears, and His body rock to and fro like a tree before the tempest, while a wail of anguish bursts from His quivering lips, as if from the depths of a broken heart. What a sight was this for angels to behold! Their loved Commander in an agony of tears! . . . In the midst of a scene of rejoicing, where all were paying Him homage, Israel's King was in tears; not silent tears of gladness, but tears and groans of insuppressible agony. . . . The tears of Jesus were not in anticipation of His own suffering. . . . It was the sight of Jerusalem that pierced the heart of Jesus—Jerusalem that had rejected the Son of God and scorned His love, that refused to be convinced by His mighty miracles, and was about to take His life. He saw what she was in her guilt of rejecting her Redeemer, and what she might have been had she accepted Him who alone could heal her wound. He had come to save her; how could He give her up?"[12] He convulsed as a rejected lover, and ached more deeply than any divorcé. His heart was broken. How terrible the ruin of cosmic terrorism!

His people substituted idols in place of Christ before the Babylonian captivity. After the Captivity they substituted legalism in place of relationship. Idols were cold and lifeless. So was legalism. They were impressed that captivity came because they had forgotten the law of God, and went to the extreme of writing so many human rules and regulations that there were more than 600 just to keep the

Sabbath. Satan is a master at getting people busy with religion as long as it is devoid of Christ. Legalism is just as bad as idols. The people were no better after the Captivity than before. Even though the laws were connected with God's law, it was a mix of the human and the divine again, which always ends up in the human *replacing* the divine. Both before and after the Captivity Christ was replaced by human ideas of worship. The Temple was just as desolate after the Captivity as before, because the hearts of the worshipers were just as devoid of Christ both times. So it was to happen again in the Christian Era.

If in the future Christ had ridden on a donkey over the brow of a Roman hill and looked out on that great city and seen the papal system, I believe He would have wept again. He loves Roman Catholics and sees in them the same kind of need He saw in the people of Judah. They are so much alike, their worship is so much alike, and the tyranny of a human system over the people is so much alike. His heart breaks for all humans caught up in any counterfeit worship that leaves Him out. He yearns to let His people know that Calvary is a gift, that salvation is free. "Come to me, all you who are weary and burdened, and I will give you rest" (Matthew 11:28). He's disturbed when He sees His people in a round of endless duties that bring no satisfaction and don't minister to deep heart needs. He yearns to come in and bring to each one all that they need in Him.

In His teaching of last-day events, and events preceding them, Jesus saw what would happen in the Christian Era, that the history of Judah would be repeated in the history of the Papacy. He pleaded, "When you see standing in the holy place 'the abomination that causes desolation,' spoken of through the prophet Daniel—let the reader understand" (Matthew 24:15). The temple in Jerusalem was desolate because the abomination of false worship replaced Christ as central. Jesus was looking to a coming abomination that would desolate the temple again. Paul saw the same desolation. The lawless one will (cf. Daniel 7:25) "oppose and exalt himself over everything that is called God or is worshiped, so that he sets himself up in God's temple, proclaiming himself to be God" (2 Thessalonians 2:4). This is the temple in heaven, as Daniel 8 shows (see verses 11–13). It comes after the temple in Jerusalem is destroyed.

Abomination That Causes Desolation

In the book of Daniel there is a rebellion, or an abomination, that causes desolation. Rebellion is an abomination. Cosmic terrorism lies behind all rebellion, and it always causes desolation. In Daniel 8:13, 14 a question and answer are given. "How long will the rebellion against the daily ministry of Christ in heaven's sanctuary continue? When will the desolating work be checked?" "It will take 2,300 evenings and mornings and then the heavenly sanctuary will be cleansed by being restored to its proper place."

Daniel 8 is the first mention of the words "rebellion [or abomination] that causes desolation," with reference to heaven's temple. The second mention is in Daniel 11:31, in the time of the Papacy (see Daniel 11:25-45), and refers to the same events as Daniel 8:13. In Daniel 11:31 the priests of the Papacy rise up to desecrate the temple fortress and abolish the daily ministry of Christ. Priestly activities replace Christ's ministry and profane from a distance the heavenly temple. This is the abomination that causes desolation. We'll consider a final reference later.

In the ancient tabernacle and temples the preincarnate Christ dwelt in the temple on earth. Through His Shekinah glory He was present on the throne in the Most Holy Place. Satan's strategy has always been to replace Christ on His throne. His attack began in the temple in heaven, and then came to the temple on earth. Since Christ ascended to heaven, the attack returns to heaven, and cosmic terrorism does everything to hide the reality of what's going on there. The Papacy has been the primary system through which Satan accomplishes this task. The temple in heaven is unaffected, which makes it different from the temple on earth. But the worshipers, who are robbed of viewing Christ's ministry for them in heaven, are the human temples desolated by the counterfeit focus on human priests in place of Christ, human forgiveness in place of Christ, and human Masses in place of Calvary.

Daniel knows about the abomination that brought desolation to the Jerusalem temple. He must have been sick about the reference to a heavenly temple being impacted by this same rebellion. Ezekiel, Daniel's contemporary, speaks of Satan's launching the cosmic terrorism in heaven. The literal translation is "By the iniquity of your trade you have profaned your holy places" (Ezekiel 28:18; "desecrated your sanctuaries," NIV ; cf. "profaned your sanctuaries," NASB, "defiled your sanctuaries," NKJV, KJV). The reference is not to his person but to the place he has desecrated, although both are involved. The holy places are the heavenly sanctuary.[13] Satan desecrated that sanctuary once while in heaven and will do so again through an earthly system. Whether present or from a distance, his attack is the same—to replace Christ by taking His place in fact or in focus.

Here's a summary of what Gabriel said to Daniel about this counterfeit system. "It's a master of intrigue that rises to power and becomes very strong. It causes astounding devastation and succeeds in everything it does. It destroys the holy people. It causes deceit to prosper and considers itself superior. It will destroy many and will oppose the Prince of princes. Yet it will be destroyed, but not by human power" (see Daniel 8:23-25). The religious or Christian garb gives it an appearance of respectability that cloaks the devil's devastating work of desolation.

How Do We Know It Is 2,300 Years?

How do we know the 2,300 evenings and mornings is 2,300 years? Gabriel said that "the vision concerns the time of the end" (Daniel 8:17), "the vision concerns the appointed time of the end" (verse 19), "the vision . . . concerns the distant future" (verse 26). Three times Gabriel points to a long way into the future, called the time of the end. Daniel is living in the time of Babylon, so the time includes the history of Babylon, the history of Media-Persia, the history of Greece, the history of pagan Rome and the history of papal Rome at least to the time of the end. Because this is vastly more than a mere 2,300 evenings and mornings, it must be 2,300 years.

It is this contextual evidence that is more persuasive than anything else in computing the length of time. The word for vision in the three-time designations above is always *hazon,* the full-length vision, of which the *mareh* of chapter 9 is the first 490 years of the larger vision. It follows, then, that if the 490 years is the first segment of the 2,300 (as seen in the previous chapter), then the 2,300 will also be years. There are two ways to work out the beginning and end of the 2,300 years. The first segment of the 2,300 years brings us to three and a half years beyond Calvary (see the reference in Daniel 9:27 to dying in the middle of the last seven years). One can work back from the Calvary date (A.D. 31) and arrive at the beginning date, which is the same as the date of the decree to rebuild Jerusalem (Artaxerxes, 457 B.C.; Daniel 9:25). Adding 2,300 years onto 457 B.C. brings us to 1844. It was that year Christ began His Second Apartment ministry in heaven's sanctuary, which is the subject of Daniel 7.

According to Daniel 8:14, something began in 1844 that counteracts the rebellion that makes desolation. This is spelled out in Daniel 7, the subject of our next chapter. This brings us to the final example of a text about the abomination that desolates. It is Daniel 12:11. "From the time that the daily sacrifice is abolished and the abomination that causes desolation is set up, there will be 1,290 days. Blessed is the one who waits for and reaches the end of the 1,335 days."

In Daniel 7 it says three times that the little horn rises after it defeats three of the 10 horns of the 10 divisions of pagan Rome (verses 8, 20, 24). The first horn (Visigoths) were defeated in 508.[14] Taking that as the starting date we have the following computation:

$$508 + 1,290 = 1798$$
$$508 + 1,335 = 1843$$

We treat the days as years, as we did in the 2,300 evenings and mornings of Daniel 8:14.

The text says "blessed" is the one who waits and comes to 1,335. Why? Because that brings us within range of 1844, or the end of the 2,300 years, the time God will do something that will make the one figuring these numbers "blessed" or "happy." Indeed, 1844 is very good news, and Satan wants to hide what happened there so as to keep attention away from his rebellion and its future. We will take this up in the next chapter.

How About the End-time Church?

Christ wept over Jerusalem because He longed to enter into a relationship with His people that would bring them joy and fulfillment. It was painful to Him because He knew He had all that they needed, or would ever desire. But they kept Him outside. I believe He weeps over the papal system too, as it distances Christ from their worship. We might feel tempted to say that they should have known better, for look at all Christ has done for humans beings. How could anyone replace Him by anyone or anything else? But we can all get so busy, even in good things, that we do not spend enough time with Him. Isn't that the greatest problem with the pace of life in these postmodern times? Does Christ weep over us too?

Christ is concerned about the end-time church. Just as He referred to the papal system in asking people to study Daniel with understanding, Christ gave a revelation of the end-time church in Revelation (see 3:14-22). It doesn't realize that its worship is worthless. It says it's rich, and increased with goods, and has need of nothing. It doesn't know that it's wretched, pitiful, poor, blind, and naked. The greatest tragedy is to feel secure and not be. More will be said about this church in another chapter, but mention is made here to compare it with Israel and the papal system. Though all are different in some matters of teaching, they share a basic experience—separation from Christ. And this is the primary thrust of cosmic terrorism. Satan and his angels specialize in breaking up relationships, particularly a relationship of dependence on Christ. They all experienced such a relationship once, and may have lived in a thrilling relationship with Him far longer than any of us. They know what a relationship with Him does for a person. So they bend every energy to break a dependent relationship on Christ. They know this is the only way they can take them captive.

"Israel had been represented as a vine which God had planted in the Promised Land. The Jews based their hope of salvation on the fact of their connection with Israel. But Jesus says, I am the real Vine. Think not that through a connection with Israel you may become partakers of the life of God, and inheritors of His promise. Through Me alone is spiritual life received."[15] A connection with

125

Israel did not save Jews from Assyrian and Babylonian captivities. Rejecting the warnings of prophets and of Christ revealed their real connection. Long before the obvious captivities they were in captivity to cosmic terrorism. Satan wrenched them from Christ. His slavery was worse than Egyptian tyranny. "You took your sons and daughters whom you bore to me and sacrificed them as food to the idols" (Ezekiel 16:20). They could mouth all day long about being Israelites, but they were really Satanites. There's no middle ground between Christ and Satan. Being neither hot nor cold is Laodicea's problem. It's called sitting on the fence, uncommitted, and devoid of Christ. "Israel was a spreading vine," independent, bringing forth fruit only for itself, and building many altars with a deceitful heart (Hosea 10:1, 2).[16]

The papal system is just as independent, with its idols, and binds members to itself. "No salvation outside the church" has been its standard through the years. It still is. Vatican II says, "Through the Church, we abide in Christ."[17] The church comes between the branch and the Vine. It follows that "the faithful must cling to their bishop, as the Church does to Christ, and Jesus Christ to the Father."[18] Anything that comes between Christ and a person robs that person of a direct connection with Christ. It's like a minister saying to a newlywed bride, "I will come on the honeymoon to assure your connection with your bridegroom." Imagine her shock and consternation. Imagine his! "Get out of here!" would not overestimate the feelings aroused. No church, idol, or boring religion has a right to come between you and Christ. This is an abomination that brings desolation. He is the bridegroom; you are the bride.

---

[1] Norman R. Gulley, *Christ Is Coming!,* pp. 102-111.
[2] *The Documents of Vatican II,* gen ed. Walter M. Abbott, S.J. (London: Geoffrey Chapman, 1967), p. 91.
[3] *Ibid.,* p. 90.
[4] *Ibid.,* p. 92.
[5] *Ibid.,* p. 93.
[6] *Ibid.,* pp. 94, 95.
[7] *Ibid.,* p. 96.
[8] *Catechism of the Catholic Church* (Liguori, Mo.: Liguori, 1994), p. 251.
[9] *Ibid.,* p. 252.
[10] *Ibid.*

[11] Ellen G. White, *The Great Controversy*, pp. 20, 21.

[12] White, *The Desire of Ages*, pp. 575, 576.

[13] *The Seventh-day Adventist Bible Commentary*, vol. 4, p. 676.

[14] W. H. Shea, *The Abundant Life Bible Amplifier: Daniel 7-12*, pp. 219-221.

[15] White, *The Great Controversy*, p. 675.

[16] God is angry when His bride is snatched from Him by Satan, (Ezekiel 16:32-43), and that's what happened in Israel and is happening in the papal system and in the end-time church. Jehovah Christ said, "Have you seen what faithless Israel has done? She has gone up on every high hill and under every spreading tree and has committed adultery there. . . . Her unfaithful sister Judah did not return to me with all her heart, but only in pretense" (Jeremiah 3:6-10).

[17] *The Documents of Vatican II*, p. 19.

[18] *Ibid.*, p. 52.

SUPREME COURT DECISION

Judgment day was Calvary. Jesus said, "'Now is the time for judgment on this world: now the prince of this world will be driven out. But I, when I am lifted up from the earth, will draw all men to myself.' He said this to show the kind of death he was going to die" (John 12:31–33).

Calvary was the determinative moment in Christ's war against cosmic terrorism. The devil operated with such subtlety and cunning craft that unfallen angels still wondered if he was right after even thousands of years of human history! All the time Satan made it appear that God was responsible for human sin just as He was responsible for the fall of angels. But Satan went too far at the cross. His campaign to crucify Christ revealed what he really wanted to do by replacing Him in heaven: to sit on His throne in His stead. Christ bore long with Satan. He didn't kill him, but he killed Christ.

At Calvary "Satan saw that his disguise was torn away. His administration was laid open before the unfallen angels and before the heavenly universe. He had revealed himself as a murderer. By shedding the blood of the Son of God, he had uprooted himself from the sympathies of the heavenly beings. Henceforth his work was restricted. Whatever attitude he might assume, he could no longer await the angels as they came from the heavenly courts, and before them accuse Christ's brethren of being clothed with the garments of blackness and the defilement of sin. The last link of sympathy between Satan and the heavenly world was broken."[1]

Why Does God Permit Evil?

God is blamed for the presence of evil in His universe. Satan makes sure of that. Through the centuries leading thinkers questioned why God permits evil to continue if He is all-powerful and all-merciful. Many decided that He is not all-powerful and all-merciful. Satan exulted. These scholars were ignorant of cosmic terrorism. They didn't know that God could have destroyed the rebels as soon as they revolted. He had the power to do it. But what would have been the fallout? Wouldn't created beings have thought Him too hasty? Wouldn't they have served Him from fear? Wouldn't they wonder if Satan was right? How come he wasn't given a chance? Is God trying to hide something? Can we trust Him? Is He really just? That's why time continues, and God waits. He wants everyone to fully understand and be fully satisfied.

Cosmic terrorism continues until it is fully exposed for what it is, and Christ is fully revealed for who He is. Total disclosure—that's the deciding factor as far as time is concerned. But wait a minute—didn't that happen at Calvary? What more could be exposed and revealed? Isn't the cross the ultimate of both? Isn't that why it will be studied throughout eternity more than anything else? Yes, I agree that Calvary will be our study throughout eternity, that there is an exhaustless depth to Christ's sacrifice that no one will ever plummet. If that's so, how come times of terror continue? Wouldn't it have been wise to have the Second Advent take place soon after Calvary and be done with it?

"Satan was not then destroyed. The angels did not even then understand all that was involved in the great controversy. The principles at stake were to be more fully revealed. And for the sake of man, Satan's existence must be continued. Man as well as angels must see the contrast between the Prince of light and the prince of darkness. He must choose whom he will serve."[2] Ever been up flat against the face of a mountain and it seemed but a wall above you? You've got to move out and put distance between you until it begins to be seen for what it is. Right? So it is with Calvary. It takes distance in time to look back and see it in perspective and grasp it for what it is. When we realize more of what God suffered on the cross it makes the hellish work of Satan even more hideous. They come as a package—the deepening understanding of Christ's sacrifice exposes more the horror of Satan's deed. Time also continues so that Satan can show to what lengths he will yet go to defeat Christ and attempt to take His place. Time continues so the universe can see what Satan will do about the cross. Time continues because God wants created beings to understand fully the nature of cosmic terrorism so it will never rise again.

The Issues in Cosmic Terrorism

In the first section of this book we noted a number of issues. It's time to add more in the context of the Supreme Court. It should never be forgotten that Satan's rebellion is simply that. He hates the Trinity and wants to take Christ's place. Now, it's true that he never announced his plans. That would never work. He wouldn't gain sympathy. Who likes a cold-blooded murderer who wants to get his own way and couldn't care less about anyone else? No, he'll gain by deception what he could never gain by announcement. He went undercover. He pretended to have the best interests of heaven's government in mind. He had a lot to say about law, for law is a reflection of God. He charged God as unfair, for the law cannot be obeyed. It was like saying created beings came out factory-imperfect. They cannot keep God's law. It's unreasonable. It's God's fault. He should have done a better job as Creator. And speaking of unreasonable, the ancient law must take into consideration the advanced level of angelic maturity. Angels don't need law. There are greater heights that they can achieve, but God keeps them back from greater freedom with this oppressive law. Now that strategy gets a following. Satan appeals to the interests of others, while secretly seeking his own selfish ends. Two attacks on God's law, both questioning His fairness.

Cosmic terrorism makes up issues on the run; throughout the battle new issues are added. Doesn't matter if they contradict. Who says lies are consistent? Here are some issues in the order introduced.[3]

1. Law of God cannot be obeyed.
2. Law of God keeps angels back from a greater future.

130

3. God keeps humans back from their full potential.
4. Lawbreakers can never be pardoned.
5. If God pardoned them, He is not a God of truth and justice, for justice destroys mercy. As a created being Christ disproved the first issue, and at Calvary He disproved the fourth and fifth. After Calvary Satan introduced a new issue.
6. Mercy destroys justice, which means that Calvary does away with the law.

Before Calvary Satan claimed God cannot forgive and still be just. After all, Satan and his angels were thrown out of heaven and there was no plan of salvation for them. He hoped to keep the human race captive by this terrorist strategy. They couldn't be saved either. But Calvary shattered this false charge. Christ died for humans. So after Calvary, what could Satan say? Plenty. Cunning and shrewd, he claimed Calvary proved his point. If Christ died to forgive others, then the law is not the big deal God made it to be. After all, mercy means the law is no longer binding, for God demonstrated on the cross that He can forgive lawbreaking. Once it was all justice without mercy. But now it's mercy, and justice is shoved to the side. So Calvary does away with the law. That lie infiltrated most Christian churches. He plucked a text of Scripture to push his point. Satan gloats when a biblical text is twisted to his purpose. Nothing like a biblical text for the saints. "You are not under law, but under grace" (Romans 6:14). That'll do it. Mercy destroys justice, Calvary does away with God's law. Freedom at last, so he claimed.

Now to the next order of business. How about mercy for humans but none for angels? That had a hearing before Calvary, at least to those who never knew how long Christ and angels pleaded with rebel angels to come back before they plunged over the precipice of their own choice. "Not coming, and that's our final answer," they scoffed. They didn't and never will. So it's not a case that God elects some and damns others. That's an idea Satan pushes with fiendish spite in the Christian Era. Satan and his terrorists killed the Savior at Calvary, proving that was their final answer. They would never have anything to do with Christ, and they want to drag everyone else with them. That's why separating persons from Christ is priority business for them.

That Calvary does away with the law is a new terrorist weapon in the Christian Age. It's very much alive in Daniel 7. The little horn changes the time in the law (see Daniel 7:25). There are two words for time in Daniel: (1) *iddan,* meaning a "span of time," such as the time, times, and half a time (1,260 years, 538-1798) that the Papacy rules over the saints (see verse 25), and (2) *zeman* (plural in text, *zim-min*), a "point in time" in "try to change the set times and the law" (law is singular in the original language).[4] The plural times refers to the recurring time in the law, or the seventh day that comes each week. The Papacy changed the seventh-day Sabbath to Sunday, the first day of the week. This was replacing God's holy day given to humans at Creation for all the world. Christ is the Lord of the Sabbath (see Mark 2:28), so Satan attacked Christ's day with a replacement of his own making.

To say the day was changed to honor Christ's resurrection on Sunday is a cunning way to give the change legitimacy. If Christ wanted such a change, He would have announced it as clearly as He announced the seventh-day commandment. If He is just, any change of His law must be made very plain to all. But Scripture is absolutely silent on this. The fact that there were first-day meetings in the New Testament overlooks the Sabbath meetings that continued. Besides, nowhere does Scripture even hint that these gatherings constituted a new Sabbath.[5]

Papal Church Changed Sabbath to Sunday

God's law is as unchangeable as He is. This means that the Sabbath is, in principle, as everlasting as God. Attempting to change the Sabbath to another day is tantamount to attempting to change God. The *Catechism of the Council of Trent for Parish Priests* records what the Catholic Church did: "The Church of God has thought it well to transfer the celebration and observance of the Sabbath to Sunday."[6] So Sunday is the creation of the Catholic Church, whereas the Sabbath is the creation of Christ.

Stephen Keenan, in *A Doctrinal Catechism,* raises the question

"Have you any other way of proving that the Church has the power to institute festivals of precept?" The answer given is "Had she not such power, she could not have done that in which all modern religionists agree with her—she could not have substituted the observance of Sunday the first day of the week, for the observance of Saturday the seventh day, a change for which there is no scriptural authority."[7]

In the *Catholic Mirror* (1893) we read, "The Catholic Church for over one thousand years before the existence of a Protestant, by virtue of her Divine mission, changed the day from Saturday to Sunday. We say by virtue of her Divine mission because He [who] has so called Himself 'the Lord of the Sabbath' . . . commanded all, without exception, 'to hear His Church,' under penalty of being classed by Him as 'the heathen and the publican.' . . . But the Protestant says: How can I receive the teachings of an apostate Church? How, we ask, have you managed to receive her teaching all your life, *in direct opposition* to your recognized teacher, the Bible, on the Sabbath question?"[8]

Gaspare de Fosso, archbishop of Reggio, in his address to the seventeenth session of the Council of Trent, January 18, 1562, cites the change of Sabbath from Saturday to Sunday as an evidence of the authority of the church. He said, "The authority of the church, then, is illustrated most clearly by the Scriptures; for while on the one hand she recommends them, declares them to be divine, offers them to us to be read, in doubtful matters explains them faithfully, and condemns whatever is contrary to them; on the other hand, the legal precepts in the Scriptures taught by the Lord have ceased by virtue of the same authority. The Sabbath, the most glorious day in the law, has been changed into the Lord's day."[9] The archbishop of Reggio "openly declared that tradition stood above Scripture. The authority of the church could therefore not be bound to the authority of the Scriptures, because the church had changed circumcision into baptism, Sabbath into Sunday, not by the command of Christ, but by its own authority."[10]

Johann Eck, opponent of Luther at Leipzig, argues for the church's superiority over Scripture. "The Scripture teaches 'Remember that you sanctify the day of the Sabbath; six days shall you labor and do all your work, but the seventh day is the Sabbath of the Lord your God,' etc. But the Church has changed the Sabbath into the Lord's (day) by its own authority, concerning which you have no scripture. Christ said to his disciples in the mount, 'I have not come to dissolve the law but to fulfill it'; and yet the church of the Apostles in the first council has boldly spoken out concerning the cessation of legal things. . . . The Scripture decrees in the [apostolic] council . . . that you abstain from . . . blood and from a strangled thing; a matter so clearly defined and expressed the Church has changed by her own authority, for she used both blood and things strangled. See the power of the Church over Scripture. The Sabbath is commanded many times by God; neither in the Gospels nor in Paul is it declared that the Sabbath has ceased; nevertheless the Church has instituted the Lord's day through the tradition of the Apostles without Scripture." [11]

Here's a new level of cosmic terrorism. It's a direct attack on God's holy law. Never before had Satan changed one of the Ten Commandments. Here's a professed Christian system changing God's law, the foundation of His throne. Here's an affront to the divine constitution of the universe. Satan's attack on the throne has entered a new level of daring.

Background to Daniel 7

In Daniel 8 the papal system desecrates the heavenly sanctuary, and Judah was a type of this rebellion (see previous chapter). In the Old Testament Satan hijacked Israel and Judah to cause no one to be ready for the coming of Christ. It was almost 100 percent successful. Only a remnant were ready for Christ to come. In the Christian Era Satan hijacked the largest Christian church and has made it his avenue of mission to the world, as Christ called Christians to be His avenue to the world. In the end-time the issue will be the Sabbath versus Sunday. Which is the Sabbath of the Lord your God? Christians will take their stand, and be divided over this central issue. It has everything to do with what constitutes true worship.

Judgment on Judah

It's instructive that the immediate background to Daniel (see 2 Kings 21-25; 2 Chronicles 33-36),[12] as well as the contemporary prophets, Jeremiah and Ezekiel,[13] documents that Judah was judged by God for desecration of His sanctuary, and for setting up of other gods in His place—the precise thrust of the little horn against Christ and His New Testament sanctuary service. It should also be kept in mind that in contrast with the secular nations mentioned in Daniel (all of which lose their dominion; see Daniel 7:12), the saints and the little horn both claim to be Christian, and either receive or lose their dominion subsequent to the judgment.[14]

Local Judgment on Babylon

We now come to Daniel 7. Did you notice when Daniel had the dream and visions of Daniel 7 (verse1)? It was the first year of Belshazzar, king of Babylon. Daniel 5, or Belshazzar's feast, is the last night of his reign. Daniel 6 is the first year of Darius the Mede, when Daniel was delivered from the lions. So chronologically speaking, the chapters are in this order: 7; 5; 6. Daniel 5 and 6 are the last two chapters of the historical section, and Daniel 7 is the first chapter of the end-time events section. The pre-Advent judgment was so important to God that He gave it to Daniel before the events of Daniel 5 and 6 had taken place. In terms of sequence the pre-Advent judgment was given before the judgment on Babylon.

I look at the judgment on Babylon in Daniel 5 as a type of the pre-Advent judgment in Daniel 7. Daniel 1-6 has a number of historical types of events to come. We already noted that worship before the image on the Plain of Dura (see Daniel 3) is a type of worship of a counterfeit day in the end-time (see Revelation 13:12-15). In the same way, the judgment of Babylon is a local judgment that typifies a global judgment to come. One took place on earth, the other takes place in heaven.

Consider Belshazzar's banquet. The king and guests drank wine. Maybe they downed too much. We don't know. At least the king ordered the gold and silver goblets that Nebuchadnezzar had taken from the Jerusalem Temple to be brought in (see Daniel 5:2, 3; cf.

1:1, 2). The king and his nobles, wives, and concubines then drank wine from the sacred Temple goblets. That was bad enough. But they did more. "As they drank the wine, they praised the gods of gold and silver, of bronze, iron, wood and stone" (Daniel 5:4). They used holy sanctuary vessels from God's Temple to worship idols! They used the vessels of the Creator to worship replacement gods!

Belshazzar should have known better. Nebuchadnezzar was driven to the fields as an animal because of pride, and after seven years he raised his eyes to heaven and his sanity returned. He acknowledged God as the Most High God and as sovereign, ruling over human kingdoms (see Daniel 4:24-37; cf. 5:18-21). Belshazzar didn't humble himself but set himself up "against the Lord of heaven" (Daniel 5:22). He failed to honor God, who held his life in His hands. In this way he mirrored the future Papacy, with its pride and counterfeit worship that hides Christ.

Belshazzar's Babylonian counterfeit worship represents the essence of spiritual Babylon's papal worship. Sacred Temple vessels used to praise idols point to mixing sacred truths from God's Word with idolatrous creations from human imagination. Idolatry, that's what it is. So in the name of Christ her Son, they praise Mary, queen of heaven, in the daily recitation of the rosary. Mixing the holy with the profane, truth with error, or temple vessels with heathen idols. This calls for judgment. So the judgment on local Babylon is a type of judgment on global Babylon.

The Day of Atonement Judgment

According to biblical typology, the pre-Advent judgment, concluding human history, is typified by the annual Day of Atonement (see Leviticus 16). That annual judgment was only for Israel and never included other nations (see verse 16). One would expect a correspondence of this in the end-time antitype (see Daniel 7). Although Daniel 7 does not name who is being judged in the pre-Advent judgment, it designates those who will receive the judgment verdict (see verses 22, 26). It's logical to assume that they're included in the judgment investigation. The two groups receiving this verdict are: (1) God's people attacked by the little horn (see verses 20-22,

25-27); and (2) the little horn, as a professedly Christian system (see verses 22, 26).

But is it legitimate to include the little horn (Papacy)? We read, "The only cases considered are those of the professed people of God,"[15] and these are defined as "all who have believed on Jesus,"[16] yet it also significantly includes "all who have ever taken upon themselves the name of Christ."[17] If two groups come to view here—that is, genuine believers and those taking on Christ's name— then the little horn corresponds to both. For the little horn has members within it who love God and the saints, whereas the system hates God and the saints.

It would seem reasonable that the judgment includes: (1) "All persons (of whatever communion) who have professed a relationship with God," as William Shea suggests;[18] and (2) the little horn, as a counterfeit system, because it masquerades as Christian—taking "the name of Christ." It should be remembered that because Israel also was composed of the genuine and the nominal, there is a correspondence between the type and the antitype. It should also be remembered that Christ mentions a pre-Advent inspection in Matthew 22:1-14, referred to as "a mixed company," for "not all who profess to be Christians are true disciples."[19] Remember that the original attack against Christ and His position in heaven was made by Lucifer while he still pretended to be a loyal angel. He works through this same guise in the attack of the little horn as a professedly Christian system.

As Baldwin puts it, "the heavenly court decrees that *his dominion shall be taken away,* and he whose rule has been destructive will in turn see his dominion totally destroyed."[20] *The Seventh-day Adventist Bible Commentary* states, "The judgment will pass sentence of extinction upon the papacy. This power will continue its war against the saints to the very last. Then its dominion over them will be forever removed, and it will be consumed."[21]

Internal contextual evidence in Daniel 7 suggests that the saints and the little horn equally share in the pre-Advent judgment verdict, which includes three interrelated acts: (1) dominion is given to the Son of Man (see Daniel 7:14; cf. verses 13, 14); (2) dominion is taken from the little horn (see verse 26); and (3) dominion is given to the saints of the Most High (verses 18, 27). These three acts represent judgment in favor of the saints (verse 26) and judgment against their little-horn enemy (verses 21, 22). It should be noted that the loss of the little horn's dominion is at the end (see verses 21, 22, 25-27), unlike the loss of dominion by the beast powers (see verse 12). Christ comes in the Second Advent "for judgment" (Malachi 3:5), which is "His coming for the execution of the judgment;"[22] i.e., the implementation of the pre-Advent verdict that destroys the little horn/beast (see Daniel 7 and Revelation 13) in Armageddon, as we will note in chapter 14.

Scriptural evidence for including the little horn in the judgment is found in Hebrews, which describes backsliding Christians (*katapatesas,* Hebrews 10:29; cf. verses 29-31) in similar terms as Daniel describes the little horn (*mirmac,* MT, *Sunpatethesetai,* LXX; Daniel 8:13, cf. verse 10)—both "trample" *(pateo)* on Christ, both have an anti-Christ thrust. It's of interest that, in speaking of these backsliding Christians, to whom Hebrews was written, Calvin likened them to the Papacy. He said, "Our business with the Papists is similar in the present day; for they confess with us that Christ is the Son of God, the Redeemer who had been promised to the world: but when we come to the reality, we find that they rob him of more than one-half of his power."[23] It's precisely this same kind of backsliding, with its rebellion against God (see Jeremiah 6:28; Ezekiel 2:3; Daniel 8:12) and desecration of His Old Testament Temple (2 Kings 21, 23; Jeremiah 23:11; Ezekiel 5:11; 8:1-18), that brought judgment on Judah in the time of Daniel.

Further scriptural evidence for including the little horn in the pre-Advent judgment is found in 2 Thessalonians 2:2-4, in which Paul speaks of a coming apostasy *(apostasia)* that opposes God, sitting in the temple of God *(naon tou Theo),* as if God. Here's a religious power usurping Christ's place in his New Testament temple. The roots of this passage are in Ezekiel 28:2, Isaiah 11:4, and Daniel 11:36. The last text speaks of the little horn. Hans LaRondelle rightly concludes that "Paul did not think of the antichrist as an atheistic power but as a staunchly religious one, who will claim to speak instead of and on behalf of Christ."[24]

Still more evidence is found in Revelation, with its reference to the true and false Christian churches—the two women of chapters 12 and 17, respectively. Also in Revelation, the three angels' messages refer to the "beast" (little horn) in the context of the pre-Advent judgment (Revelation 14:6-11). Biblical evidence suggests that the little horn is a counterfeit "Christian" system, and as such is included in the pre-Advent judgment.

Daniel 7 is the first mention of the little horn in Scripture, and each of the three times the little horn is named, Daniel immediately speaks of the judgment (verses 7, 8 followed by verses 9, 10; verses 11, 12 followed by verses 13, 14; verses 20, 21 followed by verse 22). In the light of what we have said thus far, it seems that the repeated reference to the little horn within the context of the pre-Advent judgment is significant. The little horn is judged in Daniel 7.

The Judgment of Daniel 7

After locating the little horn in the history of the nations, Daniel takes readers to the two most important moments of the judgment, the commencement and the end. The setting up of the judgment takes place in the Most Holy Place of heaven's sanctuary. "Thrones were set in place, and the Ancient of Days took his seat. . . . His throne was flaming with fire, and its wheels were all ablaze. A river of fire was flowing, coming out from before him" (verses 9, 10). The Father's throne moves into the judgment room, with thousands of attending angels, and ten thousand times ten thousand standing before Him. The court was seated and the books were opened. The court session is ready to begin.

Then Daniel's vision goes to the end of the session, and "there before me was one like a son of man, coming with the clouds of heaven. He approached the Ancient of Days and was led into his presence. He was given authority, glory and sovereign power; all peoples, nations and men of every language worshiped him. His dominion is an everlasting dominion that will not pass away, and his kingdom is one that will never be destroyed" (verses 13, 14).

King Nebuchadnezzar's image received worship from different nations (see Daniel 3:4-7), but Christ will receive worship from all nations according to the judgment verdict. Daniel is troubled and seeks understanding. A heavenly being tells him that even though four great beasts are kingdoms rising from the earth, "the saints of the Most High will receive the kingdom and possess it forever—yes, for ever and ever" (Daniel 7:17, 18). That was good news, but what about this little horn? "As I watched, this horn was waging war against the saints and defeating them, until the Ancient of Days came and pronounced judgment in favor of the saints of the Most High, and the time came when they possessed the kingdom" (verses 21, 22).

This suggests that the little horn's war against the saints was called into question by the verdict handed down at the end of the pre-Advent judgment. That leads to the saints possessing the kingdom. Then Daniel was shown the little horn again. "He will speak against the Most High and oppress his saints and try to change the set times and the laws. The saints will be handed over to him for a time, times and half a time. But the court will sit, and his power will be taken away and completely destroyed forever. Then the sovereignty, power and greatness of the kingdoms under the whole heaven will be handed over to the saints, the people of the Most High. His kingdom will be an everlasting kingdom, and all rulers will worship and obey him" (verses 25-27).

This is the Supreme Court decision of the universe. The little horn's power is taken away and the kingdoms given to the saints. In other words, the little horn will be destroyed and God's saints delivered. Before the judgment it seemed that nothing could stop the progress of the little horn against the saints. But the session in heaven reverses the condition on earth.

Judge as Intercessor

No New Testament book develops so completely the post-Resurrection ministry of Christ as does Hebrews. The keyword of Hebrews is "better"; Christ is said to be better than the services of the ancient sanctuary/temples that pointed to Him. Christ's intercession for His people is part of Christ's better ministry as compared with that of Old Testament priests, even as His better sacrifice was better than the multiple cultic sacrifices. Examination of the records (see Daniel 7:10) is only one side of the judgment. The other is the intercession, or advocacy, of Christ (cf. 1 Timothy 2:5; 1 John 2:1). Christ is there in the presence of God on our behalf (see Hebrews 9:24), where He is able to fully save, for He is ever living to intercede (see Hebrews 7:25). The two ministries of Christ are not subsequent, with the pre-Advent judgment following the intercession, but are concurrent. It is the One interceding for us who is involved in the pre-Advent judgment.

This is the advocate-intercessor portrayed in Zechariah 3, in which the cosmic controversy dimensions of the pre-Advent judgment come into focus. Joshua, representative of God's people, is in dire need. While he was dressed in filthy garments Satan accuses him (see verses 1-3). Zechariah's vision sees a law court scene with an accuser and a defender of the convicted. Joshua is referred to as "a burning stick snatched from the fire" (verse 2). Keil and Delitzsch notes that "the fire out of which Joshua had been saved like a brand was the captivity, in which both Joshua and the nation had been brought to the verge of destruction."[25] They had deserved the Captivity (see Deuteronomy 28:36-64; 29:25-28). They had rebelled against God, who gave them over to their captors (see Daniel 1:1, 2). They had nothing to recommend them, save their utter need. This could also be said of the backslidden Christians to whom Hebrews is addressed. (Both the Jews of the Captivity and Christian Jews reading Hebrews had rebelled like the little horn.) It's precisely for people who have sinned, but realize their need (the little horn never does) for Christ to intercede. So Joshua stood accused by Satan, and with clothing to prove the charges correct.

Joshua was desperate. Here he was at the judgment bar, and yet clothed in sin. Nothing like having the evidence of the crime written all over you as you stand before the judge! Later Christ would speak of the king coming in to inspect the guests, and finding "a man there who was not wearing wedding clothes" (Matthew 22:11). That man evidently thought he could make it on his own in the judgment—that he was good enough, that his garments would suffice, that his life-record was sufficient. But he was thrown out (see verse 13). Unlike this man, Joshua apparently knew his need, and could look only to God for help. Had not God led Israel back from Babylonian captivity just as He had out of Egypt? Could He not rescue them spiritually, too? Joshua had nothing to recommend him. He simply stood there with utter faith in God alone.

"Zechariah's vision of Joshua and the Angel applies with peculiar force to the experience of God's people in the closing up of the great day of atonement."[26] Therefore, Zechariah 3 is a type of the pre-Advent judgment. While Satan rebuked Joshua, Christ[27] said, "'Take off his filthy clothes.' Then he said to Joshua, 'See, I have taken away your sin, and I will put rich garments on you'" (Zechariah 3:4). Oh the wonder of salvation! No doubt Joshua uttered words such as "I delight greatly in the Lord; my soul rejoices in my God. For he has clothed me with garments of salvation and arrayed me in a robe of righteousness" (Isaiah 61:10). It's precisely this intercessor-advocate that comes to view in Hebrews, for Christ did not finish His intercession when the judgment began—He continues it, as demonstrated by Zechariah's vision. It should also be remembered that the typical daily morning and evening sacrifices were also offered on the Day of Atonement (see Exodus 29:38-42; Leviticus 6:9, 12, 13; Numbers 28:3-8).

Many end-time saints fear the present judgment as much as the coming great time of trouble. The end-time remnant needs to capture the full impact of Zechariah and Hebrews relative to the continuing intercession-advocacy of the conquering Christ during the pre-Advent judgment. Their focus must be on Christ and not on themselves. Revelation is precise: In the judgment hour the saints worship Christ as their Creator (see Revelation 14:7), realizing that just as He brought them into this world so only He can get them into the next world.[28] End-time saints are pictured as naked (see Revelation 3:18) just as Adam and Eve were at the Fall (see Genesis 3:10, 21). No fig leaves, or human works, can meet their need. Only the slain Lamb can supply the covering. Only the robe of Christ's righteousness (see Isaiah 61:10; Revelation 6:11), the wedding garment supplied by the Lord (see Matthew 22:11, 12), will suffice. The prodigal son needs the best robe to cover his tattered rags (see Luke 15:22). Christ clothes Zechariah with "rich garments" (Zechariah 3:4).

Saints pass the judgment because they are different from the little horn. They don't speak great words against Christ, or magnify themselves, or persecute the saints, or think to change God's law, or put themselves in Christ's place, casting His truth to the ground (see Daniel 7 and 8). They reflect Christ in their living. Satan "presents their sins before them to discourage them. He is constantly seeking occasion against those who are trying to obey God. Even their best and most acceptable services he seeks to make appear corrupt. By countless devices, the most subtle and the most cruel, he endeavors to secure their condemnation. Man cannot meet these charges himself. In his sin-stained garments, confessing his guilt, he stands before God. But Jesus our Advocate presents an effectual plea in behalf of all who by repentance and faith have committed the keeping of their souls to Him. He pleads their cause and vanquishes their accuser by the mighty arguments of Calvary."[29]

Calvary Is Preeminent

We are now ready to come to the heart of the pre-Advent judgment. God doesn't need this judgment or the millennial and postmillennial judgments as far as knowing who will be saved and who will be lost. He is omniscient (see Psalm 33:13-15; 56:8; 104:24; 139:2, 6; 147:4; Isaiah 44:28; 46:9, 10; Malachi 3:16; Matthew 10:29, 30; Acts 15:8; Romans 11:33; Ephesians 3:10). "The Lord knows those who are his" (2 Timothy 2:19). But He has them for the sake of the on-looking universe because of the issues of cosmic terrorism. All those viewing the judgment need to see that God is just. In the pre-Advent judgment the universe looks at the record of human works, good and bad (see Daniel 7:10). But more than that, they look to see whether individuals have accepted or rejected the saving work that Jesus did for them on the cross. Their relation to the substitutionary judgment of the covenant-Savior is determinative (cf. John 16:26, 27; 17:3).

It's precisely that, and nothing else, that determines personal destiny. God is not asking us to be preoccupied with our own perfection but with His. It's His garment of righteousness that we need. So the pre-Advent judgment is Christ-centered and not human-centered. It's not so much what individuals have or have not done per se that is decisive. Rather it's whether they have accepted or rejected what Christ has done for them when He was judged in their place at the cross (see John 12:31). It's also true that the judgment has as much to do with vindication of God as with the vindication of His followers. If God wants to open Himself up for investigation, then that's His choice. He does it to win the trust of the redeemed and the unfallen beings, so that sin will never arise again. So the judgment is for the benefit of all created beings as well as for God's human followers. That's the breadth of the eternal gospel context of the judgment. The judgment is as much good news as the gospel! The judgment would not be necessary if there were no cosmic terrorism.

The judgment does not repudiate Calvary. It's the Crucified who intercedes for us. The pre-Advent judgment is part of the unfolding in salvation-history of what was accomplished at the cross. Calvary moves inexorably to the deliverance of God's people and the destruction of their enemies because both were accomplished by Christ on the cross. It's by the authority of Calvary that Christ delivers His saints and destroys Satan and all their enemies in the coming battle of Armageddon (see Revelation 19:14-21; 20:11-15). This will be the pre-Advent implementation of the judgment verdict. The judgment verdict carries out the deliverance-destruction verdict of Calvary.

We need to understand fully Satan's scheme. What he has done on a general level in deflecting attention from the authentic heavenly sanctuary service to his counterfeit earthly priesthood (little horn), he is doing on the personal level by deflecting attention away from humanity's only Substitute to humans themselves. Looking to an earthly priesthood or to our own personhood equally deflects the gaze from Christ.

There's wondrous good news in the pre-Advent judgment, for it does not stand by itself. It's surrounded by Calvary before it, Christ's intercession during it, and Armageddon beyond it. In all three events Christ works consistently for His people and against their enemies (this is why the little horn is investigated in the judgment and receives the judgment verdict in Armageddon). In all three events Christ is "the same yesterday and today and forever" (Hebrews 13:8). What Christ accomplished on the cross is simply unfolding in all subsequent salvation-history, including the pre-Advent judgment. That's why the "hour of his judgment" is part of the "eternal gospel" (Revelation 14:6, 7). In this judgment hour it's our crucified Savior who "is able to save completely those who come to God through him, because he always lives to intercede for them" (Hebrews 7:25).

---

[1] Ellen G. White, *The Desire of Ages*, p. 761.

[2] *Ibid.*

[3] *Ibid.*, pp. 761-763.

[4] W. H. Shea, *The Abundant Life Bible Amplifier: Daniel 7-12*, p. 139.

[5] For an analysis of the New Testament first-day texts, see Norman Gulley, *Christ Is Coming!*, pp. 344-349.

[6] *Catechism of the Council of Trent for Parish Priests*, trans. by McHugh and Callan, 2nd rev. ed. (1937), p. 402; quoted in T. H. Jemison, *Christian Beliefs: Fundamental Biblical Teachings for Seventh-day Adventist College Classes* (Boise, Idaho: Pacific Press Pub. Assn., 1959), p. 289.

[7] Stephen Keenan, *A Doctrinal Catechism*, 3rd American ed., rev. (New York: T. W. Strong, late Edward Dunigan & Bro., 1876, p. 174), in the *Seventh-day Adventist Bible Students' Source Book* (Washington, D.C.: Review and Herald Pub. Assn., 1962), p. 886.

[8] *The Christian Sabbath*, 2nd ed. (Baltimore: *The Catholic Mirror*, 1893), pp. 29-33, quoted in the *Seventh-day Adventist Bible Students' Source Book*, p. 885.

[9] Gaspare (Ricciulli) de Fosso in the J. D. Mansi, ed., *Sacrorum Conciliorum . . . Collectio*, cited in the *Seventh-day Adventist Bible Students' Source Book*, p. 887.

[10] Heinrich Julius Holtzmann, *Kanon und Tradition* (Ludwigsburg: Druck und Verlag von Ferd. Riehm, 1859), p. 263, cited in the *Seventh-day Adventist Bible Students' Source Book*, p. 888.

[11] Johann Eck, *Enchiridion Locorum Communinium . . . Adversus Lutheranos* (Venice: Ioan. Antonius & Fratres de Sabio, 1533), fols. 4v, 5r, 42v. Latin. Trans. by Frank H. Yost. Cited in the *Seventh-day Adventist Bible Students' Source Book*, p. 888.

[12] During Manasseh's reign the Temple was desecrated with altars of other gods (see 2 Kings 21:4, 5), and in it pagan priests and mediums ministered and children were offered as sacrifices (see 2 Kings 23:4-24). Judah did more evil than the nations God had destroyed (see 2 Kings 21:9).

[13] Jeremiah prophesied judgments on Judah (see 7:34; 15:14; 21:5, 6; 25:9-14; 32:29; 34:2, 22; 35:15; 37:3; 52:13, 14), for Judah had forgotten God (see 2:32), become hardened in rebellion (see 6:28), and forsaken the law (see 9:13), and its prophets and priests were godless, even desecrating the Temple (see 23:11). Judgments came because "the Lord will take vengeance, vengeance for his temple" (51:11). Ezekiel prophesied God's judgment because Judah had defiled God's temple (see 5:11), even flaunting idolatry in the Temple (see 8:1-18). In vision God is pictured as coming to the Old Testament temple to judge (see 1:1, 2; 8:1).

[14] It would seem that the loss of dominion by the little horn subsequent to the judgment has more to do with the judgment than with the fact that it also is subsequent to the other nations mentioned in Daniel.

[15] White, *The Great Controversy*, p. 480.

[16] *Ibid.*, p. 483.

[17] *Ibid.*, p. 486.

[18] William H. Shea, *Selected Studies on Prophetic Interpretation* (Lincoln, Nebr.: College

View, 1982), vol. 1, p. 125.

[19] White, *Christ's Object Lessons* (Washington, D.C.: Review and Herald Pub. Assn., 1941), pp. 309, 310.

[20] Joyce G. Baldwin, *Daniel* (Leicester, U.K.: InterVarsity, 1978), p. 146.

[21] *The Seventh-day Adventist Bible Commentary,* vol. 4, p. 834.

[22] White, *The Great Controversy,* p. 425.

[23] John Calvin, *Hebrews* (Grand Rapids: Baker, 1989), p. xxviii.

[24] Hans LaRondelle, "The Middle Ages With the Scope of Apocalyptic Prophecy," *Journal of the Evangelical Theological Society* 32, no. 3 (1989): 351.

[25] C. F. Keil and F. Delitzsch, *Minor Prophets, Commentary on the Old Testament,* vol. 10, p. 252.

[26] White, *Testimonies for the Church* (Mountain View, Calif.: Pacific Press Pub. Assn., 1948), vol. 5, p. 472.

[27] The "angel of the Lord" (Zechariah 3:1-3) is Michael of Daniel 12:1, or Jesus Christ (cf. Jude 9; Revelation 12:7-11).

[28] Compare Ellen G. White's first vision, in which she saw that only those who kept their eyes on Jesus made it up the path to heaven. Those taking their gaze away from Him fell to the world below (*Early Writings* [Washington, D.C.: Review and Herald Pub. Assn., 1945], p. 14).

[29] White, *Testimonies for the Church,* vol. 5, pp. 470, 471.

CHRISTIANS AND MUSLIMS IN BATTLE

America's war on terrorism is against terror in any form anywhere, but the attack on September 11, 2001, was carried out by Muslim extremists. These Muslims hate America as if it is Satan personified. Some wonder if the present war could escalate and involve all Muslim countries rising up in an all-out jihad against America. At least Osama bin Laden would like that to happen. The fact is this is not the first time that Christians and Muslims have fought each other, and that's the topic before us.

The Crusades

There were eight crusades between 1095 and 1270. As historian Philip Schaff put it: "They were a succession of tournaments between two continents and two religions, struggling for supremacy — Europe and Asia, Christianity and Mohammedanism."[1] One aim of the Crusades was to conquer Palestine. It was a war between Christians and Muslims.

There are parallels between the Crusades and the present war on terror. With the launching of the Crusades "a new era in European history was begun,"[2] and with the launching of the war on terrorism a new era in global history began. Muslims are involved in both battles, and the allied alliance is mostly made up of so-called Christian countries. As history reports about the Crusades, "All Europe was suddenly united in a common and holy cause,"[3] and on September 11, 2001, all the free world was suddenly united in a common and just cause.

Muslims sacked St. Peter's in 841, and threatened Rome for the second time in 846. They conquered the Holy Land in 1076. "A rude and savage tribe, they heaped, with the intense fanaticism of new converts, all manner of insults and injuries upon the Christians. Many were imprisoned or sold into slavery."[4]

The First Crusade had a double purpose: to help protect the Eastern Christian church from invading Muslim Turks in their region and to capture Jerusalem so Muslims could not persecute Christian pilgrims visiting the city. The hope was that the Eastern Church could be reunited with the Western church. But the primary focus was to capture the Holy Land from the Muslims. Pope Urban II gave a stirring sermon at a synod in Clermont, France, in November 1095. Fourteen archbishops, 250 bishops, and 400 abbots heard him. He said Christ Himself will lead the warriors across the sea and mountains. All sins will be forgiven for all who participate and eternal life to all who die.[5] Eugenius (1146) even extended eternal life to parents of those who took part in the Crusades. Innocent III promised plenary indulgence to all who built ships for the Crusades, and to others who contributed in other ways. The Crusades became "a new way for the laity to atone for their sins, and to merit salvation."[6] Yet, ironically, it was the cross that became the symbol of the Crusaders, who wore it as a badge. They carried and wore the cross but hung on to the pope's promise of salvation. What a paradox!

Besides emperors, kings, and church leaders, Crusaders included a motley array of ruffians who committed the most offensive crimes under cover of church protection. Some even went on Crusades to escape creditors. From the church's point of view, the end justified the means; they promised so much to swell the ranks of the armies. It didn't matter if their promises were true or not. They were stirred by the battles that Israel engaged in, as recorded in Joshua and Judges.[7] We noted previously that it was never God's original intent that His people fight. "Jesus said, 'My kingdom is not of this world. If it were, my servants would fight to prevent my arrest by the Jews. But now my kingdom is from another place'" (John 18:36).

In the First Crusade 300,000 Crusaders perished. Huge numbers were massacred by Bulgarians, 15,000 massacred by Hungarians. Other Crusaders massacred and robbed Jews in Mainz and other cities along the Rhine. They didn't care. They gladly murdered the Christ-killers, and they murdered with impunity because of the promise of forgiveness of all sins. Their hardships included being "forced to eat horse flesh, camels, dogs, . . . and even worse." Only 20,000 men reached Jerusalem in June 1099. A futile assault was made on the city walls; boiling pitch and oil was lopped over the walls on them and showers of stones followed. The summer heat and lack of water took its toll. Dead horses were strewn across the hillsides. The weary and thirsty Crusaders made a procession round the walls of Jerusalem, hoping that they would fall like those of Jericho. The difference was that God was then fighting for His people (see Joshua 5:14-6:20), rather than His people fighting for Him. The Crusaders fought without any divine intervention. Finally reinforcements came by sea, along with workmen and supplies of tools and food.[8]

It was Friday, the anniversary of the Crucifixion, when the last assault was planned. They finally broke through into the city. "The scenes of carnage which followed belong to the many dark pages of Jerusalem's history and showed how, in the quality of mercy, the crusading knight was far below the ideal of Christian perfection. The streets were choked with the bodies of the slain. The Jews were burnt with their synagogues. The greatest slaughter was in the temple enclosure." So many were murdered that "the blood of the massacred in the temple area reached to the very knees and bridles of the horses."[9] You don't have to be a future Stalin or Hitler to kill Jews without mercy, for the same cosmic terrorism worked through them all.

The final battle of the First Crusade was against the Egyptians, the Muslims from the south. Historian Hans Mayer writes, "On 12 August 1099 battle was joined on level ground near the Egyptian harbour-fortress of Ascalon. The Egyptians were taken by surprise while still in their camp and were completely defeated. Their commander, the vizier al-Afdal (1094-1121) fled back to Egypt. On 13 August the victorious army returned in triumph to Jerusalem. The success of the crusade was now assured. The regaining of the Holy Land was an astonishing achievement."[10]

No reign of peace came with Jerusalem in Christian hands, not because of threats by Muslims so much as internal bitter intrigues. Such is religion without Christ. How Satan gloated as barbaric acts were done in the name of Christ and under the badge of the cross! Here were Crusaders who reflected his image rather than Christ's. Ninety years later, on October 2, 1187, Muslim Saladin defeated the Christians and entered Jerusalem. Once more the city was in Muslim hands. Saladin, however, was a man of chivalry. There were "no scenes of savage butchery." The inhabitants were given their liberty for a payment of money.[11] Since that date Muslims have worshiped on Mount Moriah. Saladin was one who lived his religion, but almost no other, on either side, was like him. Religious fanaticism fanned the flames during the Crusades, and both sides were caught up in the fervor and furor.

One Crusade was particularly troubling, for 30,000 girls and boys went to war with some adults, good and bad. The zeal for the Crusade was "fanned by priestly zeal," and all the children perished through hardship or shipwreck, or were sold as slaves by unscrupulous dealers and shipped to lands afar and never heard of again.[12]

In 1187, in the battle at Hattin, Muslims decimated the European Crusaders, and Jerusalem and most of the centers belonging to the Crusaders came under Muslim control. Through diplomacy with Egypt, the Papacy obtained possession of Jerusalem. But in 1244 Muslims captured the city and held it for 700 years, until the twentieth century![13]

The Crusades were a failure. Besides the loss of hundreds of thousands of lives, the Holy Land was not won, the advance of Islam was not permanently hindered, and the break of Eastern Christendom (Constantinople, 1054) from Rome was not repaired. Christian doctrines were hated by Muslims because of the terrible atrocities of the Crusaders. The system of indulgences cheapened sin and grace.[14] These last two facts show the sorry work of religion without Christ. Even though Pope Urban II said Christ Himself would lead the Crusade, the fact is that He could not. Christ is the one who wept over the city, who won people's hearts through love and not through fighting. He would never promise forgiveness of any sin and eternal life in exchange for fighting. He promises forgiveness of all sins and eternal life to those who accept Him and stay in a saving relationship of dependence on Him.

The Crusades were acts of terror instigated by the cosmic terrorism of Satan. Here again Satan promoted action in the name of religion separate from the presence and power of Christ. The carnage revealed the evil in the hearts of professed Christians. But the same can be said of Muslim carnage too. The battling Crusaders and Muslims reflected Satan more than anyone else, and in this respect they had much in common. They were religious extremists fired by false theology. The Christian Crusaders wanted to have all their sins forgiven by going to war. They were told that if they died they would have eternal life—guaranteed. The Muslims who hijacked the planes that plunged into the twin towers had the same hope. Both worked to earn eternal life, when all the time it is a free gift. They were motivated by false theology.

Christians today have a false theology that offers God's blessing to those who look after the Jews. They believe that Israel has a special role in last-day events, that the present state of Israel is a divine miracle, and hence $3 billion is given to Israel every year by the American government. Of course there are a number of reasons that America gives money to Israel, and it should not be forgotten that it gives money to the Muslim country of Egypt too. But many Muslims believe that America sides with Israel in the Israel-Palestinian conflict, and this may be true in part because of the false theology about Israel's future. So false theology fueled the Crusades and fuels the Muslim extremists' hatred of America, and may have some influence in America's pro-Israeli Middle East policy.

In the past throughout the Roman world people flocked to join the Crusades in hatred of Muslims, inspired by false theology. Today throughout the Muslim world people flock to join the cause of Osama bin Laden in hatred of America, inspired by false theology. In the shadows, engineering it all, is the consummate terrorist, Satan, who stirs up the passions, promotes false teachings, and hijacks devotees on a journey that leads to eternal destruction. This is cosmic terrorism. It hides the Savior of humans, who did not take the sword, but went to the cross to die for His enemies.

Satan's Counterfeit Religions

False religions are powerful tools in the hands of cosmic terrorism, for as substitutes they hide Christ and His cross. The Papacy and Islam do this. In chapter 9 we noted how the Papacy hides Christ and Calvary in its counterfeit sanctuary system on earth. The Qur'an demotes Jesus to one of the prophets.[15] It claims He did not die on the cross; it only looked like He did. It claims Jesus was taken to God and nothing is said about what He does.[16] So Islam also hides Christ's present work in the heavenly sanctuary. Islam claims Jesus will return again to earth in the end-time to complete His prophetic ministry, and fight the antichrist.[17] This sets Islam up for Satan's coming as Christ. The Koran rejects the Sabbath.[18]

Yahiya Emerick, author and practicing Islamic believer, claims that "according to the sayings of the prophet Muhammad, Jesus will speak to the Christians and Jews of the world and convert them to Islam. He will succeed in breaking the worship of the cross and will stop the eating of pork. . . . Jesus will be the spiritual head of a transnational government of peace." This lasts for 40 years, during which time Jesus marries, has children, dies, and is buried in Medina next to the grave of the prophet Muhammad.[19]

Both religions look to the end-time for the antichrist, as opposed to Scripture's placement of it during history, as seen in Daniel.[20] This deflects attention from the present activities of cosmic terrorism through the Papacy to a projected future. Both religions place human ideas above biblical revelation, either in traditions or the Qur'an. Both religions have a regimented works system to gain forgiveness of sins, which is a result of rejecting salvation as a gift through Christ. In reading the Qur'an I found human works throughout the book.[21]

The Papacy began in 538, only 72 years before Muhammad's first alleged vision (610). Here is a two-pronged attack on Christ by cosmic terrorism. As we consider the Crusades in Scripture keep in mind that Scripture sees the Papacy as the final counterfeit, with all other counterfeits joining her (see Revelation 13:1-4), for it is through a counterfeit Christian guise that Satan comes as Christ in the end-time—not as Muhammad or Buddha or any other religious leader. It's the Sunday law, birthed through the Papacy, that Satan comes to enforce in the end-time test on worship. This is when cosmic terrorism takes over the world. He comes to take Christ's place on earth. That's the end-game.

In 1962-1965, in preparation for the end-time, Vatican Council II reached out to all religions to bring them together. It said of Islam, "Upon the Moslems, too, the Church looks with esteem. . . . Though they do not acknowledge Jesus as God, they revere Him as a prophet. They also honor Mary, His virgin mother; at times they call on her, too, with devotion."[22]

The Crusades in Scripture

Daniel 11:23-39 presents the Crusades from the Papal perspective. This may be the hardest chapter in Scripture, and so one cannot be fully sure of the meaning of every verse. As William Shea gives the most reasonable interpretation of the passage, I will follow him in presenting it. The prince of the covenant is mentioned in verse 22. This is Christ, and the word for prince is *nagid,* the same as in Daniel 9:25, and refers to Christ during His life on earth. It's pagan Rome that destroyed, or crucified, Christ in A.D. 31.

When do verses 23-30 take place? William Shea canvasses two different options. Does verse 23 refer to the conquest of Jerusalem in A.D. 70, when the Roman army of Titus destroyed the Temple? The verse doesn't appear to mention this conquest. He next comes to the time of Constantine (275-337) when the Roman Empire converted to Christianity, but this verse doesn't fit these circumstances. With these two major events eliminated he comes to the rise of papal Rome in the sixth century A.D. So it's not pagan Rome but papal Rome that comes to view in Daniel 11:23-30. We move away from the political to the ecclesiastical period, when the church of Rome was coming into prominence.[23]

Emperor Constantine moved the capital of the Roman Empire to Constantinople (in the east) so that the church gained power in

Rome (in the west). Rather than Daniel 11:23-39 following a chronological order, Shea suggests that the verses follow a topical order as follows:

1. Verses 23-30   actual military campaigning
2. Verse 30   subversion of the system of salvation
3. Verses 32-34   persecution
4. Verses 35-39   self-exaltation

Thus these verses of Daniel 11 parallel Daniel 7 and 8. Yet only Daniel 11 has any reference to the Crusades.[24]

In Daniel 11:23-39 the king of the north is the Papacy (Christians), and the king of the south is Egypt (Muslims). Forces from Egypt participated in the fighting of the First Crusade, and the last Crusade was an unsuccessful attempt to invade Egypt. There is a thousand-year gap between the death of Christ in verse 22 and the Crusades beginning in verse 23. What a tragedy that the papal church became obsessed in possessing the places where Christ once was instead of being possessed by the present Christ. The church threw all its efforts into being in the Holy Land while doing nothing about the holy heavenly ministry of Christ.

The biblical account begins with making an agreement with deceit. I believe this may refer to the false promises made to Crusaders. It says with only a few people will the Papacy rise to power. This agrees with Daniel 7:8, in which the horn is called "a little one," and also agrees with Daniel 8:9, in which it says it started small and grew in power. It then talks about "few people" *(meh-awt),* which can mean "few" or "little." Shea points out that this could mean either few in number compared to the hordes of Muslims, or could mean "little" with reference to the Children's Crusade of A.D. 1217-1221. Either could be correct, because the Papacy grew in prestige as the leader of the Crusades. There had never been such a sustained movement of people volunteering to give themselves to fight in a cause like the Crusades. The involvement of so many people, at so many levels, in so many countries, caused the participants to look to Rome for leadership.

The plundering of Daniel 11:24 made the Papacy rich, and this in turn contributed to its rise in power. The Papacy is said to have achieved what neither its fathers nor forefathers did, and that is true: The Crusades and the wealth they produced are unparalleled in the history of pagan or papal Rome. But "only for a time," says the verse. The Crusades wouldn't go on forever. In verse 25 the Papacy and Muslims fight, both with large armies, and the Papacy defeats the Muslims. This may well have been at the conclusion of the First Crusade.

Verse 27 speaks of two kings who are rivals, and lie to each other. Shea suggests that this took place after the fall of Jerusalem in the First Crusade. Who should be king of Jerusalem? Infighting ensued in both the secular and sacred realms. There were two candidates to be king, Raymond and Godfrey. Godfrey finally obtained the position through trickery, and reigned without the title king. In the sacred realm there was rivalry for the position of patriarch of Jerusalem. Arnulf of Normandy was finally chosen, though he was not qualified for the position. But he allegedly found a relic from the cross, and this made his position secure. And then there was a question of how these two leaders of state and church should relate.[25]

In verse 28 the king of the north returns to his own country with great wealth. Four of the leaders of the First Crusade returned to their homes in Europe with riches, whereas 3,000 foot soldiers remained with Godfrey in Jerusalem. The power of the church is shown in the Crusade against the Albigenses in southern France (1208-1227). So the Papacy fought Christians as well as Muslims.

Verses 29, 30 aptly describe the final Crusade. In verse 30 there's a bad translation of the original language. In English texts it appears that ships from Egypt come against the Papacy. But as Shea points out, "against" would require the preposition 'al, whereas the text uses be or beth, which mean "with" in this context. The ships didn't come against him, but with him. They were his ships. This is how the Papacy tried to invade Egypt. The French king Louis IX led the Crusade. He stayed the winter in the island of Cyprus, and in the spring of 1249 set sail for Egypt. The battle at Mansourah in the Egyptian delta, in February 1250, was a major defeat. King Louis with his men retreated to Damietta and surrendered to the Egyptians. The king was taken prisoner and held for ransom. Eventually he was released, and with 1,400 troops traveled back to France.[26]

We have commented on verse 31 in chapter 9. This is a battle of a different kind. It's against the heavenly temple. Through the setting up of a counterfeit priestly ministry that substitutes for Christ's ministry, the Papacy deflects attention away from Christ's work in heaven's sanctuary to their own priestly ministry on earth. So, as it were, the heavenly sanctuary is cast down (see Daniel 8:11). But those who know God will firmly resist this counterfeit. The papal Crusade against the heavenly sanctuary ministry throws light on its Crusades to obtain the city of Jerusalem. In both the Papacy sought power and prestige. It did neither to come close to Christ and receive His ministry. What's the use of Crusades to the Holy Land when a counterfeit sanctuary ministry drives the Papacy? Christ has left the holy land and is in the holy sanctuary in heaven. That's the focus any church true to Him must have and give to the world. It must cause all, including Muslims and Jews, to see a Savior who ever liveth to make intercession for those who will come to Him (see Hebrews 7:25).

---

[1] Philip Schaff, *History of the Christian Church: The Middle Ages, A.D. 1049-1294* (Grand Rapids: Eerdmans, 1960), vol. 5, p. 214.

[2] *Ibid.,* p. 231.

[3] *Ibid.*

[4] *Ibid.,* p. 223.

[5] Kenneth Scott Latourette, *A History of Christianity: Beginnings to 1500,* rev. ed. (Peabody, Mass.: Prince), vol. 1, p. 410. Schaff, pp. 227-229.

[6] Schaff, p. 217.

[7] *Ibid.,* pp. 217, 218.

[8] *Ibid.,* pp. 231-239.

[9] *Ibid.,* pp. 239, 240.

[10] Hans E. Mayer, *The Crusades* 2nd ed. (Oxford, London: Oxford University, 1988), p. 57.

[11] Schaff, p. 251.

[12] *Ibid.,* pp. 266-268.

[13] Latourette, pp. 411, 412.

[14] Schaff, pp. 290, 291.

[15] Qur'an, text, translation, and commentary, Abdullah Yusuf Ali (Elmhurst, N.Y.: Tahrike Tarsile Qur'an, Inc., 2001), after as Qur'an. Qur'an 2:136, 163; 3:84.

[16] Qur'an 4:157, 158.

[17] Yahiya J. A. Emerick, *The Complete Idiot's Guide to Understanding Islam* (Indianapolis: Pearson Education Co., 2002), pp. 106-108, 206, 207.

[18] Qur'an 16:124, see also p. 689, note 2159.

[19] Emerick, pp. 108, 109.

[20] *Ibid.,* p. 106.

[21] The focus is on reward, not redemption. Hell is mentioned repeatedly throughout the Koran and often in the most lurid details. Although the reward is a garden with streams running beneath it, and that is often mentioned too, the fear of an eternal hell would be stimulus enough to cause devotees to try to save themselves. The Qur'an says, "Save yourselves and your Families from a Fire" (66:6).

[22] *The Documents of Vatican II,* p. 663.

[23] W. H. Shea, *The Abundant Life Bible Amplifier: Daniel 7-12,* pp. 195, 196.

[24] *Ibid.,* pp. 195-197.

[25] *Ibid.,* pp. 197-200.

[26] *Ibid.,* pp. 200-203.

COSMIC TERRORISM
IN THE END-TIME

Cosmic terrorism does everything to hide Christ from view by calling His justice, His Word, and His lawkeeping into question. Cosmic terrorism deflects attention from Christ as Creator and High Priest. Cosmic terrorism makes Calvary of no effect, causing saints to focus on the crisis and not Christ, and attacks the book of Revelation. Luther and Calvin both dismissed Revelation as unimportant for saints. And yet it's this book that is "the revelation of Jesus Christ," meaning a revelation from Jesus as well as a revelation about Him (Revelation 1:1). No wonder Satan hates the book and does everything to keep people from understanding it!

Have you had a difficult time with Revelation? Has it seemed a mystery? Has it been hard to make sense of symbols and beasts? You are not alone. I invite you to see Christ in the book, and focus on Him, and let the parts, as far as possible, be understood in the light of Him.

Pulling Back the Curtain

Our five chapters on Revelation must necessarily be an introduction, but that's all we need to unlock the book and see in it wondrous truth for the end-time. How to study the book involves its structure, which I have written on elsewhere.[1] In this chapter we'll look at the throne-room scenes, which is one of the four structural features of the book.

Before coming to the first throne-room scene in Revelation 4, 5, let's look at the first chapter. It's thrilling for those scared of final events and worried about all the world against them. Jesus is "the ruler of the kings of the earth" (verse 5). He "loves us and has freed us from our sins by his blood, and has made us to be a kingdom and priests to serve his God and Father" (verses 5, 6). "Look, he is coming with the clouds, and every eye will see him, even those who pierced him; and all the peoples of the earth will mourn because of him" (verse 7). These verses shout out that Christ is in control of kings on earth. He also freed us at Calvary. "Freed" is in the Greek aorist tense, meaning He freed us once for all. It does not need to be repeated. That makes repetitious masses unnecessary. We are free! Free from fear of earthly rulers, because Christ is ruler over them. And free from fear of the future, because He's coming back. Fear belongs to the other side of the cosmic controversy, not to those free in Christ through His death and through His present rule in their lives.

Then Jesus speaks, "I am the Alpha and the Omega, who is and who was, and who is to come, the Almighty" (verse 9). The Christ who spoke all worlds into existence, the Victor of Calvary, the powerful Intercessor, the soon coming King—He is almighty! That's the final word over cosmic terrorism. It's never been and never will be a match to God. He alone is almighty!

Like Daniel, John was in captivity. It could have been his first Sabbath away from worship with fellow believers. Wouldn't it be like Jesus to want to spend the first Sabbath with His last disciple of the 12? Marooned on a lonely island called Patmos, he was separated from loved ones and friends, but not from Christ. Daniel and John were both in captivity and were both beyond retirement age, but God used them to write two of the most important books on last-day events for His end-time people. They are types of the end-time people in their commitment to Christ in times of trouble. It was Sabbath, the day that is an issue in last-day events, and the Christ of creation, the almighty transcendent God, comes to visit John, and in so doing comes as the God up close. Here in the last book of the Bible, just as in the first, we find these two qualities of Christ emphasized. He's not only the mighty defender of His people, but He does so as the God up close. He's not an absentee God, as in deism. He does not need Mary or saints to get His attention. He's the God who is with us always, even to the end of the world (see Matthew 28:20). He comes to visit John.

In Revelation Christ speaks and also appears, so John hears (verse 10) and sees (verse 12) Him. John sees Jesus in the midst of the seven candlesticks (verse 13) that represent the seven churches (verse 20). Just as Christ stood in the fiery furnace with the three Hebrew worthies (see Daniel 3:25), so He stands in the midst of His churches. He wants it understood up front, and understood clearly, that He's the God up close in last-day events. No wonder Satan hates this book! He keeps this fact hidden. Study the beast and get lost in the trumpets—that's OK. But don't see Christ in the book, for he knows that once saints realize the truth about Christ, it will set them free from fear forever (see John 8:32).

John sees the "son of man" (Revelation 1:13). Here is the elder brother of the human race. Here is the One who understands what it's like to go through troubles. Here is the One on whose bosom John reclined (see John 13:23). He knows what it means to be in the presence of the God up close. This is the Savior who said, "Let not your heart be troubled." Christ knows that "Satan's craft is most successful against those who are depressed by difficulties"[2] He knows that "for the joy set before him [He] endured the cross" (Hebrews 12:2)—that's why He said to the troubled disciples: "Trust in God; trust also in me. . . . I am going there [heaven] to prepare a place for you. And if I go and prepare a place for you, I will come back and take you to be with me that you also may be where I am" (John 14:1-3). Here's the Christ who likes humans to be with Him, and likes to be with them. So He came to be with John, and John sees Him, but not as He once was in simple garment and sandaled feet. No, He has changed.

His high priestly robe goes to His feet, with golden sash. His feet are like bronze glowing in a furnace, and his voice was like the sound of rushing waters. Here's Jesus as high priest—whom Satan hides from view. There are two things very significant about Christ in this scene: (1) His eyes are like "blazing fire," and (2) out of His mouth comes a "sharp double-edged sword" (verses 13-16). These point to the future when He will vault through the heavens and rescue His people in last-day events. At that time "His eyes are like blazing fire" (Revelation 19:12) and "out of his mouth comes a sharp sword with which to strike down the nations" (verse 15). In the first scene of Christ, the readers are directed to His coming to rescue them in the great time of trouble.

In the meantime He is the God up close. He doesn't look down from heaven and call saints on His cell phone. No! "When for the truth's sake the believer stands at the bar of unrighteous tribunals, Christ stands by his side. All the reproaches that fall upon him fall upon Christ. Christ is condemned over again in the person of His disciples. When one is incarcerated in prison walls, Christ ravishes the heart with His love. When one suffers death for His sake, Christ says, 'I am he that liveth, and was dead; and, behold, I am alive forevermore . . . and have the keys of hell and of death.' Revelation 1:18."[3] Christ prefaced these words with "Do not be afraid" (verse 17).

Clearly the first chapter is full of good news. Christ is in control at the throne room of the universe. But more important, He's present up close with His people, and goes through their troubles with them. "God is our refuge and strength, an ever-present help in trouble. Therefore we will not fear, though the earth give way and the mountains fall into the heart of the sea, though its waters roar and foam and the mountains quake with their surging. . . . Be still, and know that I am God; I will be exalted among the nations, I will be exalted in the earth. The Lord Almighty is with us; the God of Jacob is our fortress" (Psalm 46:1-11).

Counterfeit Versus Genuine Worship

The end-time test is worship. That's another reason that end-time saints study the throne-room scenes where genuine worship takes place. It's spontaneous, joyous, full of heart and gratitude. It's adoration, devotion, and exultant praise. It's relationship, not ritual. There's thunderous exaltation at the homecoming of a sinner (cf. Luke 15:23, 24). Here's Christ, who rejoiceth "over you with singing" (Zephaniah 3:17). Spontaneous "I love you's" fill their worship. By contrast, cosmic terrorism's counterfeit worship is a boring, unsatisfying, and empty routine, with no response. This can happen in any religion.

Heaven's Throne Room

Christ beckoned to John, "Come up here, and I will show you what must take place after this" (Revelation 4:1). In vision John came to the throne room of heaven. Christ knew that the throne room is the best place to study things to come, including last-day events. After all, that's where cosmic terrorism began, and it was from this throne room that the first terrorists were expelled. It was the first place of victory over the devil. But more than that, on the throne is seated the Father and the Son in full majesty and power. This is the scene that cosmic terrorism hides from view through the counterfeit system on earth. The devil and his demons know the power of Those on the throne. This is the scene that no false religion views, as they struggle in a meaningless round of empty works to earn their own salvation or enlightenment. They work tirelessly to gain what no one can merit. They are busy getting nowhere. It's like being on a plane bound for paradise that plunges into perdition. The ultimate hijack. That's the tyranny of cosmic terrorism!

It's this throne that the end-time saints must see. It's from the perspective of this throne that end-time events must be studied. Christ wanted John to see what goes on at the throne, and write about what he saw and heard. He guided him to begin each of the seven segments of Revelation with this throne-room scene. This way Christ would use the book of Revelation to counteract Satan's strategy to keep the throne from human view. End-time saints must focus on the heavenly throne in order to be unafraid of earthly thrones.

The first scene is God the Father on the throne. God created "all things" through the Son (Hebrews 1:2). The Father is worshiped as Creator. Created beings cry out, "Holy, holy, holy is the Lord God Almighty, who was, and is, and is to come" (Revelation 4:8). "You are worthy, our Lord and God, to receive glory and honor and power, for you created all things, and by your will they were created and have their being" (verse 11). Here, near the beginning of the last book of the Bible, the Almighty God, the transcendent God, is worshiped as Creator, as Christ was in Genesis 1. (Cross reference Job 38:4-7.)

In Revelation 5 we come to the God up close, just as we did in

Genesis 2. In Genesis the God up close is Jesus in His creation of Adam and Eve, and in His Sabbath with them. In Revelation 5, it is Christ as Redeemer, who became man, lived as a man, and died to save the rebel race. One cannot get more up close than becoming human, taking all human sin, and dying in place of humans at the cross!

Genesis 1 and Revelation 4—Transcendent Creator God
Genesis 2 and Revelation 5—Immanent God up close

The 24 Elders

Twenty-four thrones surround God's throne. On them are seated 24 elders. Who are these 24 people who sit on thrones in God's throne room? They are dressed in white garments, symbolic of righteousness (see Revelation 3:4), and have gold crowns on their heads (see Revelation 4:2-4). Their crowns are *stephanoi,* or laurel wreaths of victory. Winners of Olympic Games wear *stephanoi.* The 24 humans were victorious on earth. Now they have thrones in the throne room of the universe! What an awesome privilege! But how did they get there? Who are they? And what is their work?

We know of only three humans in heaven: Enoch (see Genesis 5:24; Hebrews 11:5), Elijah (2 Kings 2:11, 12; Matthew 17:3), and Moses (Jude 9; Matthew 11:5). When Jesus died, the temple curtain between holy and Most Holy places split from top to bottom by some divine hand. "The earth shook and the rocks split. The tombs broke open and the bodies of many holy people who had died were raised to life. They came out of the tombs, and after Jesus' resurrection they went into the holy city and appeared to many people" (Matthew 27:51-53). "When he [Christ] ascended on high, he led captives in his train" (Ephesians 4:8). They went to the throne with Christ.

Why did Christ take humans to heaven with Him? The answer is the same as why He took Enoch, Elijah, and Moses in the Old Testament. God is on trial in the cosmic controversy. Cosmic terrorism says God is unjust. The presence of human beings in heaven gives evidence that God has nothing to hide and is pleased to have the human race represented, along with all the inhabitants of other worlds and angels as observers in the unfolding of the cosmic controversy. Out of the redeemed humans in heaven, Christ chose 24 to have a special ministry beyond observation. They were to serve as priests to minister along with Him in His ministry as the high priest. In the earthly tabernacle there were 24 groups of priests (see 1 Chronicles 24:1-18; 25:9-31). For example, Zacharias, father of John the Baptist, was in the eighth group (see Luke 1:5, 8, 9). These ministered with the high priest on earth.

One thing is sure—these priests are not human intercessors. They are not saints to whom Christians pray. That is the counterfeit system. Nor do they plead with Christ, as Mary is alleged to do. That is the counterfeit system too. The 24 elders are merely helpers, and nothing more. We always find them worshiping Christ, and praising Him for what He has done. They do hold golden bowls full of incense, which are the prayers of the saints (see Revelation 5:8), but nowhere do they answer these prayers and act as coworkers in Christ's intercessory ministry. They sing to Christ and declare that He has "made them [the redeemed] to be a kingdom and priests to serve our God" (verse 10). Serving God is sufficient. They do not serve humans. There's only one mediator between God and man, and that is Jesus (see 1 Timothy 2:5). They are servant-priests who worship and praise Christ.

But how about the priests in the Old Testament? And how about the "royal priesthood" of Christians in the New Testament? How are they different from the priests in the counterfeit system, and how do they compare to the 24 priests in heaven? These questions deserve passing mention. The priestly ministry of the 24 orders of priests only typified Christ's coming better priestly ministry (see the book of Hebrews). They functioned in the sanctuary/temples for believers. But the nation of Israel had a different priestly function. They were to witness to the world. In that sense they were "a kingdom of priests and a holy nation" (Exodus 19:6), words used of Christians now. "You are a chosen people, a royal priesthood, a holy nation, a people belonging to God, that you may declare the praises of him who called you out of darkness into his wonderful light" (1 Peter 2:9).

Telling unbelievers the good news of what Christ has done in the life is praising Him for His death and intercession, whether done in Israel or today. God has always had a priesthood of believers in this sense, the remnant who revel in relating His love to others and do so in response to Him, just like those at the throne. These witnesses catch the spirit of the throne-room scenes, because they gaze on the Christ who is there and on what is happening there, and pour forth heart songs of grateful praise. We sing these songs on earth before we do in heaven and the new earth. By complete contrast, the counterfeit is a substitute system to earn salvation through connection to priests and not to Christ. It's the human in place of the divine. It's empty. How can its celebrants enter into the spontaneous, joyous, exuberant worship at the throne room, exalting, praising, and adoring God and Christ for the free gift of salvation? But the 24 elders can, and do.

It's significant, then, that before coming to the throne-room scenes of worship, John writes, "To him who loves us and has freed us from our sins by his blood, and has made us to be a kingdom and priests to serve his God and Father" (Revelation 1:5, 6). The two are inseparable, free salvation and gratitude for the gift. True worship on earth joins the worship of the throne-room scenes. No wonder they are so important to the book of Revelation and to us. Just as Christ couldn't be a high priest without having a sacrifice to minister (see Hebrews 8:1-3), He chose not to minister in heaven's sanctuary without other human priests, who do not take His place as in the counterfeit system. You don't need interceding saints in heaven when 24 elders sing that no one except Christ is worthy!

Only Christ Is Worthy

John wept because no one was found in heaven or on earth who could open the scroll at the throne (see Revelation 5:1-4). An elder pointed John to Christ. Christ came to get the scroll. "The twenty-four elders fell down before the Lamb. . . . They sang a new song: 'You are worthy to take the scroll and to open its seals, because you were slain, and with your blood you purchased men for God from every tribe and language and people and nation. You have made them to be a kingdom and priests to serve our God, and they will reign on earth'" (verses 8-10). There's no question in the minds of the 24 elders. They were not co-redeemers. There's no need of other mediators. There's only one Christ, and no one else is worthy to open the scroll. No one else is worthy to minister as high priest, for no one else died to provide the sacrifice that must be ministered. Clearly the 24 elders do not put themselves in a special relationship with Christ, for He redeemed them, and they are only there in heaven because of Him. They serve only at His pleasure.

At heaven's throne God the Father and the Son receive adoration and worship as the Creator and Redeemer of humans. God the Father is worthy of worship as the Creator, and Jesus is worthy of worship as the Creator-Redeemer. In the next to the last verse both the Father and Son are worshiped: "To him who sits on the throne and to the Lamb be praise and honor and glory and power, for ever and ever!" (verse 13).

So here, in the beginning of the book of Revelation, those around the throne of heaven worship God as Creator and Redeemer. Near the end of the book of Revelation, in the end-time, those on earth are called to worship God as Creator. "Worship him who made the heavens, the earth, the sea and the springs of water" (Revelation 14:7). And the end-time saints worship their Redeemer and Deliverer: "Hallelujah! Salvation and glory and power belong to our God, for true and just are his judgments" (Revelation 19:1, 2). End-time saints sing out, "Salvation belongs to our God, who sits on the throne, and to the Lamb" (Revelation 7:10). The elders fall down on their faces before the throne and worship God, saying, "Amen! Praise and glory and wisdom and thanks and honor and power and strength be to our God for ever and ever. Amen!" (verse 12).

Translated saints after the Second Advent are "before the throne of God and serve him day and night in his temple; and he who sits on the throne will spread his tent over them. Never again will they hunger; never again will they thirst. The sun will not beat upon them, nor any scorching heat. For the Lamb at the center of the throne will be their shepherd; he will lead them to springs of living water. And God will wipe away every tear from their eyes" (verses 15-17). What a beautiful description of the Shepherd Christ who continues in heaven to be a caring, compassionate God up close—forever! It seems that the 24 elders serve in the temple until the close of probation just as the translated saints will serve in the temple during the millennium.

Redeemed in heaven now, and translated redeemed after the Second Advent, praise God and worship Him as Creator and Redeemer. It's a heartfelt adoration that comes from utter gratitude for salvation and love for the Savior. God is the focus of their worship, no one and nothing else. The counterfeit replaces Christ with other priests, Mary, and saints. Christ pulls back the curtain to reveal what goes on at the throne so that the reality of the Creator-Redeemer and the joyful worship cause end-time saints to be lifted above themselves and enraptured in the gift of salvation in final events. In spirit, they join those at the throne in worship of the almighty.

No longer bound by fear or looking to their own works to get through the end-time (which is no different from those who try to earn their salvation), they revel in the freedom of salvation. Caught up in praise of the Redeemer, they realize that salvation from the world includes salvation through final events. Caught up in the joy and freedom of that thought, their praise echoes heaven's songs. It's Christ's saving power and presence in this worship that alone keeps the saints from the end-time counterfeit worship.

Other Throne-Room Scenes

There are seven throne-room scenes in Revelation that open a new segment of the book. Before coming to study past and future events in history, Christ wants the readers to first look up to God at the throne. He is in control. Here is the Father and the Victor at Calvary. He won back the right to own the world. He defeated the enemy. He is the King-Priest, the only mediator of humans. He is more than able to take end-time saints through the great time of trouble, because He already conquered for them in a greater time of trouble.

A throne-room scene is found in 4; 5; 8:1-6; 11:19; 15:1-8; 16:17-17:3; 19:1-10 and 21:5-11. Each one keeps the focus of the readers directed upward before looking outward. It's only from the throne room that we look out unafraid. When spending time at the throne room each day, we can more easily face rulers on earth. When meditating on the throne room each day, this world loses its appeal. Worshiping God at the throne each day is a foretaste of heaven. When Christ at the throne is real to end-time saints, they enter the unknown with a known destiny. Looking at Christ there tells them that He did not come to earth and go through His final events just to return to heaven. That's why He took so many humans with Him, and will take the rest when He returns. He went through final events solely to take *us* through final events and bring us home to be with Him. His going through final events for us makes our final events look like a picnic. He went through final events for us so that He can go through our final events *with* us. The view of the 24 elders at the throne gives encouragement. It's only a matter of time until we join them.

Second Throne-Room Scene

The second throne-room scene is Revelation 8:1-6. Seven angels stand before God at the throne (verse 2). "Another angel, who had a golden censer, came and stood at the altar. He was given much incense to offer, with the prayers of all the saints, on the golden altar before the throne. The smoke of the incense, together with the prayers of the saints, went up before God from the angel's hand. Then the angel took the censer, filled it with fire from the altar, and hurled it on the earth; and there came peals of thunder, rumblings, flashes of lightning and an earthquake. Then the seven angels who had the seven trumpets prepared to sound them" (verses 3-6).

What a view! Christ has angel helpers just as He has the 24 elders. Did you notice what the angel does? He comes to the altar of incense in the holy place with a golden censer and offers incense with the prayers of all the saints. In the last throne-room scene we saw the 24 elders with golden bowls full of incense, which are the prayers of the saints (see Revelation 5:8). Evidently this angel and the 24 elders are doing the same work as God's helpers at the throne. They minister together in the heavenly sanctuary. But there's one thing the 24 elders do not do: they do not hurl fire to earth in judgment. This reminds us of the angel of death in the Exodus.

Third Throne-Room Scene

The third throne-room scene is Revelation 11:19. "Then God's temple in heaven was opened, and within his temple was seen the ark of his covenant. And there came flashes of lightning, rumblings, peals of thunder, an earthquake and a great hailstorm." The second throne-room scene was in the holy place, as was the first throne-room scene where the throne was before the seven lamps (see Revelation 4:5). Revelation 5 was the inauguration of Christ as high priest in heaven's sanctuary. He was found worthy to open the seals, and begin His ministry.

Now the third throne-room scene peers into the Most Holy Place, where the throne is. This is not to suggest that the throne was not in the first two scenes, but underlines the movable throne. It moved into the Most Holy Place. We saw God moving into the Most Holy Place in Daniel 7:9, 10. It's a throne described as having wheels (see Ezekiel 1, 10). The throne in heaven is the ark of His covenant. God's covenant with humans, to be their God, their Savior, and their friend, is linked to the Ten Commandments found inside the ark of the covenant. That's the law Satan fought against in heaven, and changed on earth. But it remains the basis of God's throne, the constitution of the universe, and His relationship with humans. That's why Christ summed up the Ten Commandments as love to God and love to others (see Matthew 22:37-40).

The law reflects the Godhead. Each loves the other two, and in so doing They love Each Other. Here is the essence of the covenant relationship. That's what we see at the throne where Christ shares His work with the 24 elders and angels. He loves them, and they love Him, for this is the God who loved the world so much that He gave Jesus to it (see John 3:16). Christ did not just visit us. He became one of us. He is an eternal gift. He came willingly for a rebel race because His love for them is incomprehensible, unshakable, and eternal. That's why Christ promises, "If you love me, you will obey what I command." And immediately after saying that, He said, "And I will ask the Father, and he will give you another Counselor to be with you forever. . . . I will not leave you as orphans; I will come to you" (John 14:15-18). The Father went through great suffering and anguish with His Son, and the Holy Spirit comforts and sustains and "intercedes for us with groans that words cannot express" (Romans 8:26). All of Them live to help us, not to receive our worship. We cannot help worshiping Them because our hearts are overflowing with Their wondrous love. They deserve far more adoration than eternity can ever give.

All of this is hidden from view by cosmic terrorism. Satan cannot enjoy the love of God that he once reveled in, and he does everything in his power to keep humans from experiencing this love. So he repackages the law as a bunch of rules and regulations that restrict. They are arbitrary and prove that God does not love humans, and keeps them back from experiencing full freedom. That's why Christ pulls back the curtain and lets humans see the joy and exultant celebration and adoration in heartfelt worship at the throne. Nothing regimented or legal there.

They cannot help worshiping in the full light of the glory and majesty of God, and gazing on Jesus who came at the risk of failure and eternal loss to redeem a race of rebels. He didn't have to come. He couldn't help it. Love drove Him to give everything for humans, whom He has always deeply and dearly loved with all His heart. And in taking this plunge He could have failed and lost the utter joys of being at the throne. This breaks the hearts of created beings as they gladly, freely, and with all their hearts love Him in return. No wonder they shout aloud and sing with gusto about the worthiness of the Father and the Son!

Fourth Throne-Room Scene

The fourth throne-room scene is Revelation 15. As in the second throne-room scene, there are seven angels, this time with seven last plagues. They went forth from the temple to deliver the plagues, which is appropriate, for it is in the temple that the pre-Advent judgment verdict is given (see Daniel 7:13, 14). Again it is angels, and not the 24 elders, that do the work of judgment. The plagues are one part of the implementations of the judgment verdict. The temple is called "the tabernacle of the Testimony" (Revelation 15:5), which refers to the law. For it is the law that the little horn changed on earth (see

Daniel 7:25), and it's that power that is judged.

While the plagues are delivered smoke from the glory and power of God fills the temple, so that no one can enter it. Evidently all angels, the elders, and every other created being leave the temple. It must be a time of great sadness for God, and the changed circumstances at the throne remind one of the darkness that hovered over Calvary when Jesus was dying (see Luke 23:44). This strange work of judgment must be a terrible experience for God, as these are His children, and it wrenches His heart. Maybe the Godhead weeps in the darkness as Christ wept over Jerusalem.

This throne-room scene is in the form of a chiasm, for the beginning and ending of the scene are about the plagues. Between these two ends is a later scene after the Second Advent. There is a sea of glass mixed with fire. It's like an ocean at sunset. On the shore stand those victorious over the papal system, the beast, and his image of Revelation 13:11-17, which is the same power as the little horn of Daniel 7. These are the ones who kept God's law, including the Sabbath changed by the little horn. God gives them harps, and they sing the Song of Moses the servant of God and the Song of the Lamb. What music comes from this great throng from "every nation, tribe, language and people" (Revelation 14:6) joining together for the first time and singing in the language of heaven. A mighty chorus of praise thunders to the heavens, "Great and marvelous are your deeds, Lord God Almighty. Just and true are your ways, King of the ages. Who will not fear you, O Lord, and bring glory to your name? For you alone are holy. All nations will come and worship before you, for your righteous acts have been revealed" (Revelation 15:3, 4).

What a tumultuous testimony to the greatness, goodness, and justice of God! Having come through the greatest time of trouble, with all the world against them and a death decree to prove it, the translated group have nothing but adoration and praise for God. They loudly and joyously proclaim that God the Father, Son, and Holy Spirit are exonerated of all charges by cosmic terrorism. They have felt the hatred of the devil and the love of God, and there's no comparison. They will forever praise and worship the Father, the Son, and the Holy Spirit. In the first throne-room scene the 24 elders and

171

angels proclaimed that only Christ is worthy, and now the translated redeemed proclaim that only God is holy. These are convictions drawn from willing hearts as they give themselves in full devotion and adoration to the incomparable Kings at the throne of the universe.

Fifth Throne-Room Scene

The fifth throne-room scene is Revelation 16:17-17:3. As often happens in Revelation, the conclusion is given first, and then the details come later. This is the Hebrew way of thinking that we noted in Daniel 7-9. The judgment of the little horn is given first in Daniel 7. So in this throne-room scene there comes out of the temple a loud voice saying, "It is done!" What a long time the Godhead patiently waited to declare the end of the conflict on Planet Earth! There's still a millennium and its aftermath to go before it is all over, but at least the battle is finished for God's people. "It is done!" is now added to the "It is finished" of Calvary—two great conclusions, the latter dependent on the first, for without the "It is finished" God could never say "It is done." It's nothing that the redeemed have done that counts; it's what the Redeemer has done that is determinative and decisive! That's why throughout eternity the saints will celebrate Calvary above every other event in cosmic history. For that was judgment day for Christ (see John 12:31, 32). He took the judgment that belonged to humans. He stood in their place. The full fury of God's wrath against sin fell on Him. There Jesus "poured out his life unto death, and was numbered with the transgressors" (Isaiah 53:12). At Calvary Father, Son, and Holy Spirit suffered together to the depths that only eternal love for Each Other and humans can comprehend.

The judgment during the seventh plague and the judgment on the papal power, both in view in this temple scene, pale into insignificance compared to the judgment Christ bore on the cross for every human. One of the plague angels beckoned John to come and see the judgment on the papal power. Here's the disciple who took the mother of Jesus at His request as they watched Jesus suffer at Calvary (see John 19:26, 27). He was there when Christ cried out, "It is finished." He must have thought of that moment when he heard the loud voice from the throne say, "It is done!"

Sixth Throne-Room Scene

The sixth throne-room scene is Revelation 19:1-10. In the New International Version of the Bible this segment of the chapter is appropriately titled "Hallelujah!" The second segment of the chapter (verses 14-21) is the Second Advent judgment on the two beasts of Revelation 13. As is usual in Hebrew thought, the throne-room scene gives the conclusion of the judgment before giving the judgment. It shows the rapturous response to the judgment in the Second Advent. Chronologically the judgment on earth comes first, and the hallelujahs follow in heaven after the Second Advent.

"I heard what sounded like the roar of a great multitude in heaven shouting: 'Hallelujah! Salvation and glory and power belong to our God, for true and just are his judgments. He has condemned the great prostitute who corrupted the earth by her adulteries. He has avenged on her the blood of his servants'" (Revelation 19:1, 2). Revelation 18:20 says, "God has judged her for the way she treated you." The judgment on Babylon is the subject of both chapters. This is true also in the judgment on the two beasts of Revelation 13. That's the papal power and all who join with her to form a global terrorism against God's end-time people.

The "great multitude" shouting these jubilant praises is the same "great multitude" that lives through the great time of trouble, and live to see Jesus come (see Revelation 7:9, 14; 14:1-3). The 24 elders fall down and worship God seated on the throne crying out, "Amen, Hallelujah!" They respond to the great multitude, as if saying, "They are right! Hallelujah to God!" for they watched God's up-close love for His persecuted people during the great time of trouble. They observed the fantastic rescue of His people in the Second Advent. Then a voice came from the throne: "Praise our God, all you his servants, you who fear him, both small and great!" (Revelation 19:5). We do not know who called for this praise, but the voice said "our" God, perhaps suggesting a created being. It seems spontaneous. Whether one of the 24 elders, or Gabriel, or a temple angel, it doesn't matter. Look at the response: "Then I heard what sounded like a great multitude, like the roar of rushing waters and like loud peals of thunder, shouting: 'Hallelujah! For our Lord

God Almighty reigns. Let us rejoice and be glad and give him glory! For the wedding of the Lamb has come, and his bride has made herself ready. Fine linen, bright and clean, was given her to wear" (verses 6-8).

That's really worth shouting about! A wedding of Christ and the redeemed. Here is the ultimate description of a God up close! Satan bent every energy to discredit Him, and cause distrust and distance between humans and Christ. But end-time saints know better. They didn't fall for the lie. They sensed Him with them in the trenches during the great time of trouble. "Lo, I am with you alway, even unto the end of the world" (Matthew 28:20, KJV) was true. "Never will I leave you; never will I forsake you" (Hebrews 13:5) proved Satan false. In thunderous acclamation they ready themselves for the wedding!

Extra Throne-Room Scene

The extra throne-room scene is Revelation 7:9-16. I call it extra, because it doesn't introduce a new segment of Revelation as the other seven do. It's a parallel scene with the sixth throne-room scene. In both we find a "great multitude," the end-time saints who go through the great time of trouble and live to see Jesus come. This great multitude stand before the throne after the Second Advent. None have anything to say about themselves. Some persons think that end-time saints must reach a higher level of perfection, because they live after the close of probation. But those who go through the experience have nothing to say about that. There's only one gospel, the "everlasting gospel" that end-time saints proclaim (see Revelation 14:6). They cry in a loud voice, "Salvation belongs to our God, who sits on the throne, and to the Lamb" (Revelation 7:10).

Created beings fall down with "their faces before the throne and [worship] God, saying, 'Amen! Praise and glory and wisdom and thanks and honor and power and strength be to our God for ever and ever. Amen!'" (verses 11, 12). A stunning second to the praise given by end-time saints. No doubt about it—no one gets credit for salvation besides the Savior. Only the Lamb is worthy! It's Satan's scheme to get saints preoccupied with matters of perfection instead of with dependence on the Savior. Dependence brings all the necessary perfection, for it is Christ's perfection that comes through the relationship. Worthy is the Lamb—alone!

The elders say that the great multitude in white (see verse 9) come through "the great tribulation" (verse 14) or the great time of trouble.[5] They come white in the blood of the Lamb. Without the Lamb they couldn't stand before Him at the throne. "Nothing in my hands I bring, simply to Thy cross I cling" describes the experience of the redeemed.

The Seventh Throne-Room Scene

The seventh throne-room scene is Revelation 21:5-11. Here's the last throne-room scene. It's context is the creation of the new heavens and the new earth. The chiastic structure of Scripture has the first two chapters in Genesis about the creation of the old heavens and earth, and the last two chapters of Revelation about the new creation and descriptions of the new earth. Christ is speaking from the throne, saying, " 'I am making everything new!' Then he said, 'Write this down, for these words are trustworthy and true' " (verse 5). It's of interest that the veracity of His words is emphasized in the context of the new creation, compared to Satan's calling His words in question in the context of the first creation (see Genesis 3:1-5).

"He said to me: 'It is done. I am the Alpha and the Omega, the Beginning and the End. To him who is thirsty I will give to drink without cost from the spring of the water of life. He who overcomes will inherit all this, and I will be his God and he will be my son' " (Revelation 21:6, 7). This "It is done" refers to the end of cosmic terrorism and the beginning of a new earth free from sin and sinners. That day is coming, for God's word is sure. The second death will be the end of the long terrible treacherous trail of terror. Cosmic terrorism will never rear its ugly head again! Then a plague angel wants to show John the bride of the Lamb as before he showed the demise of Babylon. There it is—better than anything engineered by humans, a colossal city, the New Jerusalem, filled with city homes for all the redeemed. "It shone with the glory of God, and its brilliance was like that of a very precious jewel, like a jasper, clear as crystal" (verse 11). Here's the fulfillment of Christ's promise to troubled disciples. "Do not let your hearts be troubled. Trust in God; trust also in me. . . . I am going there to prepare a place for you. . . . I will come back and take you to be with me that you also may be where I am" (John 14:1-3).

The throne-room scenes give insight into the kind of God those around the throne know Him to be, including the end-time redeemed. The testimony of all is unanimous. The Trinity are awesome, and worthy of praise and adoration forever. How tragic that Lucifer, who occupied his own throne next to Christ's throne and knew best how wondrous and marvelous are the Trinity, should launch the cancer of terrorism from the very center where resplendent love was so freely manifest. What tragedy that he thought he could do better, but really wanted Christ's throne. How fantastic that Christ looks out on the redeemed and says, "To him who overcomes I will give the right to sit with me on my throne, just as I overcame and sat down with my Father on his throne" (Revelation 3:21). How incredible! The throne that Satan wanted to grasp and usurp in Christ's place, Christ gives to the redeemed to share with Him forever!

---

[1] Many Christians believe that the first three chapters have to do with the churches in the Christian Era, and chapters 4 onward have to do with the final seven years between the secret rapture and the Second Advent, or the age of Israel. But, as in Daniel, God's structure divides the book into history (chapters 1-11) and last-day events (13-21), with chapter 12 as the apex on the cosmic controversy. The central verses of this chapter are on Calvary (verses 9-13), for history and last-day events are best understood in the light of Calvary. The other two structures are (1) sanctuary: as one goes through the book one follows Christ in His journey from Calvary, into His heavenly sanctuary ministry in the first apartment, which ends with the historical segment of the book (see 11:19), and then He enters the Second Apartment ministry in the last-day events segment of the book; and (2) festivals: as one reads through the book one goes through a Jewish festival calendar year (Passover, Pentecost, Trumpets, Atonement, and Tabernacles). All structures prove that the book is one unit, traverses through history, and is not divided, as most Christians believe. For further study, see *Christ Is Coming!*, pp. 62-70.

[2] Ellen G. White, *The Desire of Ages*, p. 662.

[3] *Ibid.*, p. 669.

[4] *Ibid.*, pp. 19, 20.

[5] There's only one time of trouble referred to as "the" great tribulation in Revelation, and that's the great time of trouble that the translated remnant go through. That's why the great multitude (see Revelation 7:9, 14) seem to be the 144,000 named group that sing a song that no one else (of the redeemed) can sing (see Revelation 14:1-3), because it's the song of their experience during the great time of trouble (*The Great Controversy*, p. 649). If

that's correct, then it seems that Revelation particularly focuses on the redeemed of the end-time without forgetting the redeemed of all time, for Christ went through the greatest time of trouble ever, and has a message of comfort for those who will go through the great time of trouble. Christ spoke of an unequaled time of trouble in Matthew 24:21. As Matthew 24 has a double reference to a near time and an end-time, could this verse (verse 21) refer to both the greatest time of trouble in duration (538-1798) and the greatest time of trouble in intensity (great time of trouble)?

GLOBAL TERROR

What do you do when all the world is against you? What if you are commanded to break the Sabbath? What if a death decree enforces the command? What if you cannot buy or sell? All this is coming. What do you do then? This is the global terror that threatens God's saints in the end-time, and is the reason most are petrified of last-day events. Many would rather die and go to heaven via resurrection. How about you?

We saw the importance of focus on God and Christ in heaven's throne room in the last chapter. Paul adds, "God raised us up with Christ and seated us with him in the heavenly realms in Christ Jesus" (Ephesians 2:6). "Since, then, you have been raised with Christ, set your hearts on things above, where Christ is seated at the right hand of God" (Colossians 3:1). Christians can rejoice because they are in Christ at the throne, and can in Him see last-day events from that perspective. The things of that throne room are more real to them than the passing things of earth. When we spend time at the throne in daily worship we can experience this reality.

Context Is Vital

Revelation 13 is the worst chapter in the Bible for most end-time saints. Too bad it's in the book, say some; others shrug their shoulders and try not to think of the future. Denial—it's like burying one's head in the sand. Is there a better way, a way that brings hope out of doom? There is. It's important to study Revelation 13 in its biblical context and get the full picture, instead of only part. Of course it's Satan's studied strategy to fixate the saints on Revelation 13 so they lose heart. That suits his purposes well, and he's done remarkably well. Here he's up to his hiding game again. He hides the context and buries the saints in fear, for then he knows he has them. He hijacks their freedom by keeping them focused on the crisis that hides the Christ. It's his ace card that he uses in a thousand ways.

Revelation 12

Revelation 12 to 14 form a literary unit. The full picture begins with Revelation 12. I'm glad it comes before chapter 13. It's good news, and provides the background for understanding the bad news of Revelation 13. Let's see how. Revelation 12 presents cosmic terrorism in only 17 verses. Brief, bold, basic insights into four of its battles. These major battles define the controversy: heaven (verses 7, 8), time of Christ (verses 9-11), papal persecution (verses 13-16), and the end-time (verse 17). The end-time battle is the subject of Revelation 13. So in Revelation 12 we have the battle that launched the controversy in heaven, the battle that decided the controversy at Calvary, the battle against Christians for 1,260 years, and the final global battle against the saints.

Let's consider the first battle. Satan pretended to help make heaven a better place for believers. He mingled among angel believers as if seeking their good. "While claiming for himself perfect loyalty to God, he urged that changes in the order and laws of heaven were necessary for the stability of the divine government. Thus while working to excite opposition to the law of God and to instill his own discontent into the minds of the angels under him, he was ostensibly seeking to remove dissatisfaction and to reconcile disaffected angels to the order of heaven. While secretly fomenting discord and rebellion, he with consummate craft caused it to appear as his sole purpose to promote loyalty and to preserve harmony and peace."[1] Talk about a Christian guise. Even in heaven there was a lamblike cover for the dragon's real purpose. There's nothing new in his strategy in the end-time, when lamblike America acts as a dragon (see Revelation 13:11-17).

Look what Satan schemed in heaven. "Not content with his position, though honored above the heavenly host, he ventured to covet homage due alone to the Creator. Instead of seeking to make God supreme in the affections and allegiance of all created beings, it was his endeavor to secure their service and loyalty to himself. And coveting the glory with which the infinite Father had invested His Son, this prince of angels aspired to power that was the prerogative of Christ alone."[2] Satan wants to be worshiped. He's out to rob Christ of His worship and take it to himself. That's why the end-time battle is over worship. Eight times worship is mentioned in Revelation 13, 14. (Revelation 13:4 [twice], 8, 12, 15; 14:7, 9, 11). That's why in the end-time Satan is worshiped (see Revelation 13:4). He will use the Papacy and America to accomplish this end. What he could not do in heaven, he will almost accomplish on earth. Whereas two thirds of the angels resisted him in heaven (see Revelation 12:4), only a remnant of humans resist him in the end-time. That's what Revelation 13 is all about.

Look at the remnant. A woman wears a crown. It's the very first verse of Revelation 12. It's a *stephanos* crown, a laurel wreath of victory worn by winners in the ancient Greek Olympics. It's the gold medal of today. The woman, representing God's church (see Jeremiah 6:2), enters with the evidence of victory. The crown of victory begins this important context to Revelation 13. Victory comes to those who worship Christ. They are only few in numbers—but they wear the crown. This victory shouts out in defiance of the global conglomerate that seeks to destroy them in Revelation 13. It's a world without the crown that comes to annihilate them. It's a world that depends on earthly kings to get the job done. It's a world that depends on earthly crowns without the only crown that counts.

Consider the first three battles. There is "war in heaven. Michael and his angels fought against the dragon, and the dragon and his angels fought back. But he was not strong enough, and they lost their place in heaven" (Revelation 12:7, 8). Victory came to those who worshiped Christ. In the second battle, "The great dragon was hurled down—that ancient serpent called the devil or Satan, who leads the whole world astray. He was hurled to the earth, and his angels with him" (verse 9). This is in human history. He's leading the whole world astray. When did this happen? As noted previously this took place at Calvary (see verses 9-13). "They overcame him by the blood of the Lamb and by the word of their testimony; they did not love their lives so much as to shrink from death" (verse 11). Victory at Calvary! That's why the woman wears the victor's crown. Satan's demise is assured through the death of Christ.

The third battle wages for 1,260 years, from 538 to 1798. "When the dragon saw that he had been hurled to the earth [at Calvary], he pursued the woman who had given birth to the male child [Christ, mentioned in verses 4, 5]. The woman was given the two wings of a great eagle, so that she might fly to the place prepared for her in the desert, where she would be taken care of for a time, times and half a time, out of the serpent's reach" (verses 13, 14). "The woman fled into the desert to a place prepared for her by God, where she might be taken care of for 1,260 days" (verse 6).

Satan's attack on Christians comes after his defeat at Calvary. Because of his loss at the cross he is mad at the true church. If he can capture them, he can make the cross of none effect. If he can claim all humans as his, then the cross was a waste of time. So he schemed. Did he kill Christians during this long period? Yes. That's when Christian blood flowed freely. But God still took care of His people. Nothing, not even death, could separate them from Him (see Romans 8:38, 39). Abiding in Him, they were kept safe for heaven—safe for eternal victory. They were stored away in God's great "layaway" plan for heaven. That's what counts. Saints stood solid, unmoved, unshaken. That's victory. Satan couldn't get them to join his side. They remained loyal to Christ, who remained true to them. They were cared for and kept for heaven and forever. Things of the present, the fleeting and passing, couldn't move them away from Christ. They worshiped Him. They refused to bow to papal anathemas. They rejected all worship of the papal system.

But Satan threw all he had into the battle. It waged long and hard. "Then from his mouth the serpent spewed water like a river to overtake the woman and sweep her away with the torrent" (Revelation 12:15). Waters represent "peoples, multitudes, nations and languages" (Revelation 17:15). Right? Where were they?

Populated Europe is where the battle raged, as people—so-called Christian people—ranted and raved in rage against God's remnant. That remnant felt that all the Christian world was against them. That's always the way it is for the remnant.

Remember when Elijah stood alone facing the 450 prophets of Baal and 400 prophets of Asherah on Mount Carmel in that great test of worship in his day (see 1 Kings 18:19)? Which God should be worshiped—the God of heaven or the counterfeit god of Baal? The Baal worshipers were all Israelites. They were apostate Jews facing Elijah in a test on worship. In the same way apostate Protestantism enforces their idea of worship (see Revelation 13:11–17) on the end-time Elijah people whom God said would come before His second coming (see Malachi 4:5). The parallel is precise: apostates out to destroy the saints.

But the God who stepped in and saved the day for Elijah stepped in and saved the day for the persecuted church in Europe. Instead of the flood of persecution, like a swollen and rushing river, drowning the church, "the earth helped the woman by opening its mouth and swallowing the river that the dragon had spewed out of his mouth" (Revelation 12:16). When did this happen? Whereas "waters" represent peoples, "earth" is a comparatively unpopulated area. And in 1798 that was America.

Jesus spoke of this time in His teaching on last-day events. With the 1,260 years still future He said, "For then there will be great distress, unequaled from the beginning of the world until now—and never to be equaled again. If those days had not been cut short, no one would survive, but for the sake of the elect those days will be shortened" (Matthew 24:21, 22). Were those days cut short before 1798? The *Mayflower* came over to America in 1620, which led to the Declaration of Independence in 1776, just 22 years before 1798! Here was a free country, separate from Europe, an asylum for persecuted Pilgrims. The papal persecution was indeed cut short.

Do you know what happened on the *Mayflower?* Somewhere across the Atlantic Peregrine White was born, direct ancestor of James White, the husband of Ellen G. White. Fleeing from church persecution, the Whites came to the New World, the world into which the Seventh-day Adventist Church would be born, and from which it would enter the entire world. Out of Christians fleeing from church persecution would come a new end-time church, a church that would become just as global as the Catholic Church, a church that would be center stage in end-time events when the Papacy and this church would face each other over the matter of worship. This end-time church, like the church throughout all time, keeps all God's commandments and has the testimony of Jesus (see Revelation 12:17). The fact that the devil is mad against this kind of church indicates that the churches he uses in the end-time do not keep all the commandments of God nor cherish the testimony of Jesus.

What Is the Difference Between True and False Worship?

Revelation 13 is a chapter about false worship (see verses 4, 8, 12-15). But what distinguishes false from true worship? The true church are "those who obey God's commandments and hold to the testimony of Jesus" (Revelation 12:17). The testimony of Jesus is the "spirit of prophecy" (Revelation 19:10). God's remnant have always kept His commandments and been true to the prophetic gift in their midst, whether in the Old Testament or Christian Eras. But what does the "spirit of prophecy" mean? It's far more than the end-time gift through Ellen G. White. It includes that of course. But it's also the entire gift of prophecy found in Scripture. It's clear that this includes the messages given by Jesus. Hebrews puts it well: "In the past God spoke to our forefathers through the prophets at many times and in various ways, but in these last days he has spoken to us by his Son" (Hebrews 1:1, 2).

So end-time saints "obey God's commandments and remain faithful to Jesus" (Revelation 14:12). Put another way, the true church obeys all God's commandments and what Jesus has taught, in contrast to the false church that does neither. So the commandments of God and the truth taught by Jesus will be central to the end-time test over worship. That's why Hans LaRondelle is right when he says, "God's expanded testimony places the church before the authority of God's Son (see Hebrews 1:1, 2; 2:1-4; 10:26-31; 12:22-29)."[3]

The book of Revelation is a revelation of Jesus. Jesus will be revealed in His end-time saints who, in opposition to the world, will stand true to the Word of God and to the teachings of Jesus. The world will reject the Word of God and the teachings of Jesus. So the final end-time test of worship involves whether Jesus is the focus of worship or not. The world will worship the papal power and Satan (see Revelation 13:4). The saints will worship Christ (see Revelation 14:7). What will take place on the global scale is but the same as happened to John on the local level. John, the writer of Revelation, was banished to "the island of Patmos because of the word of God and the testimony of Jesus" (Revelation 1:9). The words "testimony of Jesus" occur five times in Revelation (1:2, 9; 12:17; 19:10; 20:4). John stood true to the "Word of God" (John 1:1)—the term *word* or *words* occur numerous times in Revelation (1:9; 17:17; 19:9, 13)—and to the testimony "about" and "given by" Jesus. These two phrases occur together. It is God's Word, and the final revelation of the Word of God (Jesus), that gives authoritative revelation to humans and constitutes the basis of true worship. Any deviance from God's Word or the teaching of Jesus is the basis of counterfeit worship.

Christ and His disciples kept the Sabbath (see Luke 4:16; 23:54, 56), and He declared that His sacrifice finished the payment for sin (see John 19:30). Biblical writers affirm that the Sabbath rest remains for all time (Hebrews 4:9, 10; Isaiah 66:22, 23) and that the sacrifice of Jesus was once for all time (see Hebrews 9:26; Isaiah 53:3-12). Sunday replaced the eternal Sabbath, and recrucifying Christ in the Mass replaced the "once for all, completed sacrifice" of Christ. The church that truly experiences the Sabbath rest, and hence experiences a resting in Christ's completed and all-sufficient atonement, faces the church that keeps a man-made day of worship and relies on human-made repetitions of Calvary. You cannot get any different than that! The one rests in Christ alone; the other rests in their man-made substitutes for the teaching of Jesus. The one is true to the Word of God and the teaching of Jesus; the other isn't. Relationship to the Written and Living Words of God makes the decisive difference in the end-time global test of worship.

Four battles: heaven, Calvary, the 1,260 years, and the end-time. Just as Christ won the first three battles so He'll win the end-time battle of Revelation 12:17, when Satan is mad against the end-time remnant. That madness is seen in Revelation 13 with its global worship of Satan and the Papacy, enforced by America with signs (see Revelation 13:13, 14), a death decree (see verse 15), and an inability to buy or sell (see verse 17) for those not complying. In spite of these measures, it's the woman who wears the crown, and not those attempting to destroy her.

Revelation 13

In Revelation 13 we come to a chapter full of religiopolitical warfare. We come to global Christianity caught up in a power struggle, to Christians dominating the world. How utterly foreign to Christ's beatitude "Blessed are the meek, for they will inherit the earth" (Matthew 5:5)! No meekness here. Force overtakes faith, the power of the dragon determines the devotion given. False worship, that's what it is. Worship the beast (see Revelation 13:4), worship his image (see verse 15), and worship the devil (see verse 4). But no worship of God.

The worship of Christ as Creator of all things (see Revelation 14:7), including His coming kingdom (see 1 Thessalonians 4:16-18; Revelation 21:1-3), is shoved aside in the mad dash for Christians to build their kingdom on earth. Christians rush to do the impossible. The kingdom comes from above and not from below. This is Christianity taken over by the enemy. This is cosmic terrorism in near global triumph. This is Christianity in name only, but in reality it's a clever avenue through which the devil works, for the Christian guise gives it acceptability in Christian circles. Lamblike and dragonlike (see Revelation 13:11) describes the whole history presented in the chapter, and not just America in the end-time. Christian in name but devilish in mission—this is Christianity persecuting true Christians (see verse 7). Past persecution will become global persecution, even ending in a death decree (see verse 15).

Christ warned, "Then you will be handed over to be persecuted and put to death, and you will be hated by all nations because of me. At that time many will turn away from the faith and will betray and hate each other, and many false prophets will appear and deceive many people. Because of the increase of wickedness, the love of most will grow cold, but he who stands firm to the end will be saved" (Matthew 24:9-13). John spoke of that day too. He gives the rest of the story. He looks to the millennium, and to a special honor granted to those who die in the end-time: "I saw thrones on which were seated those who had been given authority to judge. And I saw the souls of those who had been beheaded because of their testimony for Jesus and because of the word of God. They had not worshiped the beast or his image and had not received his mark on their foreheads or their hands. They came to life and reigned with Christ a thousand years" (Revelation 20:4). What a privilege to sit with Christ on His throne and reign for a thousand years!

Christians spilling Christian blood in the name of Christ! What ever happened to grace? It is thrown to the winds. For some it is no longer amazing grace but amazing grief. Jesus sent Christians to make disciples of all nations (see Matthew 28:19), not to dominate all nations and the saints. "Not by the decisions of courts or councils or legislative assemblies, not by the patronage of worldly great men, is the kingdom of Christ established, but by the implanting of Christ's nature in humanity through the work of the Holy Spirit."[4] It's the kingdom of grace that God works to establish in the present. In his book *What's So Amazing About Grace,* Philip Yancey says, "The church's single most important contribution" is to "offer grace."[5] Yet, when on airplanes he asks passengers what "evangelical Christian" means to them, he says, "In reply, mostly I hear political descriptions: of strident pro-life activists, or gay-rights opponents, or proposals for censoring the Internet. I hear references to the Moral Majority, an organization disbanded years ago. Not once—*not once*—have I heard a description redolent of grace. Apparently that is not the aroma Christians give off in the world."[6]

Kenneth Myers, in the book *Power Religion: The Selling Out of the Evangelical Church,* comments, "Surely we ought to be more preoccupied with serving our neighbors than with ruling them. The involvement of Christians in cultural and civic life ought to be motivated by love of neighbor, not by self-interest—not even by the corporate self-interest of the evangelical movement."[7] Frank Peretti reminds us that "history tells the sorry tale of the dismal failure of politicized religion and even of the masses who used and abused it to their own impoverishment."[8] Revelation 13 is the ultimate attempt to force an alleged Christian religion on the world, with signs, miracles (see Revelation 13:13, 14), and a death decree (see verse 15) to persuade.

The Two Beasts of Revelation 13

Satan conquered almost the entire world before the flood. He lacked only eight people (see Genesis 7:7). Revelation 13 shows that he'll try again in the end-time. He has most of the world. To get all of the world he must capture Christians. He approaches Christians through the appearance of Christian worship. That's the thrust of Revelation 13.

Satan leads Christian churches to unite in the end-time. I have traced this history in *Christ Is Coming!* and will not repeat it here.[9] Churches are uniting to face a common enemy, just as America united to face terrorism. The enemy is secularism, humanism, godlessness, and religious fanaticism that foster and feed the kind of terrorism outbreaks we see around the world today. The union is evident in Revelation 13. The whole world worships the papal power and worships the devil. "Men worshiped the dragon [devil] because he had given authority to the beast, and they also worshiped the beast" (verse 4).

There's a counterfeit Trinity in the end-time. The devil counterfeits the Father and gives authority to the Papacy, just as the Father gave authority to Christ (see Revelation 2:27). The earth beast forces the world to worship the Papacy (see Revelation 13:12), just as the Holy Spirit brings glory to Christ (see John 16:14). Satan is the counterfeit Father, the papal power is the counterfeit Christ, and the power that rises from the earth, or America, becomes the counterfeit Holy Spirit by bringing glory to the papal system. It's America, and apostate Protestantism in America, that bring glory to the papal system. This comes about by a national Sunday law that honors the counterfeit Sabbath invented by the Papacy. This becomes an international Sunday law, for all over the world people will be forced to worship this idol Sabbath, and in doing so "all the world wondered after the [papal] beast" (Revelation 13:3, KJV).

The final human-made idol stands tall over the modern Plain of Dura (see Daniel 3:1-27). All are forced to bow down and worship (just as Nebuchadnezzar required), and nearly all obey. This is the final pre-Advent jihad carried out by the satanic al-Qaeda terrorist organization. The few who don't bow, because Sabbath is the seventh day, are the modern Hebrew worthies. Are they thrown into a modern fiery furnace? Yes, and Christ enters and stays with them all the way!

Who forces the world to fall down and worship this final false idol? America and its apostate Protestantism performs "great and miraculous signs even causing fire to come down from heaven" (Revelation 13:13). Here's a false Mount Carmel (see 1 Kings 18:19-40). You remember the genuine one. "The god who answers by fire—he is God" (verse 24). "Then the fire of the Lord fell. . . . When all the people saw this, they fell prostrate and cried 'The Lord—he is God! The Lord—he is God!'" (verses 38, 39). From the modern Mount Carmel ring out the words "If God supports Sunday, let the fire fall!" and unseen terrorist angels throw down flames. Miracles will deceive the world (see Revelation 13:14). "Seeing is believing" just as it was in Eden when Eve saw that the fruit was good to eat (see Genesis 3:6). Satan captures the world. In America an image to the first beast (see Revelation 13:15) is an image to the Papacy, which is a union of church and state. When church and state unite, they enforce Sunday and order death for those who do not comply (see verse 15).

The human race worships Satan in this last pre-Advent act of defiance against Christ (see verse 4). Satan ascends the throne on earth that he was unable to take in heaven. The remnant who remain standing tall are those who have Christ ruling on the throne of their hearts, who worship Him as King of kings and Lord of lords, and who have no fear of the world and its decrees.

The War on Terrorism Since September 11

America could never fulfill its role of forcing all the world to accept Sunday while the U.S.S.R. was a superpower. With the collapse of Communism, and the breakup of the Soviet republic into separate countries, America remains the only superpower. The attack on America on September 11, 2001, catapulted America into global leadership undreamed-of the day before. The military might of America has been demonstrated in the swift collapse of the Taliban and of Saddam's Iraq, leaving nations around the world in shock. There's no other country anywhere near America's amazing capability in sophisticated delivery systems and precision accuracy. Even in the allied alliance, none can contribute at the advanced level of America's military machine, and none is anywhere near able to pay for such a system. America is pouring into the war on terrorism $30 million a day, or $1 billion a month. At the time of this writing, President George W. Bush wants to spend $80 billion in the war and homeland security during the next fiscal year. In a league of its own, America is not just a superpower; it's a superstar with no rival!

Since the attack, Americans have been willing to give up some of their freedoms in order to have security. Life has changed in the land of the free. Even wiretapping is not off limits for the government to detect potential terrorists. Americans are disturbed that people who come on visitors' visas can overstay their visit, and not be detected. They want something done about the thousands in the country beyond their legal time. A national identification system has been debated, and is still ongoing. August Gribbin of the Washington *Times* stated that the "White House has ruled out creating a national identity card system as a counter terrorist measure," yet noted that "the Arlington-based American Association of Motor Vehicle Administrators confirms that 24 states and the U.S. military have adopted its recommendation for creating a standard driver's licenses and more are interested. The suggested cards have computer-readable stripes and bar codes that contain a digitized photo and data about the card's owner. The codes on the cards could be read by the same kind of scanners found in grocery stores. There is no question the technology for implementing a national identity system is here." [10]

We know that the finger ID method is being used in the country. No two fingerprints are the same, not even those of identical twins. So for most people, except some of the older generation, this system is a good one. I know a business owner who uses the system for workers to get into his factory. Others have talked about the eye as being another ID marker. Undoubtedly there'll be many more ideas brought to the table. We don't know what the final system will be, but we know that around the world there will be a way of identifying who cannot buy or sell and thus fulfilling the prophecy of Revelation 13. The war on terrorism heightens the need to have such a system, and given that things could get worse, people may well be willing to give up more freedoms to have a fail-safe identification system to provide security.

The Good News Behind Revelation 13

The global war on terrorism gives America a position of unprecedented prominence and prestige. It gives her a war that can continue into the indefinite future. Nations that battle with terrorism look to America in a way not possible before September 11, 2001. No one can predict the future, but at least America has catapulted into a strategic leadership role in the world that can fulfill the prophecies of Revelation 13. The two beasts of Revelation 13 are wild beasts. They are wild in their terrorism against God, His heavenly sanctuary, and His people. They are wild because they oppose God's holy Sabbath, and bow in worship to this false idol, and false Christ, on the final Plain of Dura. So far it's bad news.

The good news begins when we realize the importance of the biblical roots for Revelation 13. Revelation 13 is rooted in Daniel 7. The sea beast (papal power) is the same as the little horn (see outline below). They both oppose God, His heavenly sanctuary, and His people. Daniel 7 is the root passage behind Revelation 13. The papal power is dominant in both. This should never be forgotten. There are two death decrees in the end-time: the death decree for those who do not bow to the Sunday idol (see Revelation 13:15), and the death decree of the pre-Advent judgment verdict (see Daniel 7:21, 22; 25-27). These are two judgment verdicts, one on earth and one in heaven. The good news is that the pre-Advent judgment verdict in heaven precedes the death decree on earth. That's why none of God's people die for not bowing to the Sunday idol. As in Daniel, those who don't bow in worship come out of the fiery furnace alive.

Revelation 13 focuses on end-time events on earth, whereas Daniel 7 focuses on end-time events in heaven. The verdict of heaven overthrows the verdict on earth, its idol, and the system that sponsors both. So don't be afraid of a world power that will command you to bow down or die. That's the greatest time of trouble that Adventists fear so much. Fear no more. Look up. It's far better than you think. Look at your adversary in the light of your Advocate. Face up, enemy—what's the use of ruling the world when your kingdom is about to be destroyed? What's the use of being worshiped by the world if the worshipers are about to perish? Above all else, ask yourself, reader, What's the use of a human death decree against you when there is a divine death decree against your enemy?

Revelation 13
Sea beast—*therion* = wild beast

> Blasphemous, verse 1
> Proud, against God and the heavenly sanctuary, verse 5.
> Wars against the saints, verse 7

Daniel 7
Little horn

> Boastful, 7:8
> Against God, oppresses the saints, 7:25
> Against heavenly sanctuary, 8:11

Revelation 13
Earth beast—*therion* = wild beast

> Lamblike but speaks and acts as a dragon, verses 11, 12
> Forces world to worship sea beast, verse 12
> Deceives the world through false Christian miracles, verses 13, 14
> Death decree to those not complying to forced worship, verse 15
> Cannot buy or sell if not complying to forced worship, verses 16, 17

[1] Ellen G. White, *Patriarchs and Prophets,* p. 38.

[2] *Ibid.,* p. 35.

[3] Hans LaRondelle, *How to Understand the End-Time Prophecies of the Bible* (Sarasota, Fla.: First Impressions, 1997), p. 282.

[4] White, *The Desire of Ages,* p. 509.

[5] Philip Yancey, *What's So Amazing About Grace?* (Grand Rapids: Zondervan, 1997), pp. 15, 31.

[6] *Ibid.,* p. 31.

[7] Kenneth A. Myers, *Power Religion: The Selling Out of the Evangelical Church,* ed. Michael Scott Horton, (Chicago: Moody, 1992), p. 55.

[8] Frank Peretti in Ravi Zacharias, *Deliver Us From Evil: Restoring the Soul in a Disintegrating Culture* (Dallas: Word, 1996), p. xvii.

[9] Norman R. Gulley, *Christ Is Coming!,* pp. 112-126.

[10] August Gribbin, Washington *Times,* Sept. 27, 2001.

FINAL BATTLE

It was the Communist revolutionary Lenin who said, "Give me one generation of youth, and I will transform the entire world." Now an entire generation of youth has been given to a woman named J. K. Rowling and her four books on witchcraft, known as the Harry Potter series. Many parents are concerned about the influence of these books, in which the boy Harry lives in a world of witches and wizards. Other parents and educators are elated that kids are reading again. Finally something has grabbed their attention away from television and videos. What do you think?

Journalist and Counselor Isobel Webster from Lincolnshire, England, says, "Harry Potter encourages us to dream of being a savior-figure."[1] The inward look is consistent with the New Age view that we are becoming gods. That's Satan's lie. As the supreme terrorist he wants to throw people back on their own supposed resources because he knows he can take them captive when they do.

God said to Israel, "When you enter the land the Lord your God is giving you, do not learn to imitate the detestable ways of the nations there. Let no one be found among you who sacrifices his son or daughter in the fire, who practices divination or sorcery, interprets omens, engages in witchcraft, or casts spells, or who is a medium or spiritist or who consults the dead. Anyone who does these things is detestable to the Lord, and because of these detestable practices the Lord your God will drive out those nations before you" (Deuteronomy 18:9-12). God places witchcraft with pagan practices. Because the land was filled with these things, He promises to drive the people out before Israel.

God not only rejects witchcraft but knows His people cannot be successful against these forces without Him driving them out for them. Again we see that it was never God's purpose that His people fight. He promised to fight for them. Because when they depended on themselves they ended up succumbing to these practices, for these practices were other forms of self-dependence. In last-day events God wants His people to give up on self-dependence and depend on Him alone!

There's so much emphasis today on self-help seminars, and "you are what you think" approaches to success. Although I share the sentiments of right thoughts and focus, I don't believe a person does this on their own. There's no magic in looking to Christ rather than the crisis, for example. It's only Christ who can help us do this, so it's not our determination to achieve this but our dependence on Him to achieve it *through* us. There's no solo work in the Christian walk any more than we go through final events alone. Remember the thrust of cosmic terrorism is to break our dependence on Christ. We cannot fight spiritual battles alone. Christ gains our victory as we daily depend upon Him by taking time to be with Him, practicing His presence, reading about Him, worshiping Him. Now that's the battle! "Abide in me" (John 15:4, NKJV), and bear "much fruit" for "apart from me you can do nothing" (John 15:5 NIV). There's no battle for a Christian to fight alone when Christ promises to never leave us (see Hebrews 13:5), to be "in [us]" (Colossians 1:27), and with us to the end of the world (see Matthew 28:20).

Look Up!

As we saw in the last chapter, the good news about the great time of trouble that so many Adventists fear is not the death decree verdict against end-time saints, but the preceding death decree against the enemies of God's people in the pre-Advent judgment. That's why the pre-Advent judgment is linked to the everlasting gospel in the first angel's message (see Revelation 14:6, 7). The angel has "the eternal gospel" to take to the whole world, proclaiming, "Fear God and give him glory, because the hour of his judgment has come. Worship him who made the heavens, the earth, the sea, and the springs of water" (verses 6, 7).

As we saw in chapter 12, victorious saints on earth echo the worship of created beings at the throne. They are lifted into the heights in adoration and devotion to Christ their Creator-Redeemer. They reverence Him. They worship Him. He is everything to them. Their minds and hearts are full of Him, as they see Him on the throne of the universe, and they know that He is the only one who brought them into the world. He first created Adam and Eve. Then He gave all humans life when they were born. He keeps their heart ticking when they sleep. They live because of Him. And just as He brought them into this world, so He alone can get them into the next world. Humans contribute nothing in both cases. The only difference now is that humans are alive to either turn down or accept the gift. Going through final events is as much a gift as Calvary, for it takes both to get to heaven. The knowledge of the gift gives great joy and gratitude beyond any fear of those who seek to take it away in end-time tests.

In worshiping Him as the Creator who made the heavens and the earth, the sea, and the springs of water, end-time saints repeat a portion of the Sabbath command (see Exodus 20:11). They remember that it was not humans but the Sabbath that was the crowning climax of creation. The first full day of life for humans was a day of resting in Christ in deep fellowship with their Creator, the God up close. Likewise in the end-time, the Sabbath test on the modern plain of Dura is not simply knowing that Sunday is a counterfeit idol, nor that the seventh day is the Sabbath, but it is experiencing the Sabbath as a resting in Christ. One would rather die than give up the Sabbath because one would rather die than give up Christ. It's an experience in which self-dependence has been fully replaced by Christ-dependence.

The final pre-Advent battle against cosmic terrorism is not a battle that end-time saints fight. Christ will do the fighting for them. Their part is to relax, rest fully in Him, and let Him do the fighting. That battle is the hardest for self-dependent humans. That's why they must die daily, as Paul put it (see 1 Corinthians 15:31). They have to come to the place where they pray the prayer of Christ, "Not my will, but yours be done" (Luke 22:42). The only way Jesus went through His final events was in total dependence upon His Father. That's why it was so heart-wrenching for Him when He felt God-forsaken (see Matthew 27:46). His separation from God was for us. It was our sins that drove the wedge between Them as far as Christ's experience of suffering loneliness is concerned. The Father had not left Him, but it felt as if He had. Christ plunged into the eternal separation from God so that we will never have to do the same.

"It would be well for us to spend a thoughtful hour each day in contemplation of the life of Christ. We should take it point by point, and let the imagination grasp each scene, especially the closing ones. As we thus dwell upon His great sacrifice for us, our confidence in Him will be more constant, our love will be quickened, and we shall be more deeply imbued with His spirit. If we would be saved at last, we must learn the lesson of penitence and humiliation at the foot of the cross. As we associate together, we may be a blessing to one another. If we are Christ's, our sweetest thoughts will be of Him. We shall love to talk of Him; and as we speak to one another of His love, our hearts will be softened by divine influences. Beholding the beauty of His character, we shall be 'changed into the same image from glory to glory.' 2 Corinthians 3:18."[2]

Everyone who triumphs through final events will do so because they are not fixated on final events but focused on Christ's final events for them. End-time saints must put all their energies into contemplating Christ at Calvary and Christ at the throne. That's their battle. It will take planning each day. It will take filling the mind with reading on the cross and the throne scenes, as we did in the book of Revelation. It will take time thinking about Him and talking about Him, too. Express your joy in Christ, and it will grow.

There's no better way to crumble self-dependence than to look to the throne room and to see Christ there in all His majesty and glory, to see the transcendent all-powerful God, the one well able to carry saints through every coming crisis. Isaiah saw Him. "I saw the Lord seated on a throne, high and exalted, and the train of his robe filled the temple. Above him were seraphs, each with six wings: With two wings they covered their faces, with two they covered their feet, and with two they were flying. And they were calling to one another: 'Holy, holy, holy is the Lord Almighty; the whole earth is full of his glory.' At the sound of their voices the doorposts and thresholds shook and the temple was filled with smoke. 'Woe to me!' I cried. 'I am ruined! For I am a man of unclean lips, and I live among a people of unclean lips, and my eyes have seen the King, the Lord Almighty'" (Isaiah 6:1-5).

Look Back

It's good to go over the mighty deeds Christ did for His people in ancient times. The prophets constantly reminded Israel and Judah of what He had done for them. But the people soon forgot, and allowed the deeds of humans to fill their minds. Today we are no different. Most saints spend more time with the newspaper and TV than with God's Word. Their minds are saturated with the deeds of humans. No wonder they think of end-time events in terms of what they have to go through, how much suffering there will be for them; no wonder they question how they can make it. It's time to fill the minds with the deeds of Christ and allow those deeds to transform the mind with a vision of Christ. Stephen recited the mighty deeds of God, and when the religious leaders were furious with him and about to stone him to death he was unafraid. Final events were not for him a matter of fear. "Stephen, full of the Holy Spirit, looked up to heaven and saw the glory of God, and Jesus standing at the right hand of God. 'Look,' he said, 'I see heaven open and the Son of Man standing at the right hand of God'" (Acts 7:55, 56). What a way to die. When you know the truth, the truth sets you free (see John 8:32). The truth of God and Christ on the throne, what They have done and are doing and will do, sets us free from fearing final events.

One of the events Stephen mentioned was the Exodus (see Acts 7:36). There was no way Israel contributed to that deliverance. They did not open up the way through the Red Sea, keep the two walls of water back, provide dry ground for a passage, and destroy the Egyptian army. We have said that the journey through final events is a repetition of the Exodus. The way out of Egypt and the way out of final events is the same. God provides for His saints what they can never provide for themselves. The battle is His, and the victory is His gift.

This transforms worship. It's no longer routine. It's revelry. David experienced it. "The Lord is my strength and my shield; my heart trusts in him, and I am helped. My heart leaps for joy and I will give thanks to him in song" (Psalm 28:7). The psalms are rich in adoration, praise, and devotion to God. Spending time with the psalms lifts readers into the atmosphere of genuine devotion to God. The way we sing can be an outside indicator of our heart. If it's spontaneous and full of joy, it's adoration and worship. This comes from meditating on God and His mighty acts.

That's what happened after the Exodus deliverance. It's called the Song of Moses. "Then Moses and the Israelites sang this song to the Lord: 'I will sing to the Lord, for he is highly exalted. The horse and its rider he has hurled into the sea. The Lord is my strength and my song; he has become my salvation. He is my God, and I will praise him'" (Exodus 15:1, 2). He is a personal God. "Who among the gods is like you, O Lord? Who is like you—majestic in holiness, awesome in glory, working wonders? You stretched out your right hand and the earth swallowed them. In your unfailing love you will lead the people you have redeemed. In your strength you will guide them to your holy dwelling" (verses 12, 13).

The final exodus through last-day events inspires singing throughout eternity. It's called the Song of Moses and the song of the Lamb (see Revelation 15:3). "Great and marvelous are your deeds, Lord God Almighty" (verse 3). Both songs exult in the mighty saving acts of God. There's no mention of human acts. Humans rested in Christ their deliverer. That's the only work they can contribute, for exodus deliverance is like Calvary deliverance, where Christ provides the gift that humans cannot give or earn. That's why Moses referred to the Exodus as redemption. It's not until the truth dawns on us that going through last-day events is like Calvary that we'll no more fear this coming gift than we do the gift of the cross.

Pre-Advent Armageddon

Armageddon is a part of the final exodus. It's the implementation of the pre-Advent verdict. It brings destruction of the worldwide enemy against God's people, and deliverance to God's people. It's exodus on a global scale. Scripture puts the battle in the setting of a worldwide campaign to capture the planet through spiritualism, which gets us back to Harry Potter.

Spiritualism is sweeping the world today, and preparing to hijack humanity in a last desperate effort to conquer the world for Satan. I will not repeat here what I wrote in *Christ Is Coming!* about this movement, but it is vital that we understand Satan's terrorist strategy to take over the planet before Christ returns.[3]

"Then I saw three evil spirits that looked like frogs; they came out of the mouth of the dragon [paganism], out of the mouth of the beast [Papacy], and out of the mouth of the false prophet [apostate Protestantism]. They are spirits of demons performing miraculous signs and they go out to the kings of the whole world, to gather them for the battle on the great day of God Almighty. 'Behold I come like a thief! Blessed is he who stays awake and keeps his clothes with him, so that he may not go naked and be shamefully exposed.' Then they gathered the kings together to the place that in Hebrew is called Armageddon" (Revelation 16:13-16).

This passage needs to be studied together with Revelation 13 and 14. In Revelation 13 there's a counterfeit trinity of Satan—the Papacy and America with apostate Protestantism. In Revelation 16 Satan's counterfeit three angels have a mission to deceive through miracles, the same deceptive work described in Revelation 13:12-17. In Revelation 14 God's three angels have a message to point to Christ in last-day events (see verses 6-13). He is the Creator. He is given dominion in the judgment (see verse 7; Daniel 7:13, 14). He is given the judgment verdict to destroy the enemy and to deliver His people (see verses 21, 22, 25-27). He will defeat Babylon (see Revelation 14:8; 18:1-20) and its counterfeit worship in the end-time (see Revelation 14:9-13; 19:14-21). It is Christ who does these mighty acts even as it was Christ who did the mighty acts, in the Exodus (see Exodus 14:19; 23:20; Deuteronomy 4:37, 38; Acts 7:30, 32). In this final exodus the Egyptian army is now global spiritualism, hordes of evil spirits, demons under the devil. It is Christ, and Christ alone, who can meet them and defeat them on the basis of Calvary. This is what Armageddon is all about. It's the final pre-Advent battle between Christ and Satan.

First Armageddon Battle in the Old Testament

The Exodus followed captivity in Egypt. The first battle of Armageddon followed 20 years of captivity in Canaan. King Jabin treated the Israelites cruelly. He had 900 iron chariots. The captives cried to the Lord for help (see Judges 4:1-3). The prophet Deborah said to Barak, " 'Go! This is the day the Lord has given Sisera into your hands. Has not the Lord gone ahead of you?' . . . At Barak's advance, the Lord routed Sisera and all his chariots. . . . All the troops of Sisera fell by the sword; not a man was left" (verses 14-16). The question is Whose sword? The sword of God or the swords of the Israelites?

The song of victory describes the plight of Israel. "When they chose new gods, war came to the city gates, and not a shield or spear was seen among forty thousand in Israel" (Judges 5:8). Captivity came because they forgot the God of the Exodus. They did not have weapons to defend themselves either. It's unlikely they could get arms while in captivity. So the sword is the sword of God, who responded to their cry and wanted to remind them that He had not changed. He was still the God of the Exodus.

What prospects did they have against 900 iron chariots? No military analyst would give them a chance. Here was a walking army pitched against sleek machines that could surround and decimate them. But it was the other way round. Angels with greater swiftness were no match for the enemy! No wonder the emphasis is on God fighting for them and totally wiping out the enemy, just as in the Exodus.

No wonder they sang after the battle just as Israel did after the Exodus. "Kings came, they fought; the kings of Canaan fought at Taanach by the waters of Megiddo, but they carried off no silver, no plunder. From the heavens the stars fought, from their courses they fought against Sisera. The river Kishon swept them away" (verses 19-21). Here are heavenly beings fighting, and the river sweeps the enemy away. Arthur E. Cundall says, "The massed armies of the kings of the Canaanite city-states were met by the might of the forces of nature, operating at the behest of Israel's God. The violent storm and the turbulence of the swollen Kishon were the chief architects of victory and the gallant ten thousand Israelites receive no mention in this section."[4] Men in chariots destroyed by water as they were in the Red Sea. Unarmed Israelites delivered both times. What parallels! Superior war machines mean nothing to God. The whole world against His end-time saints will mean nothing either.

Interlude: Another Deception

Another deception of cosmic terrorism hides the truth about Armageddon through false theology. False theology always works. False theology fueled the Crusades on both sides, it brings all the world to false worship in the end-time, and it hides the truth of God's end-time plan with a counterfeit plan of final events.

Armageddon (see Revelation 16:12-16) is interpreted by most Christians as a literal battle in Palestine involving Jews and Russia. We'll not get into the details of this scenario, but here's a summary. During the last seven years between the rapture of the church and heaven, the Jews will rebuild the temple, and Russia will invade Palestine (Armageddon), with God miraculously delivering Israel from Russia. In gratitude the Jews become Christians and convert the world in the second half of the seven years. Suffice it to say that there's nothing in Scripture to substantiate these views. Yet the *Left Behind* books are popular!

What a shock to Christians one day when they find there's no rapture, secret or otherwise! Satan hijacks these Christians with a lie, and makes them think they do not need to prepare for times of trouble. They do not need to spend time looking up at the throne room, gazing on Christ, for after all, He'll rapture them out before it gets rough. That's cosmic terrorism, getting Christians hooked on a trip too early, to keep them unprepared for what's coming.

False theology lies behind the gathering of Jews from the world into literal Israel. It hides the gathering of people from the world into spiritual Israel, which includes the Seventh-day Adventist Church. That's cosmic terrorism. It deflects attention from a global Armageddon to a local Armageddon in Palestine.

By contrast, there are two global gatherings today. Spirits of demons working through three religious avenues (paganism, the Papacy, and apostate Protestantism) gather people to fight in Armageddon. And the three angels messages through the Seventh-day Adventist Church gather people to let God fight for them in Armageddon. Both gatherings are worldwide, and demons are involved. So Armageddon is not just a secular battle between two nations in the Middle East. Besides this, in the middle of the Armageddon passage, sandwiched between the two verses about the battle (see verses 14, 16), Christ says, "Behold, I come like a thief! Blessed is he who stays awake and keeps his clothes with him, so that he may not go naked and be shamefully exposed" (verse 15). This message is a shortened form but repetition of the Laodicean message, or Christ's message to the end-time church (see Revelation 3:14-22). These are the saints who go through Armageddon, and so need their robe on to be clothed in Christ, totally dependent on Him alone. Being raptured is not the dependence this text teaches. It's a horrible deception destined to bring drastic discouragement to millions of Christians. That's cosmic terrorism.

End-Time Battle of Armageddon

If only these millions could study Scripture, and allow typology to inform them of true theology. God's total destruction of the enemy and deliverance of His people in the first battle of Armageddon in Scripture is a local type of the final pre-Advent battle of Armageddon. Armageddon is to implement the double verdict of the pre-Advent judgment, to destroy the enemy and deliver God's people. This is the final outworking of the double verdict of Calvary where the death of Jesus destroys the enemy and delivers His people. Both the pre-Advent judgment and the pre-Advent Armageddon are the working out in heaven and in human history of what took place at the cross.

The context for the final battle is the drying up of the river Euphrates and the coming of the kings of the east (see Revelation 16:12). We'll take up the kings of the east near the end of the chapter. In the Red Sea and Kishon River the waters were the instrument of death to the enemies. What does the drying up of the river Euphrates mean? The future battlefield is the world, because the two sides are everywhere. So no sea or river can be involved this time. At best a river can represent symbolically what happens. The drying up of the Euphrates River relates in part to history and in part to prophetic symbolism.

First to the history. The literal city of Babylon was the capital of the nation where Judah spent 70 years in captivity. Babylon fell into the hands of Cyrus, king of Persia, in 539 B.C. without a battle because the diversion of the Euphrates River left a dry bed for the army to cross over and enter the city.[5] Symbolically waters represent people (see Revelation 17:15), and the drying up of the river Euphrates represents the destruction of spiritual Babylon, enemy of God's people. God calls Cyrus His "shepherd" (Isaiah 44:28) and His "anointed" (Isaiah 45:1). He brought the captivity of Judah to an end just as Armageddon will bring the great time of trouble captivity to an end. Cyrus is a type of Christ. Judah did not fight to be released; nor will end-time saints.

Darius the Mede (see Daniel 6:1; 9:1; 11:1) was a coregent under Cyrus (553-530 B.C.). Three kings[6] after Cyrus brings us to Xerxes (486-465 B.C.), grandson of Cyrus. He is the king at the time of Esther. A death decree to kill all the Jews (see Esther 3:13, 14) is a type of the final death decree (see Revelation 13:15). But God miraculously intervened. The fiery furnace (see Daniel 3:22, 23) the lions' den (see Daniel 6:24) of Daniel, and Haman's gallows (see Esther 7:10) of Esther are types of Armageddon because the enemy was destroyed and God's people delivered.

When the Battle Takes Place

After the close of probation, "Satan has full control of the finally impenitent. . . . The Spirit of God, persistently resisted, has been at last withdrawn."[7] That's trouble enough. Imagine nearly the whole world demon-possessed. What an angry mob this motley crew, reflecting the image of the devil! What a revelation to the universe of the result of Satan's rule! The universe sees what Satan would have done if he had ousted Christ from His throne in heaven. By contrast the followers of Christ are calm, radiate His love, and worship Him as they look up to the throne and rejoice, sensing the day of redemption nearing. The stunning contrast between the two groups is stark and clear!

But that's not all. Just as a single angel brought death to firstborn Egyptians in the Exodus, the "same destructive power exercised by holy angels when God commands, will be exercised by evil angels when He permits. There are forces now ready, and only waiting the divine permission, to spread desolation everywhere."[8] Looks like they go berserk! Here's the horror of cosmic terrorism. Billions of wicked humans demon possessed—demons causing havoc everywhere, and humans passing a death decree on the saints to wipe them out in one day (see Revelation 13:15). Here's the magnitude of satanic deception. The lamblike veneer is torn off, and the dragon appears in all his horror, the consummate terrorist who delights to destroy.

It's too late to change then. Some sat on the fence, uncommitted, members of Laodicea, neither hot nor cold. Now stone-cold, they have no hope. That's the tragedy of the terrorists' lie—that one can live for Christ and for self. It doesn't work. It never did. But now it's too late. Demon-possessed people are doomed to eternal death. Christ weeps as He beholds a race of humans devoid of anything good. The image of God in them is fully erased. They could have been like Him—free, happy, and fulfilled.

The plague angels come out of the temple after the pre-Advent judgment verdict. The plagues are part of the implementation of the verdict against spiritual Babylon. They are devastating, "the most awful scourges that have ever been known to mortals."[9] They wreak havoc on the wicked and the world, but not on God's people. "While the wicked are dying from hunger and pestilence, angels will shield the righteous and supply their wants."[10] What a difference between Satan's angels and God's angel's. On both levels, angelic and human, the wrecks of cosmic terrorism and revelers in redemption go through the great time of trouble together. How different the journey and how different the destiny.

The wicked hate the saints. They've become like Satan. They

cannot wait to kill them. Some saints, confined to prison as was John on the Island of Patmos, suffer tests and trials. But I don't wish to dwell on these, because that's precisely what Satan does to hijack pilgrims from Christ, and what he's done so well in the church. Rather I want to focus on what Jesus focused on—the joy set before Him (see Hebrews 12:2). They long for the coming of Christ. But in the meantime, "dungeon walls cannot cut off the communication between their souls and Christ. One who sees their every weakness, who is acquainted with every trial, is above all earthly powers; and angels will come to them in lonely cells, bringing light and peace from heaven."[11]

The greatest need in the great time of trouble is to see it as heaven sees it. That's why saints must look up to the throne, and look at last-day events as seen from the throne. "Could men see with heavenly vision, they would behold companies of angels that excel in strength stationed about those who have kept the word of Christ's patience. With sympathizing tenderness, angels have witnessed their distress and have heard their prayers. They are waiting the word of their Commander to snatch them from their peril."[12]

"As the wrestling ones urge their petitions before God, the veil separating them from the unseen seems almost withdrawn. The heavens glow with the dawning of eternal day, and like the melody of angel songs the words fall upon the ear: 'Stand fast to your allegiance. Help is coming.' Christ, the almighty Victor, holds out to His weary soldiers a crown of immortal glory; and His voice comes from the gates ajar: 'Lo, I am with you. Be not afraid. I am acquainted with all your sorrows; I have borne your griefs. You are not warring against untried enemies. I have fought the battle in your behalf, and in My name you are more than conquerors.'"[13]

Preparation for the battle is the sixth plague (see Revelation 16:12) and the battle occurs during the seventh plague.

Finale of the Battle

"From the sky huge hailstones of about a hundred pounds each fell upon men" (verse 21). One hundred pounds! Imagine the devastation. They fall on the wicked only and not on the saints. Again

God uses nature as a weapon, as He did in the Red Sea and in the Kishon River. This goads the wicked to put the saints to death. But the date has been set, and they must wait.

Let's pause here and go back to heaven just before the battle begins. Everything is astir. It's closing time. The Second Advent is about to take place. Does God the Father call the Son and say, "Jesus, will You go and implement the pre-Advent judgment verdict and then bring them home? I need a rest. The judgment was too long"? Is this why all Second Advent pictures have Christ coming alone with the angels? Does the father in the story of the prodigal son hear of his son's return and say, "If he can get cleaned up, and work out an appropriate apology, and knock on my office door in meekness, then I may open it and see him"? No, he looks for his return every day, and on the day he sees his beloved son, he leaves home and runs down the road to enfold him in his strong arms of love, cover him with his robe, give him a new ring, put sandals on his feet, and bring him home with great rejoicing and shouts of joy. "Let's celebrate! My son's come home!"

Back on earth the date arrives for the death decree. The wicked ache for revenge. Why should these few favorites escape the plagues while millions of wicked perish? With hellish laughs they snarl, "We'll show them. We'll be their plague." Around the world they dash out to slaughter the saints.

Up in heaven all is ready. The hour for the death decree nears. The Father says to the Son, "Let's go and bring them home." Vaulting through the heavens, in the nick of time, come the Kings of the east to rescue the redeemed. The wicked are destroyed and God's people delivered. The double verdict of Calvary and of the pre-Advent judgment is fully actualized in the battle of Armageddon (cf. Joel 2:1-17, Revelation 14:14-20; 19:14-21).

You see, coming from the east is a description of coming from heaven (see Revelation 7:2). The Father and the Son are the Kings of the east. But how do we know They come together? Is there biblical evidence? Yes, there is. It's in Revelation 5 and 6. God the Father is seated on His throne (see Revelation 5:1). The Lamb, Christ, comes to God at the throne (verse 7), and the chapter ends with a song: "To him who sits on the throne [Father] and to the Lamb be praise and honor and glory and power, for ever and ever!" (verse 13). They are seated together, Father and Son.

There were no chapter divisions when the texts were written, and Revelation 5 and 6 belong together as a literary unit. Revelation 6 ends with the Second Advent. The wicked will call to the mountains and rocks, "Fall on us and hide us from the face of him who sits on the throne and from the wrath of the Lamb!" (Revelation 6:16). There you have it, the Father and the Son! They come together in the Second Advent. Did Jesus Himself ever talk about this? Yes. He said, "In the future you will see the Son of Man sitting at the right hand of the Mighty One and coming on the clouds of heaven" (Matthew 26:64).

---

[1] Isobel Webster, "Your Teenager and the World of Harry Potter," *Messenger* 106, no. 12/13, (June 8, 2001): 6.

[2] Ellen G. White, *The Desire of Ages,* p. 83

[3] Norman R. Gulley, *Christ Is Coming!,* pp. 127-131.

[4] Arthur E. Cundall, in *Judges,* gen. ed. D. J. Wiseman, *Tyndale Old Testament Commentaries* (Downers Grove, Ill: InterVarsity, 1968), vol. 7, p. 99.

[5] D. J. Wiseman, *The International Standard Bible Encyclopedia,* fully revised, gen. ed. G. W. Bromiley, "Babylon" (Grand Rapids: Eerdmans, 1979), vol. 1, p. 389.

[6] Cambyses (530-522 B.C.) and Darius I (or Darius the Great, 522-486 B. C.) came between Cyrus and Xerxes. So the book of Esther comes after Daniel 6. For a helpful background see *The Seventh-day Adventist Bible Commentary,* vol. 3, pp. 51-64.

[7] White, *The Great Controversy,* p. 614.

[8] *Ibid.*

[9] *Ibid.,* pp. 628, 629.

[10] *Ibid.,* p. 629.

[11] *Ibid.,* p. 627.

[12] *Ibid.,* p. 630.

[13] *Ibid.,* pp. 632, 633.

THE OTHER SECOND ADVENT

J oy." Isn't that a Christian attribute (see Galatians 5:22, 23)? Aren't Christians supposed to be happy? Don't they have the blessed hope? Why so many joyless Christians—especially as they face final events on Planet Earth?

"H. L. Mencken," writes Philip Yancey, "described a Puritan as a person with a haunting fear that someone, somewhere is happy; today, many people would apply the same caricature to evangelicals or fundamentalists. Where does this reputation of upright joylessness come from? A column by humorist Erma Bombeck provides a clue: 'In church the other Sunday I was intent on a small child who was turning around smiling at everyone. He wasn't gurgling, spitting, humming, kicking, tearing the hymnals, or rummaging through his mother's handbag. He was just smiling. Finally his mother jerked him about and in a stage whisper that could be heard in a little theater off Broadway said, "Stop that grinning! You're in church!" With that, she gave him a belt and as the tears rolled down his cheeks added, "That's better," and returned to her prayers. . . .'

"Then Bombeck continued, 'Suddenly I was angry. It occurred to me the entire world is in tears, and if you're not, then you'd better get with it. I wanted to grab this child with the tear-stained face close to me and tell him about my God. The happy God. The smiling God. The God who had to have a sense of humor to have created the likes of us.'"[1]

As noted before, Satan hides God from the view of many Christians. If you believe in a God of hell, then He gives unfair punishment like this child received. Satan hides the truth about Christ's life on earth. He lived a loving life only because He's God. It's only human to sin and be unloving. Or He deceives humans to think the forms of religion are acceptable while denying its power, so practice is more important than persons, as in the case of this mom. He hides the truth about the Holy Spirit, and makes *doing* more important than *being*.

The Most Forgotten Member of the Godhead

Have you noticed that God the Father and God the Son dominate our discussion so far? We find the same fact in much of the Bible. That's because cosmic terrorism is directed preeminently against Christ; the Father gathered the angels to tell the truth about Christ when the controversy began. But the Holy Spirit is equally involved, and Satan's attack is leveled at Him in a different way: Just forget Him, or think of Him as a ghost—that will do it. In other words He's not a Person, just an extension of God, a communication medium.

In reality, the Holy Spirit is a self-effacing person who in Scripture focuses on the other two members of the Godhead. It's Jesus who speaks of the other Comforter to come after His ascension (see John 14:15-18), the Spirit of truth who leads into all truth (see John 16:12, 13). It's the book of Acts that shows His leadership in the early church. But the consummate terrorist has the answer. He attacks the book of the Holy Spirit because it reveals the truth about God and the truth about cosmic terrorism. Satan claims Scripture was authored by many human writers. We talked about this earlier, but add some more insights here. It's a human book, not the Holy Spirit's. The fact of so many different churches claiming to have the truth, yet differing so much in their understanding, is credit to the success of Satan's studied strategy. It's worked.

We Are One in the Spirit?

Being one in the Spirit has become more important than differences in doctrines today. It discounts the Spirit of truth. Experience is placed above truth. And that suits Satan's plan perfectly.

Experience is inward-looking, and becomes the standard of life. "If it feels good, do it" is popular in a world without God, and just as usable by Christians who look within instead of to Scripture. If Christians look to experience, to speaking in tongues, to miracles more than to what God says about Christian experience, they are open to experiences that God's Word condemns. So many are gullibly throwing themselves to the control of a different spirit, believing it to be the Holy Spirit. Though they know it not, Satan has them. That's cosmic terrorism.

My book *Christ Is Coming!* includes a chapter on spiritualism as Satan's final ace card in the end-time. For a very long time he has honed a plan to sweep the entire world into the trap of false Christian experience.[2] Another chapter looks into Satan's final bid for world domination and shows how successful he will be.[3] I will not repeat these matters here, but only say that cosmic terrorism takes on unprecedented proportions in the end-time. While the world is now absorbed with the war on terrorism Satan works behind the scenes on the greatest terrorism takeover of all time, next to the days before the Flood. While he is behind all terrorism, humanism, and the ills of the world, he'll take over the planet in an apparently Christian way. He comes as Christ. Christians will find this experience more powerful than any biblical text that says we do not meet Him on earth (see Matthew 24:26, 27) but in the sky (see 1 Thessalonians 4:16-18). After all, that book was written only by humans. Here's Christ Himself, and surely this is the greatest evidence of all (cf. 2 Corinthians 11:14).

Satan has given a counterfeit spirit to many Christians for a long time to prepare them for a counterfeit Christ. It's time to study the Holy Spirit and His Word, the truths that Jesus said He would bring to His people. Jesus said, "I have much more to say to you, more than you can now bear. But when he, the Spirit of truth, comes, he will guide you into all truth. He will not speak on his own; he will speak only what he hears, and he will tell you what is to come" (John 16:12, 13).

The Truth About the Holy Spirit

Did you know that the book of Acts will be repeated again?

"Study carefully in the book of Acts the experiences of Paul and the other apostles, for God's people in our day must pass through similar experiences."[4] Just as the book of Acts begins with Pentecost (see Acts 2), so the coming Pentecost arrives at the beginning of the journey through final events. There's a wonderful parallel involved. The Holy Spirit comes in both Pentecosts, in the former rain (see Acts 2) and the latter rain (see Joel 2:28, 29) to lead and guide the saints.

The Holy Spirit is mentioned at least 70 times in the book of Acts.[5] Although Jesus appeared to Paul (see 9:5, 17), visions were given (see 16:9; 18:9) and angels aided humans (see 12:7), the Holy Spirit is the predominant administrator of the early church. Christ gave commandments through the Holy Spirit (see verse 2). The Spirit baptized (see verse 5), empowered (see verse 8), was poured out (see 2:17, 33) and fell on humans (see 10:44-47). He gave utterance (see 2:4), was considered the spokesman (see 1:16; 4:25; 28:25), and filled Christians (see 2:4; 4:8, 31; 6:3, 5; 7:55; 11:22-24).

The Holy Spirit was recognized as the leader of the church. He directed in the ordination of Saul and Barnabas (see 13:2, 3) and sent them out on a missionary journey (see verse 4). He gave direction not to enter Asia (see 16:6, 7). The Spirit directed Philip to the eunuch (see 8:29) and then carried him to his next assignment (see verse 39). The Spirit spoke to Peter (see 10:19; 11:12), gave a message to Paul through Agabus (see 11:28; 21:10, 11), and spoke to Paul in every city concerning his future afflictions and imprisonments (see 20:22, 23). And the Christians at Tyre conveyed a message from the Holy Spirit to Paul not to go to Jerusalem (see 21:4).

It's interesting to note that Paul sometimes received direct communication from the Holy Spirit, and at other times through other Christians. The Holy Spirit was producing a consciousness of His leadership among them all. In fact, in a letter of direction to the church, the leaders at the first recorded General Conference meeting of the early church wrote, "For it seemed good to the Holy Spirit, and to us, to lay upon you no greater burden than these necessary things" (15:28, NKJV). They had the right order—the Holy Spirit first, and human leaders next. We find the Spirit opening Thyatira's heart to Paul's speaking (see 16:14), and Peter, John, and

Paul laying hands on those yet ignorant of the Holy Spirit that they might receive His leadership (see 8:15-17; 19:6).

The burden of the early church was to follow the Holy Spirit and that all members be filled with His presence. Although imprisonment (see 4:3; 5:18; 12:4; 16:23, 24; 22:24; 24:27), stonings (see 14:19), and beatings (see 5:40; 16:23; 21:32) plagued Christians, yet the leadership of the Holy Spirit showed itself stronger than Satan's opposition. Cosmic terrorism is no match for God the Holy Spirit! Tremendous numbers joined the church—3,000 at Pentecost (see 2:41), 5,000 just two chapters later (see 4:4), and "more than ever believers were added to the Lord, multitudes both of men and women" one chapter later (5:14, RSV). By the next chapter, "the word of God increased; and the number of the disciples multiplied greatly in Jerusalem, and a great many of the priests were obedient to the faith" (6:7, RSV). Beyond the shores of Palestine the results were the same. Throughout Macedonia "the churches were strengthened in the faith, and they increased in numbers daily" (16:5, RSV).

In Thessalonica men of fury shouted, "These that have turned the world upside down are come hither also" (17:6, KJV). The world had been shaken to its roots, not by these men, but by the Holy Spirit through these men. He, and not they, had built up the church for "in the comfort of the Holy Spirit it was multiplied" (9:31, RSV).

And who were these men, anyway? Peter the coward and Paul the persecutor—not very likely candidates for such unpopular work. But when the Holy Spirit filled these men, they were changed. And what a transformation! The coward became a man of conviction. The persecutor became a proclaimer. That's what the Holy Spirit does. Indeed, Paul knew from experience that the change within humans "comes from the Lord who is the Spirit" (2 Corinthians 3:18, RSV).

All Christ's disciples had let Him down in His greatest hour of need. But not now. Frightened men strode forth fearlessly to turn the world upside down. Bold preaching of the risen Christ shattered the status quo. Signs and miracles, including whole groups and even resurrections (see Acts 20:9-12), called into question the present order. The book of Acts throbs with the life-giving power of the

Holy Spirit. Acts proclaims His acts, not those of the disciples. The Holy Spirit made the decisive difference. The book could be re-named "Acts of the Holy Spirit," an observation recorded as early as the fourth century by Church Father Chrysostom.[6]

Coming Pentecost

Scared saints, take courage! The coming outpouring of God's Spirit will transform you, too! You'll be shocked, amazed, as-tounded. You'll rejoice. Look, "As the time comes for it [the message of the third angel] to be given with greatest power, the Lord will work through humble instruments, leading the minds of those who consecrate themselves to His service. The laborers will be qualified rather by the unction of His Spirit than by the train-ing of literary institutions. Men of faith and prayer will be con-strained to go forth with holy zeal, declaring the words which God gives to them."[7]

God will use trained people too—if they are humble—just as He used Paul. God is willing to use anyone willing to be used. That's the good news. "Many . . . will be seen hurrying hither and thither, con-strained by the Spirit of God to bring the light to others. The truth, the Word of God, is as a fire in their bones, filling them with a burning de-sire to enlighten those who sit in darkness. Many, even among the un-educated, now proclaim the words of the Lord. Children are impelled by the Spirit to go forth and declare the message from heaven. The Spirit is poured out upon all who will yield to its promptings, and, cast-ing off all man's machinery, his binding rules and cautious methods, they will declare the truth with the might of the Spirit's power. Multitudes will receive the faith and join the armies of the Lord."[8]

"Servants of God, with their faces lighted up and shining with holy consecration, will hasten from place to place to proclaim the message from heaven. By thousands of voices, all over the earth, the warning will be given. Miracles will be wrought, the sick will be healed, and signs and wonders will follow the believers. Satan also works with lying wonders, even bringing down fire from heaven in the sight of men. Thus the inhabitants of the earth will be brought to take their stand."[9]

The Thief in the Night

Together with this glorious coming Pentecost, Scripture warns of Christ's coming as a thief-in-the-night. Here are two members of the Godhead who are coming in final events. The arrival of both is vital for the saints. In the middle of the Armageddon passage of Revelation 16:12-16, Christ says, "Behold, I come like a thief! Blessed is he who stays awake and keeps his clothes with him, so that he may not go naked and be shamefully exposed" (verse 15). In chapter 14 we noted this is a condensed repetition of the message given to the last church of Laodicea (see Revelation 3:14-22). The end-time church lacks discernment, so Christ offers it eyesalve so that it can see spiritually. It thinks it's all right and has no needs, but it's a candidate for the thief-in-the-night experience because Christ is outside.

The lady in church unloving to her child had "a form of godliness but denying its power" (2 Timothy 3:5). It's this power, the power of the Holy Spirit (former rain), that was missing, and is missing when Christ is outside the life. What's the use of all the emphasis on experience when it is experience without Christ? It's through His Word that Christ comes into the life. Through His Word the former rain floods the life, bringing Christ within. Christ said, "The world cannot accept him, because it neither sees him nor knows him. But you know him, for he lives with you and will be in you. I will not leave you as orphans; I will come to you" (John 14:15, 18). The world, devoid of the Holy Spirit, is described by Jesus in the same terms He used to describe His end-time church: They do not see (discern) nor know the Holy Spirit, and He does not abide in them. So the form of religion without Christ is no different in kind from the veneer of Satan when he pretends to be Christ. Both have Christ outside, but not within. Entrance to heaven is "Christ in you, the hope of glory" (Colossians 1:27).

Christ standing outside sets one up for the thief-in-the-night experience. Christ standing outside describes the foolish virgins of Matthew 25, who were unready for Christ's coming. Christ outside describes the many who "will turn away from the faith and will betray and hate each other" (Matthew 24:10).

Christ warned that His return will be like a thief in the night (Matthew 24:43; Luke 12:39). Paul (see 1 Thessalonians 5:2, 4), Peter (see 2 Peter 3:10), and John in Revelation (Revelation 3:3) speak of the sudden coming of Christ as a thief. But is it really possible for Seventh-day Adventists to experience the thief-in-the-night unreadiness for Christ's return? After all, they expect Christ to come after the Sunday law, death decree, and plagues. How could they ever be taken by surprise? We won't be surprised if we think only of the Second Advent. But if the thief-in-the-night experience takes place before His coming, that's a different matter.

Remember the prophetic promise "I will send you the prophet Elijah before that great and dreadful day of the Lord comes" (Malachi 4:5)? Out trot the Old Testament teachers with a chart of final events relative to the First Advent. Before the Advent they placed Elijah's coming, so at least they can wait until Elijah comes. Then they'll know Christ is coming. The chart will be their guide.

One day Christ's disciples asked Him a question about that chart. "'Why then do the teachers of the law say that Elijah must come first?' Jesus replied, 'To be sure, Elijah comes and will restore all things. But I tell you, Elijah has already come, and they did not recognize him, but have done to him everything they wished. In the same way the Son of Man is going to suffer at their hands.' Then the disciples understood that he was talking to them about John the Baptist" (Matthew 17:10-13).

Imagine, they clung to their coming-events charts and missed both events—the coming of Elijah and Christ! It doesn't get any worse than that! Two events charted—and both missed. The chart really wasn't worth very much, was it?

We need to settle something. The thief-in-the-night experience isn't at Christ's coming. That's too late. After the Sunday law, death decree, great time of trouble, plagues, and the launching of Armageddon, the Second Advent is expected. But what if the thief-in-the-night experience takes place before all those events?

"I saw that many were neglecting the preparation so needful, and were looking to the time of 'refreshing' and the 'latter rain' to fit them to stand in the day of the Lord and to live in His sight. Oh, how many I saw in the time of trouble, without a shelter! They had neglected the needful preparation."[10] The latter rain empowers the messengers but doesn't prepare them. To be unready for the latter rain is like missing a train that takes one through the end-time journey. To be unready for the latter rain is to be left behind. To be unready for the latter rain is the thief-in-the-night experience. We must be ready before the latter rain comes. When does the latter rain come? It comes at the same time as the Sunday law. There's no time to get ready for the latter rain when the Sunday law comes.

Sunday is not being agitated publicly right now. It suits Satan's plan to work quietly in the background. He knows Seventh-day Adventists expect a national Sunday law and an International Sunday law. Satan wants Adventists to be unprepared when Sunday laws break upon the scene. Then they'll be unready for the latter rain and will experience the thief in the night.

"Wait a minute," complains one. "It isn't fair that Adventists have the thief-in-the-night experience back at the latter rain. That's earlier than for other Christians, for the period from Sunday law to the close of probation is still time for them to accept the Sabbath truth (see Revelation 18:1-4). So it appears that Adventists must be ready at the beginning of the early time of trouble, whereas other Christians can come in even near the end of that period.

"That's only a superficial way to look at it," replies another. "Think of it this way. The invitation is, 'Come out of her, my people' (verse 4). These people are already Christ's people, and are therefore ready for His coming. They're ready now just as Adventists must be. The only thing they need to do is to see the Sabbath and accept it. It takes only a short time for truth to dawn. By contrast, it takes a long time to get to know Christ. Those who don't know Him, even if they are Adventists, will be lost (see John 17:3). There simply isn't sufficient time to get to know Him. This is one reason there's been a long delay before the latter rain comes (see Revelation 7:1-4). God doesn't want 'anyone to perish, but everyone to come to repentance. But the day of the Lord will come like a thief. The heavens will disappear with a roar; the elements will be destroyed by fire, and the earth and everything in it will be laid bare' (2 Peter 3:9, 10)."

Clearly Peter places the thief in the night at the Advent, and not at some time before. But readiness, or unreadiness, takes place before the Advent. Ten virgins waiting for the return of Christ were found unready (see Matthew 25:1-13). They were the same as the other five, except in one respect. They lacked oil. Their lamps were "going out" (verse 8, not "gone out," as in KJV). They had little of the Holy Spirit when they needed much. Superficial—that's what Laodicea is. Neither hot (filled) nor cold (empty), Revelation 3:15, 16). Those ready must be filled with the former rain. The thief-in-the-night experience is linked to the Second Advent because it's then that people find out they're unready. Jesus warned, "Many will say to me on that day, 'Lord, Lord, did we not prophesy in your name, and in your name drive out demons and perform many miracles?' Then I will tell them plainly, 'I never knew you. Away from me, you evildoers!'" (Matthew 7:22, 23; cf. Luke 13:26, 27).

Here's the bottom line. To be ready for the second coming of Christ one must be ready for the second coming of the Holy Spirit. It's the Holy Spirit's second Pentecost, His second coming! To be unready for the second coming of the Holy Spirit is to be unready for the second coming of Christ. That's the thief in the night.

Sunday law	Close of	Second
Latter Rain	Probation	Advent
Thief in the Night		

```
  !_____!_____!
                  Armageddon
```

Satan's Attack Before the Coming Pentecost

Consider Satan's attack before the coming Pentecost. Cosmic terrorism has a two-pronged attack in its strategy against the latter rain. On the one hand he keeps Christians occupied (Adventists and others) so that they will not be ready to receive the latter rain and hence experience the thief in the night. The second strategy is to send a counterfeit of the latter rain before the true latter rain so that Christians will turn down the true gift because they think they already have it.

"Notwithstanding the widespread declension of faith and piety, there are true followers of Christ in these churches. Before the final visitation of God's judgments upon the earth there will be among the people of the Lord such a revival of primitive godliness as has not been witnessed since apostolic times. The Spirit and power of God will be poured out upon His children. At that time many will separate themselves from those churches in which the love of this world has supplanted love for God and His word. Many, both of ministers and people, will gladly accept those great truths which God has caused to be proclaimed at this time to prepare a people for the Lord's second coming. The enemy of souls decides to hinder this work; and before the time for such a movement shall come, he will endeavor to prevent it by introducing a counterfeit. In those churches which he can bring under his deceptive power he will make it appear that God's special blessing is poured out; there will be manifest what is thought to be great religious interest. Multitudes will exult that God is working marvelously for them, when the work is that of another spirit. Under a religious guise, Satan will seek to extend his influence over the Christian world."[11] This is happening all over the world today.

Satan is a diligent student of Scripture and the first Pentecost, and I'm sure he's read *The Great Controversy* many times. He's a strategist, and the more he knows about his enemy's moves, the more he can counteract Him. He always does this ahead of time, and gets the advantage. He is unscrupulous in his scheming. He knows Pentecost is coming. He knows he's no match for God the Holy Spirit, so he steals a march on Him by doing what he does best—deceiving people with a counterfeit so they won't be interested in the genuine. That's cosmic terrorism: Palm off the counterfeit for the real, and snatch eternity from them. He cannot have eternity himself, so why should they? He acts like a spoiled brat, but is a dangerous thug that no society would want loose on their streets. But he's there in the darkened shadows, unseen, out to capture the entire Christian world. How successful will he be?

Here's the strategy. First he attacks the work of the Holy Spirit, His Word (Scripture), just as He attacked Christ, His Word ("you will die if you eat"), in Eden. Getting humans to doubt the Word, he promises greater freedom but gains control. In order "to take the place of the Word of God he holds out spiritual manifestations. Here is a channel wholly under his control; by this means he can make the world believe what he will."[12] Give false messages through channeled Bibles. Nothing like having Jesus speak words that fill in His lost years from 12 to 30, and nothing like a modern revelation to counteract the other one. He palms off some of these as from Jesus, though he alleges the scriptures aren't from Him, but are mere human accounts. Channeled Bibles are the final word, just as he claims for the Koran, for we have the originals intact—and both denigrate Christ and Calvary. What a deception! Give them messages through apparitions of Mary, give them visitations of demons impersonating dead loved ones who bring them comfort, and give them a feeling of God up close when it's really the dragon about to destroy. That's cosmic terrorism.

In fact, this is the final pre-Advent takeover bid by cosmic terrorism. He doesn't come terrorizing—yet, but gives a warm feeling of being loved through electrical currents coming down healers' arms, through personal messages from respected dead ones affirming, "You are doing the right thing, for up in heaven all keep Sunday, and doctrines are not so important as religious feeling. Spirituality is what we call it up here. Spirituality is more important than knowledge." Today spirituality is in. The globe is literally bathed with the spiritual through the New Age movement in the world and the charismatic movement in the church. Today the song "We are one in the Spirit and one in the Lord" embraces all religions, for messages from different religious leaders from heaven say the same thing. "All roads lead to heaven, so travel your own road. You are on the right path if you experience spiritual manifestations like tongues, prophetic words of knowledge, miracles, a burning in your bosom, and spirit-guides in yoga meditation. Each one receives different manifestations, so seek the one you desire and be ready to receive whatever comes."[13]

Countless multitudes seek and find. They think it is the real thing. Scripture is unimportant when you have a spiritual manifestation. After all, Scripture is the human writers' recounting their own spiritual manifestation. Scripture is merely their response to their manifestation to inspire others to have the same encounter. Even countless conservative Christians today believe that Scripture is not revelation, but Christ is. To have your own encounter with Christ is the important thing. All these degrade Scripture. Other revelations take its place as God's revelation to humanity.

Without Scripture as God's revelation there's no way to test the spirits (see 1 John 4:1). That gives Satan full freedom to deceive. Many charismatics claim to have a prophetic word, and their miracles seem to suggest their authenticity. Christ warned that end-time "false Christs and false prophets will appear and perform great signs and miracles to deceive even the elect" (see Matthew 24:24). Paul warns that the "coming of the lawless one will be in accordance with the work of Satan displayed in all kinds of counterfeit miracles, signs and wonders, and in every sort of evil that deceives those who are perishing. They perish because they refused to love the truth and so be saved" (2 Thessalonians 2:9).

They don't love biblical truth. What counts is to have a spiritual manifestation. Spirituality is claimed as the goal of religion. Experience is superior to anything else.[14] And even "the apostles, as personated by these lying spirits, are made to contradict what they wrote at the dictation of the Holy Spirit when on earth. . . . Satan is making the world believe that the Bible is a mere fiction, or at least a book suited to the infancy of the race, but now to be lightly regarded, or cast aside as obsolete."[15] Paul said, "The Spirit clearly says that in later times some will abandon the faith and follow deceiving spirits and things taught by demons" (1 Timothy 4:1). "Satan well knows that all whom he can lead to neglect prayer and the searching of the Scriptures, will be overcome by his attacks."[16]

God's preparation of His people is different. He leads them out of themselves to Scripture, where they fall in love with the truth. The Holy Spirit comes to glorify Christ (see John 16:14), not self. He frees people from mere subjective spirituality as the Spirit of truth. The Holy Spirit comes to expose the scheme of the enemy through the illumination of Scripture and not through personal messages that contradict Scripture. That's why it's so important that we know thoroughly the biblical doctrine of the state of the dead, and realize that some leaders of other churches are beginning to see the deception of the enemy.[17] Sunday sacredness and the idea that people do not die are the two bases for Satan's final delusion that takes the world captive.[18] Both are documented by spiritual manifestations, and a biblically illiterate generation of Christians, along with the rest of the world, have no protection from this terrorist trap.

The Final Pre-Advent Fling of Cosmic Terrorism

An age of power is coming! It's the time of the latter rain up to probation's close (see Daniel 12:1). God sends miracles and wonders. So does Satan. It's not business as usual. Here's the final pre-Advent showdown between cosmic terrorism and God. Here's the final chance to win converts to both sides. Nothing is held back. Nothing like it has ever been seen on the planet. What happened at Pentecost takes place on a global scale, and with greater power, and Satan is present to make it of none effect. In fury he flings his energies into the fray with those of his fiends. They must conquer this last attempt to present God's view, and their best weapons are the ones mentioned above.

Satan has the world, and he has many Christians. He's out to get the saints. If he can trap them, he'll conquer the world, sit on the throne, and tell Christ that He doesn't need to return. No one is waiting for Him. Many members never will receive the latter rain. But that's not all. They'll resist the latter rain, just as Jews resisted John the Baptist and Christ (see Matthew 17:10-13). What we are about to read is the hardest part of teaching last-day events for me, and it must be much more so for Christ. I love my church, and He loves it with a much deeper love as the Creator-Savior. "There is to be in the [Seventh-day Adventist] churches a wonderful manifestation of the power of God, but it will not move upon those who have not humbled themselves before the Lord, and opened the door of the heart by confession and repentance. In the manifestation of that power which lightens the earth with the glory of God, they will see only something which in their blindness they think dangerous, something which will arouse their fears, and they will brace themselves to resist it. Because the Lord does not work according to their ideas and expectations they will oppose the work. 'Why,' they say, 'should we not know the Spirit of God, when we have been in the work so many years?' "[19]

So the thief-in-the-night is not just being unready for the latter rain but includes resisting the latter rain. What a tragedy! Imagine members resisting the very power of God that comes to take them through final events. There's no greater blindness than that! That's why Christ offers Laodicea, the end-time church, eyesalve so it can see. The problem is Laodicea doesn't think it's blind, doesn't realize it lacks discernment, and thinks it needs nothing (see Revelation 3:17-20).

It's déjà vu, for Jews resisted Christ because He didn't come according to their expectations. He came as a humble teacher-Savior, without any earthly kingdom, when they expected Him to come as a conquering king to liberate them from the hated Romans. "Only those living up to the light they have will receive greater light. Unless we are daily advancing in the exemplification of the active Christian virtues, we shall not recognize the manifestations of the Holy Spirit in the latter rain. It may be falling on hearts all around us, but we shall not discern or receive it."[20] "Every precaution must be taken to prevent spiritual declension, lest the great day of the Lord overtake us as a thief-in-the-night."[21]

How Many Adventists Experience the Thief in the Night?

"As the storm approaches, a large class who have professed faith in the third angel's message, but have not been sanctified through obedience to the truth, abandon their position and join the ranks of opposition."[22] Sounds like an exodus. But how large is large, and does this apply to the end-time? The answer is specific and staggering. "When the law of God is made void [Sunday law], the church will be sifted by fiery trials, and a larger proportion than we now anticipate will give heed to seducing spirits and doctrines of devils. Instead of being strengthened when brought into strait places, many prove that they are not living branches of the True Vine; they bore no fruit, and the husbandman taketh them away."[23] That's a specific prophecy about the effect of the Sunday law upon many Seventh-day Adventists. A larger proportion than we now anticipate will be overcome by fallen spirits and their doctrines. They'll give up at precisely the time when they need to be ready to receive the latter rain to take them through final events. It doesn't get more tragic than that! (cf. 1 Timothy 4:1).

But how many capitulate? "When the religion of Christ is most held in contempt, when His law is most despised, then should our zeal be the warmest and our courage and firmness the most unflinching. To stand in defense of truth and righteousness when the majority forsake us, to fight the battles of the Lord when champions are few—this will be our test. At this time we must gather warmth from the coldness of others, courage from their cowardice, and loyalty from their treason." [24]

Does that mean that the majority leave the church? "The church may appear as about to fall, but it does not fall. It remains, while the sinners in Zion will be sifted out—the chaff separated from the precious wheat. This is a terrible ordeal, but nevertheless it must take place." [25]

How to Prepare for the Latter Rain

Because the thief-in-the-night takes place for Seventh-day Adventists at the coming of the latter rain, it's the very next event. There's no event that comes before the latter rain. That's why it comes without any warning. That's why we must know how to get ready now!

How then should we prepare for the Spirit? " 'Ask ye of the Lord rain in the time of the latter rain.' Do not rest satisfied that in the ordinary course of the season, rain will fall. Ask for it. The growth and perfection of the seed rests not with the husbandman. God alone can ripen the harvest. But man's cooperation is required. God's work for us demands the action of our mind, the exercise of our faith. We must seek His favors with the whole heart if the showers of grace are to come to us." [26] Are we daily praying for the latter rain to come?

Look how the disciples prepared for the first Pentecost. "As the disciples waited for the fulfillment of the promise, they humbled their hearts in true repentance and confessed their unbelief. . . . As they meditated upon His pure, holy life they felt that no toil would be too hard, no sacrifice too great, if only they could bear witness in their lives to the loveliness of Christ's character. Oh, if they could but have the last three years to live over, they thought, how differently they would act! If they could only see the Master again, how earnestly they would strive to show Him how deeply they loved Him, and how sincerely they sorrowed for having grieved Him by a word or an act of unbelief! But they were comforted by the thought that they were forgiven." [27]

Notice the Christ-centered focus. They studied His life. They longed to reveal Him. They yearned to show their love for Him. That's when the Spirit comes. "The Spirit is constantly seeking to draw the attention of men to the great offering that was made on the cross of Calvary, to unfold the love of God to the world, and to open to the convicted soul the precious things of the Scriptures." [28] As we study His life, long to be like Him, yearn to show Him how much we love Him—that's when we're ready for the latter rain.

During the early history of our church, Sunday laws were agitated in the 1880s and served as a warning to get Adventists ready. Yet God brought a message about Christ to the delegates at the Minneapolis General Conference session, but not about Sunday laws. Their witnessing had stressed the law and unique beliefs but had left Christ out of the presentations. Like Laodicea, Christ was outside, longing to come into their teaching, but first into their lives. They needed the filling of the former rain. They were like the foolish virgins, satisfied with little when they could have had so much of the Holy Spirit and Christ's indwelling presence and power.

You might have seen the picture depicting the way from Eden lost to Eden restored. The law filled the center, with Calvary shunted off to the side. Ellen White ordered a new picture, entitled *Christ the Way*. This one had the law in the background and Calvary placed in the center. The first 40 years of our church history focused on the law, for after all, the Sabbath was a new discovery and important to us, and we wanted to share it. But it was often done without a proper place given to Christ, so that believers became as dry as the hills of Gilboa. The new focus looked at the law in the context of Christ. Floods fell on dry ground, life sprang up, and saints re-vived. The function of the Holy Spirit is always to bring attention to Christ and Calvary.

The sudden inbreaking of the early time of trouble and the Sunday law launches the final journey. One has to be ready for the launch, just as much as for a space trip. It's too late to enter the shut-tle when the countdown has started. When the Sunday laws and Holy Spirit come, it will be too late to take the journey. Now's the only time to get on board.

How the First Translated Man Prepared

Enoch needed Christ just as much as we do. Look what the preincarnate Christ told him. " 'Come unto me, all ye that labour and are heavy-laden, and I will give you rest. Take my yoke upon you, and learn of me; for I am meek and lowly in heart; and ye shall find rest unto your souls. For my yoke is easy, and my burden is light.' What an invitation! It was this invitation that Christ gave to Enoch before the world was destroyed by a flood." [29]

I believe it was his understanding of Christ's love for the rebel race that made all the difference in his life. He didn't keep God's law le-galistically and get translated. He fell in love with Christ and commit-ted himself wholly to Him. "Enoch learned from the lips of Adam the painful story of the fall, and the precious story of God's condescend-ing grace in the gift of his Son as the world's Redeemer." [30]

"It was no easier for Enoch to live a righteous life in his day than it is for us at the present time. The world at that time was no more favorable to growth in grace and holiness than it is now, but Enoch devoted time to prayer and communion with God, and this enabled him to escape the corruption that is in the world through lust. It was his devotion to God that fitted him for translation." [31]

Devotion, not duty, guided his steps. Relationship, not rules, blessed his life. Christ, not a creed, gave him the victory. As Paul later said, "For to me, to live is Christ" (Philippians 1:21). That's the way it's always been with those in love with the Savior. He's the only way home. Enoch had a secret, and it's the way you'll go through final events. "He educated his mind and heart to ever feel that he was in the presence of God, and when in perplexity his prayers would ascend to God to keep him."[32] That's what the mother with the baby hadn't learned in our opening paragraphs.

Enoch sought God. "He chose to be separate from them (the wicked), and spent much of his time in solitude, giving himself to reflection and prayer. He waited before God, and prayed to know His will more perfectly, that he might perform it. God communed with Enoch through His angels, and gave him divine instruction."[33] He received the love of the truth because he knew the Lover who is the truth.

No Secret Rapture Advent

The secret rapture scenario is popular today. The film *Left Behind* and the *Left Behind* books captured the headlines. But it's not in Scripture. In 1830, just before Seventh-day Adventists would focus on the true Second Advent, a counterfeit secret rapture advent originated from a vision received by Margaret MacDonald in Glasgow, Scotland.[34] It claimed Holy Spirit-filled Christians would be raptured while others would remain to be purified through the tribulation. That's a deception of cosmic terrorism, for no Christian can go through the final tribulation without the latter rain, let alone be purified. Furthermore, if God suddenly raptured Christians, imagine the multiplied plane crashes into buildings; cars, trucks, and trains smashing into buildings and people; and horrible pileups around the world! Planes plunging into the twin towers would seem small by comparison. Such a doctrine makes God into the worst terrorist of all time!

The Latter Rain Takes Saints Through Final Events

The latter rain seals God's people, so they're strengthened to stand. The sealing is "a settling into the truth, both intellectually and spiritually, so they cannot be moved."[35] "And God is faithful; he will not let you be tempted beyond what you can bear. But when you are tempted, he will also provide a way out so that you can stand up under it" (1 Corinthians 10:13). That's true, even when Satan comes as Christ (cf. 2 Corinthians 11:14). The latter rain Holy Spirit comes to seal and empower God's people (1) to give the final invitation and (2) to stand through the great time of trouble.

The latter rain doesn't come to give eternal life. Everyone saved throughout the Christian Era has been saved under the former rain, and during the Old Testament by the Spirit before the first Pentecost. Nor does the latter rain come to prepare the saints to be ready. They must be ready under the former rain. The latter rain comes to equip them to pass through final events, and triumph in the Second Advent. Jesus promised, "Never will I leave you; never will I forsake you" (Hebrews 13:5), for "Lo, I am with you always, even unto the end of the age" (Matthew 28:20, NKJV).

To be ready for the Second Advent of the Holy Spirit is the only way to be ready for the second coming of Christ. Are you ready for the first Second Advent? It's the very next event!

[1] Philip Yancey, *What's So Amazing About Grace?* pp. 31, 32.

[2] Norman R. Gulley, *Christ Is Coming!,* pp. 127-131.

[3] *Ibid.,* pp. 476-483.

[4] Ellen G. White, *Last Day Events* (Boise, Idaho: Pacific Press Pub. Assn., 1992), p. 148.

[5] W. H. Griffith Thomas, *The Holy Spirit of God* (Grand Rapids: Eerdmans, 1964), p. 39.

[6] Chrysostom, in *The Nicene and Post-Nicene Fathers* (Grand Rapids: Eerdmans, 1989), First Series, Vol. II, p. 7.

[7] White, *The Great Controversy,* p. 606.

[8] White, *Evangelism* (Washington, D.C.: Review and Herald Pub. Assn., 1946), p. 700.

[9] White, *The Great Controversy,* p. 612.

[10] White, *Early Writings,* p. 71.

[11] White, *The Great Controversy,* p. 464.

[12] *Ibid.,* p. 557.

[13] For further reading, illustrations, and sources, see Gulley, pp. 112-126, 159-204.

[14] For an in-depth study of this attack on Scripture, see Norman R. Gulley, *Systematic Theology: Prolegomena* (Berrien Springs, Mich.: Andrews University Press, 2003), vol. 1.

[15] White, *The Great Controversy,* p. 557.

[16] *Ibid.,* p. 519.

[17] Gulley, *Christ Is Coming!* pp. 253-258, 276-298.

[18] White, *The Great Controversy,* p. 588.

[19] White, *Last Day Events,* pp. 209, 210.

[20] White, *Testimonies to Ministers* (Mountain View, Calif.: Pacific Press Pub. Assn., 1923), p. 507.

[21] *Ibid.,* p. 510.

[22] White, *The Great Controversy,* p. 608.

[23] White, in *General Conference Bulletin,* Apr. 13, 1891, p. 257.

[24] White, *Testimonies for the Church,* vol. 5, p. 136.

[25] White, *Selected Messages* (Washington, D.C.: Review and Herald Pub. Assn., 1958), book 2, p. 380.

[26] White, *Testimonies to Ministers,* p. 508.

[27] White, *The Acts of the Apostles* (Mountain View, Calif.: Pacific Press Pub. Assn., 1911), p. 36.

[28] *Ibid.,* p. 52.

[29] White, "Our Privileges in Christ Jesus," *Signs of the Times,* Oct. 4, 1899.

[30] White, "The Great Controversy: Seth and Enoch," *Signs of the Times,* Feb. 20, 1879.

[31] White, "Lessons From the Life of Enoch," *Advent Review and Sabbath Herald,* Apr. 15, 1909.

[32] White, *Last Day Events,* p. 71.

[33] White, "The Great Controversy," *Signs of the Times,* Feb. 20, 1879.

[34] In March–April 1830 Margaret MacDonald received a series of visions on the Second Coming and sent one to Edward Irving. In September 1830 *The Morning Watch,* official quarterly publication of the Irvingites, published her vision. A letter describing this vision was published by Robert Norton, who considers her to be the first to speak of a secret rapture, in *The Memoirs of James and George MacDonald of Port Glasgow,* brothers of Margaret (London: John F. Shaw, 1840), pp. 171-176. See also Dave MacPherson, *The Unbelievable Pre-Tribulation Origin* (Kansas City, Kans.: Heart of American Bible Society, 1973), pp. 59-62, 105-108.

[35] *The Seventh-day Adventist Bible Commentary,* Ellen G. White comments, vol. 4, p. 1161.

BACK AT THE WHITE HOUSE AGAIN

Those who give up truth in the end-time (see Matthew 24:10; 1 Timothy 4:1) are those who have Christ outside their lives, those unready for the coming of the latter rain, and those who experience the thief in the night. They'll call "to the mountains and rocks, 'Fall on us and hide us from the face of him who sits on the throne and from the wrath of the Lamb!'" (Revelation 6:16). All those against Christ will do the same.

"A life of rebellion against God has unfitted them for heaven. Its purity, holiness, and peace would be torture to them; the glory of God would be a consuming fire. They would long to flee from that holy place. They would welcome destruction, that they might be hidden from the face of Him who died to redeem them. The destiny of the wicked is fixed by their own choice. Their exclusion from heaven is voluntary with themselves, and just and merciful on the part of God."[1]

Heaven would be eternal hell to those unfitted for the presence of the God who is love. Those who kept Christ outside will not feel the need of heaven either. For what's heaven without Christ? What's heaven without reveling in the unselfish life of the Redeemer, and worshiping Him for Calvary? What's heaven without the unselfish joys of adoration and praise for the joys of forgiveness, without seeing the One whom you love the best and reveling in thanks for ravishing you with His love on earth?

Going to church without Christ, to the workplace without Christ, in the secret moments of your life without Christ, is to choose to be without Him forever. Christianity is Christ and not the Christian, is a relationship and not mere rules, is a Person and not mere practice. The offering without the Lamb was Cain's problem. And his influence led to the world's destruction at the Flood![2]

The Sabbath test reveals the heart. Jesus said the law is love to God and love to others (see Matthew 22:37-40; cf. Galatians 5:14). The Sabbath is resting in Christ, the one we love the best. Those with Christ outside may go to church on Sabbath, but they never experience the Sabbath joy of resting in Him. And resting in Him is the only way through final events.

Saints Overjoyed

By contrast, end-time saints look up and say, "This is the Lord, we trusted in him; let us rejoice and be glad in his salvation" (Isaiah 25:9). "Those who have loved Him and waited for Him, He will crown with glory and honor and immortality. . . . 'Come, ye blessed of my Father, inherit the kingdom prepared for you from the foundation of the world.' Matthew 25:34."[3]

"With unutterable love, Jesus welcomes his faithful ones to the joy of their Lord. The Savior's joy is in seeing in the kingdom of glory the souls that have been saved by His agony and humiliation."[4]

"Before entering the city of God, the Savior bestows upon His followers the emblems of victory, and invests them with the insignia of their royal state. The glittering ranks are drawn up in the form of a hollow square about their King. . . . Upon the heads of the overcomers, Jesus with His own right hand places the crown of glory. . . . In every hand are placed the victor's palm and the shining harp. Then, as the commanding angels strike the note, every hand sweeps the harp strings with skillful touch, making sweet music in rich, melodious strains. . . . Before the ransomed throng is the holy city. Jesus opens wide the pearly gates, and the nations that have kept the truth enter in."[5]

A mighty wave of love sweeps across the redeemed. They're caught up in a mighty chorus. The music sweeps across the teeming millions as they sing, "How great is the love the Father has lavished on us, that we should be called children of God!" (1 John 3:1). "For

God so loved the world that he gave his one and only Son, that whoever believes in him shall not perish but have eternal life" (John 3:16). They keep singing the words, rising to higher notes each time until the very gates of heaven shake with the glad refrain. "Redeemed, how I love to proclaim it, redeemed by the blood of the Lamb, redeemed through His infinite mercy, His child and forever I am."

"Oh wonderful redemption! long talked of, long hoped for, contemplated with eager anticipation, but never fully understood."[6] "Oh, how glorious it will be to see Him and be welcomed as His redeemed ones! Long have we waited, but our hope is not to grow dim. If we can but see the King in His beauty we shall be forever blessed. I feel as if I must cry, 'Homeward bound!'"[7] End-time saints now understand how Ellen White felt. She'd seen Jesus in vision. Now they see Him too. How they thrill as He places a crown on their head, and says, "Well done, My beloved, welcome home, enter the kingdom prepared for you." Beautiful Savior. How could You die for us? How could You leave heaven for the rebel planet? You really must love us! Thoughts race through minds as they behold the King in His glory, and hear Him say again, "Welcome home, My children. I've longed for this day with all My heart. No more troubles and tears in this place. You'll be safe and secure forevermore." And with that we shout, "Alleluia, glory to the Lamb who was slain," as we enter through the gates.

At the Throne

All the saints participate in the millennial judgment to see why family and friends are not there. Christ wants to answer every question. As in the pre-Advent judgment it's not so much what people have done or not done as it is whether they accepted Christ's judgment for them at Calvary. That's the crucial decision. Saints observe how Christ suffered with anguish and deep sorrow as He pleaded with these rebels, but they kept Him outside. They wanted to live without Him, and so in love He sadly let them go.

Revelation focuses on end-time saints, either those who are translated, or those who die. This doesn't forget that the redeemed from all ages are at the throne, but the book of Revelation singles out the end-time generation, for it's that generation that's afraid of the end-time, and Revelation is written to remove that fear. Thus the 144,000 named group alone can sing the song of their experience in the great time of trouble (see Revelation 14:1-3), and are the same as the great multitude who go through the great tribulation (see Revelation 7:9-14). Just as the translated end-time saints are singled out, so are the end-time martyrs. "I saw thrones on which were seated those who have been given authority to judge. And I saw the souls of those who had been beheaded because of their testimony for Jesus and because of the word of God. They had not worshiped the beast or his image and had not received his mark on their foreheads or their hands. They came to life and reigned with Christ a thousand years" (Revelation 20:4). "They will be priests of God and of Christ," (verse 6). These martyrs died during the early time of trouble when the beast and his image rule (see Revelation 13:1-4, 7, 11-14).

Although Revelation was written for all Christians, it has particular focus on end-time saints because Jesus, visiting with John in exile on Patmos, was thinking of them especially. The book gives specific courage to them. It's a revelation of Christ's great love for end-time saints because they need it. Now isn't that an incentive to study the book as a special message for you!

Armageddon, Part II

Satan and his angels watch the New Jerusalem come down from heaven. It seems incredible to them that God would move the white house of the universe from heaven to earth. Satan couldn't fathom how the Father, the Holy Spirit, and angels would want to come at Christ's request. Satan fought to become God in heaven. Now even God vacates that special place. Such a difference between self and self-lessness. He shook his head in utter disbelief. "There's one thing for sure," he mused. "God must be stupid. I'd never do such a silly thing!"

But there's no more time for thinking. It's time for action. Christ calls the wicked from their graves. Seeing the billions come forth, Satan rushes around taking credit for their new life. He and his demons work with frenzied speed to galvanize the billions for battle. "We are far more than those in the city," he boasts. "We are more than able to take it by storm, overthrow those within, and set up the kingdom wrenched from us." The wicked have no choice. They throw in their lot with him. Some have come up in a different resurrection than they planned. Their only hope now is to follow Satan as he leads them against the city.

Here's phase two of Armageddon (called Gog and Magog in Revelation 20:7-9). This time it's in the Middle East. They'll march toward the New Jerusalem in Palestine. Many great generals of all time organize the troops, and manufacture weapons. This takes time. The redeemed watch from the safety of their homes in the city. The signal is given; the trudging feet of billions move across the face of the planet. They surround the city (see verse 9), feeling well able to accomplish their design, for their overwhelming numbers suggest an easy victory. As in the beginning of the cosmic controversy on Planet Earth, so now again at its end humans put stock in what they see. But in this act they stand confronted with their problem: self-dependence.

The Final Revelation

Before the final onslaught, the massive army is stopped in its tracks by the manifest presence of God, and before Him all view their lives. God gives them a replay of the major moments when He came as the light to enlighten each one (cf. John 1:9). They view Christ's attempts to save them and see each time they refused His pleas.

At the end of this replay of their lives, some taking more time than others perhaps (for some have lived hundreds of years), there comes the final moment of truth when each person realizes that God is just. How? Across the screen of the heavens, in full three-dimensional color replay, is portrayed the final events of Christ. The redeemed, unfallen, and lost are glued to the presentation.

"And now before the swaying multitude are revealed the final scenes—the patient Sufferer treading the path to Calvary; the Prince of heaven hanging upon the cross; the haughty priests and the jeering rabble deriding His expiring agony. . . . The awful spectacle appears just as it was. Satan, his angels, and his subjects have no power to turn from the picture of their own work."[8]

Satan is now unmasked before lost humans, just as he was unmasked before unfallen worlds at Calvary. But at the same time, God is fully revealed as never before and even Satan and his angels, together with all creatures, unfallen and fallen, saved and lost, bow the knee (Romans 14:11; Isaiah 45:22, 23) and exclaim, "Great and marvelous are your deeds, Lord God Almighty. Just and true are your ways, King of the ages. Who will not fear you, O Lord, and bring glory to your name? For you alone are holy. All nations will come and worship before you, for your righteous acts have been revealed" (Revelation 15:3, 4). Paul says, "We will all stand before God's judgment seat. It is written: 'As surely as I live,' says the Lord, 'Every knee will bow before me; every tongue will confess to God'" (Romans 14:10, 11 from Isaiah 45:23).

The fact that fallen angels and fallen humans are involved is mentioned by Paul in Philippians 2:10, 11, for "at the name of Jesus every knee should bow, in heaven and on earth and under the earth, and every tongue confess that Jesus Christ is Lord." The phrase "in heaven and on earth and under the earth" is based on a Hebrew idiom representing the whole creation (see Exodus 20:4; cf. its use in Revelation 5:3). Not until this moment is reached will the truth of the cross be understood by all who have lived. But then it will be so completely revealed that the question of God's justice will be forever solved. Never again will sin or sinners be a part of the universe. The powerful love of Calvary has won out at last. Every created being finds in the cross the truth about Jesus. God is seen as fully just. He couldn't simply forgive sin. Christ had to die for sin. No sin has ever been forgiven, but all sinners can be forgiven. Such love at terrible cost to Himself reveals that no one had to be lost. Love simply allows created beings the freedom to make the ultimate choice: accept or reject Calvary.

So ends the third judgment. The pre-Advent was for the onlooking universe and some translated humans and angels to behold. The millennial judgment was for the redeemed to observe. The post-millennial is for the lost to see. Through these three judgments all created beings, unfallen and fallen, have opportunity to see that God is just. They see that He has dealt equally and fairly with all, that the only difference between the saved and the lost is whether they accepted Calvary or not. God doesn't force His gift, even His greatest gift. Apart from Calvary there's no salvation. The lost see they are unfitted for heaven. No selfish person would be happy there. They see, too late, that sin is self-destructive.

They perish. Satan is the last to die. Christ stands in the deep recesses of the city and sobs. They are all His children. Satan and the angels were among His first children. He'll miss them forever. Those looking on exclaim quietly, "He said to love your enemies, and He surely did."

There's a new heaven, a new earth, a new Jerusalem, and new young redeemed. All will be in the prime of life, and all the same generation, for as time rolls on, what's the difference between 10,000 and 20, and 10,000 and 90? Gone are all differences cultural, racial, religious, and generational. No more Monday mornings, and no more struggle to stretch your pay. No more maxed out credit cards, high mortgage payments, or rent. No more cancer, weight problems, fatigue, or death. No more nightmares, fear, and depression. No more critics and people who don't understand. No more devil and demons and their horrible, unmerciful, and callous attacks. Cosmic terrorism is gone. The battle is won. Calvary determined the outcome. You revel in the security that Jesus attained for you through the agony of being brutalized, battered, and beaten by the greatest abuser and his fiends and cronies. You're here in peace because He plunged into the cosmic war at the risk of failure and eternal loss.

Calvary Forever

Once our great time of trouble is over, and the memory of sin and sinners is no more, we'll continue to study the great time of trouble that Christ endured for us. It's in seeing what He went through that makes us realize heaven is cheap enough, that our trials were nothing compared to His.

"In this life we can only begin to understand the wonderful theme of redemption. With our finite comprehension we may consider most earnestly the shame and the glory, the life and the death, the justice and the mercy, that meet in the cross; yet with the utmost stretch of our mental powers we fail to grasp its full significance. The length and the breadth, the depth and the height, of redeeming love are but dimly comprehended. The plan of redemption will not be fully understood, even when the ransomed see as they are seen and know as they are known; but through the eternal ages new truth will continually unfold to the wondering and delighted mind. . . . The cross of Christ will be the science and the song of the redeemed through all eternity."[9]

One day you're sitting on the shore. The sea of life stretches before you. You revel in the reality and rest of redemption. Final events were nothing compared to eternity with the Father, the Holy Spirit, Christ, angels, and the redeemed. You've never had such freedom, such joy, such fulfillment. No more lonely days. No more heartaches. No more emptiness. As you look out across the water, you see a shadow. You half-turn and see sandaled feet with crucifixion marks. "I've come to spend time with you," Jesus says softly. He places His arm around your shoulder, and sits down with you. Think of the joy you'll have then! Just the two of you for as much time as you wish. There's no rush. You can ask Him all the questions you want. He tells you how much He loves you. He says you matter to Him. He says that He would have died just for you if all the rest had turned Him down. You thrill to the deep and personal commitment and compassion of Christ and worship Him in loving devotion. You realize that this is just like the first Sabbath with Adam and Eve. You know that relationship with Christ is the essence of Christianity, and to break it was the aim of cosmic terrorism. You praise Christ for never breaking a relationship with anyone, and revel in the deepening love you find in Him for you.

★ ★ ★

"Let us fix our eyes on Jesus, the author and perfecter of our faith, who for the joy set before him endured the cross" (Hebrews 12:2). He fixed His gaze on the goal and endured. He longs to be your God up close and help you do the same. Cosmic terrorism is no match for those who abide in Christ (see John 15:5), for by beholding Him we are changed (see 2 Corinthians 3:18). "For in the day of trouble he will keep" you "safe in his dwelling" (Psalm 27:5), for He promised, "I will be with" you; "in trouble, I will deliver" you (Psalm 91:15). "Those who follow Christ are ever safe under His watchcare. Angels that excel in strength are sent from heaven to protect them. The wicked one cannot break through the guard which God has stationed about His people."[10] Christ "would sooner send every angel out of heaven to protect His people than leave one soul that trusts in Him to be overcome by Satan."[11]

---

[1] Ellen G. White, *The Great Controversy*, p. 543.

[2] *Ibid.*

[3] White, *The Acts of the Apostles*, p. 34.

[4] White, *The Great Controversy*, p. 647.

[5] White, *Last Day Events*, p. 282.

[6] White, *The Great Controversy*, p. 645.

[7] White, *Testimonies for the Church*, vol. 8, p. 253.

[8] White, *The Great Controversy*, p. 666.

[9] *Ibid.*, p. 651.

[10] *Ibid.*, p. 517.

[11] *Ibid.*, p. 560.